CIPS Study Matters

Level 6

Graduate Diploma in Purchasing and Supply

Strategic Supply Chain Management

Second Edition

David R Harris
Chevin Consultants Ltd

Neil Botten
Westminster Business School, University of Westminster

THE
CHARTERED INSTITUTE OF
PURCHASING & SUPPLY®

Published by

The Chartered Institute of Purchasing and Supply
Easton House, Easton on the Hill, Stamford, Lincolnshire PE9 3NZ
Tel: +44 (0) 1780 756 777
Fax: +44 (0) 1780 751 610
Email: info@cips.org
Website: http://www.cips.org

© The Chartered Institute of Purchasing and Supply 2006, 2009

First published July 2006
Second edition published June 2009

Technical reviewer: Joe Sanderson, University of Birmingham

Instructional design and publishing project management by Wordhouse Ltd, Reading, UK

Content management system, instructional editing and pre-press by Echelon Learning Ltd, London, UK

Index prepared by Indexing Specialists (UK) Ltd, Hove, UK

ISBN 978-1-86124-188-7

Contents

Introduction

This course book has been designed to assist you in studying for the CIPS Strategic Supply Chain Management unit in the level 6 Graduate Diploma in Purchasing and Supply. The book covers all topics in the official CIPS unit content document, as illustrated in the table beginning on page xi.

Gaining competitive advantage through the strategic management of supply chains is one of the most topical issues in purchasing. This course book looks at the strategic context of purchasing decisions and evaluates a number of different strategic approaches to purchasing.

Studying this module

This module links the operational supply chain with the overall corporate strategies of organisations. It is important to think at a higher level to make this link.

In summary, strategic supply chain thinking is about a state of mind. You do not need to be working at a senior level to study the module, but you do need to understand the important links between operational and tactical actions and strategy.

To help develop a greater awareness of strategic supply chain management and working at a more strategic level, look at how companies, industries and sectors behave. Draw from content in newspapers, the journal *Supply Management*, the internet and television. Also consider whether you can use the models in this course book and those covered previously to help structure your decision making. Your aim is to help elevate your thinking from a purely day-to-day process to a more strategic level.

How to use this book

The course book will take you step by step through the unit content in a series of carefully planned 'study sessions' and provides you with learning activities, self-assessment questions and revision questions to help you master the subject matter. The guide should help you organise and carry out your studies in a methodical, logical and effective way, but if you have your own study preferences you will find it a flexible resource too.

Before you begin using this course book, make sure you are familiar with any advice provided by CIPS on such things as study skills, revision techniques or support and how to handle formal assessments.

If you are on a taught course, it will be up to your tutor to explain how to use the book – when to read the study sessions, when to tackle the activities and questions, and so on.

If you are on a self-study course, or studying independently, you can use the course book in the following way:

- Scan the whole book to get a feel for the nature and content of the subject matter.
- Plan your overall study schedule so that you allow enough time to complete all 20 study sessions well before your examinations – in other words, leaving plenty of time for revision.
- For each session, set aside enough time for reading the text, tackling all the learning activities and self-assessment questions, and the revision question at the end of the session, and for the suggested further reading. Guidance on roughly how long you should set aside for studying each session is given at the beginning of the session.

Now let's take a look at the structure and content of the individual study sessions.

Overview of the study sessions

The course book breaks the content down into 20 sessions, which vary from three to six or seven hours' duration each. However, we are not advising you to study for this sort of time without a break! The sessions are simply a convenient way of breaking the syllabus into manageable chunks. Most people would try to study one or two sessions a week, taking one or two breaks within each session. You will quickly find out what suits you best.

Each session begins with a brief **introduction** which sets out the areas of the syllabus being covered and explains, if necessary, how the session fits in with the topics that come before and after.

After the introduction there is a statement of the **session learning objectives**. The objectives are designed to help you understand exactly what you should be able to do after you've studied the session. You might find it helpful to tick them off as you progress through the session. You will also find them useful during revision. There is one session learning objective for each numbered subsection of the session.

After this, there is a brief section reproducing the learning objectives and indicative content from the official **unit content document**. This will help you to understand exactly which part of the syllabus you are studying in the current session.

Following this, there are **prior knowledge** and **resources** sections if necessary. These will let you know if there are any topics you need to be familiar with before tackling each particular session, or any special resources you might need, such as a calculator or graph paper.

Then the main part of the study session begins, with the first of the numbered main subsections. At regular intervals in each study session, we have provided you with **learning activities**, which are designed to get you actively involved in the learning process. You should always try to complete the activities – usually on a separate sheet of your own paper – before reading on. You will learn much more effectively if you are actively involved in doing something as you study, rather than just passively reading the text in front of you. The feedback or answers to the activities are provided at the end of the session. Do not be tempted to skip the activity.

We also provide a number of **self-assessment questions** in each study session. These are to help you to decide for yourself whether or not you have achieved the learning objectives set out at the beginning of the session. As with the activities, you should always tackle them – usually on a separate sheet of paper. Don't be tempted to skip them. The feedback or answers are again at the end of the session. If you still do not understand a topic having attempted the self-assessment question, always try to re-read the relevant passages in the textbook readings or session, or follow the advice on further reading at the end of the session. If this still doesn't work, you should contact the CIPS Membership and Qualification Advice team.

For most of the learning activities and self-assessment questions you will need to use separate sheets of paper for your answers or responses. Some of the activities or questions require you to complete a table or form, in which case you could write your response in the course book itself, or photocopy the page.

At the end of the session are three final sections.

The first is the **summary**. Use it to remind yourself or check off what you have just studied, or later on during revision.

Then follows the **suggested further reading** section. This section, if it appears, contains recommendations for further reading which you can follow up if you would like to read alternative treatments of the topics. If for any reason you are having difficulty understanding the course book on a particular topic, try one of the alternative treatments recommended. If you are keen to read around and beyond the syllabus, to help you pick up extra points in the examination for example, you may like to try some of the additional readings recommended. If this section does not appear at the end of a session, it usually means that further reading for the session topics is not necessary.

At the end of the session we direct you to a **revision question**, which you will find in a separate section at the end of the course book. Feedback on the questions is also given.

Reading lists

CIPS produces an official reading list, which recommends essential and desirable texts for augmenting your studies. This reading list is available on the CIPS website or from the CIPS Bookshop. This course book is one of the essential texts for this unit. In this section we describe the main characteristics of the other essential texts for this unit, which you are strongly urged to buy and use throughout your course.

The other essential texts are:

Exploring Corporate Strategy (Text and Cases version) by Gerry Johnson, Kevan Scholes and Richard Whittington published by Pearson in 2007.

This is an excellent strategy text, which contains detailed coverage of all the strategy concepts and models used in this text. You should buy this book, or borrow a copy from a library, as it contains a number of diagrams referred to in this text.

Supply Chain Management, 1st edition, by Birgit Dam Jespersen and Tage Skjott-Larsen published by Copenhagen: Copenhagen Business School in 2005.

This is an interesting research paper, covering a number of key issues relating to strategic supply chain management. Though very light on theoretical content, it does contain a number of useful case studies.

Second edition amendments

This edition of the course book includes a number of changes in order to bring it into line with the current unit content. These mainly relate to the public sector, ethics and corporate social responsibility, stakeholders, hybrid/leagility approaches, how supply chains might achieve competitive advantage by supporting corporate strategy, and the emergent approach to strategy development. In line with unit changes and to focus on examination-related challenges, a number of new self-assessment and learning activities have been added.

Unit content coverage

In this section we reproduce the whole of the official CIPS unit content document for this unit. The overall unit characteristics and statements of practice for the unit are given first. Then, in the table that follows, the learning objectives and indicative content are given in the left hand column. In the right hand column are the study sessions in which you will find coverage of the various topics.

Unit characteristics

The supply chain manager is responsible for specific activities and processes which can contribute to achieving corporate strategic goals.

This unit is designed to provide students with an understanding of strategic aspects of supply chain management.

Students will analyse the supply chain to identify where value is added within it, identifying where and how strategic competitive advantage can be achieved.

Students will be able to propose a range of innovative proposals which will allow supply chain stakeholders to effectively interact and contribute towards developing and exploiting opportunities to grow and expand the business, through new product and service development, innovation, diversification and differentiation strategies.

Statements of practice

On completion of this unit, students will be able to:

- Analyse the concept of strategy and the process of developing corporate strategy
- Identify how strategy is converted into action through effective alignment and implementation
- Explain the contribution of strategic supply chain management to corporate strategy
- Understand the nature of supply chains
- Assess the role of strategic supply chain management in achieving competitive advantage
- Distinguish and assess various models of supply chain structures and relationships

Learning objectives and indicative content

1.0 The concept of strategy and the process of developing corporate strategy (Weighting 25%)

1.1 Evaluate the concepts of strategy, strategic planning, deliberate and emergent strategies and strategic management.   Study session 1

- Definitions of strategy (Grant, Ohmae, Johnson and Scholes, Mintzberg)
- Strategic planning models (Ansoff, Bryson, Mintzberg)
- Rational and incremental approaches to formulating strategy
- Deliberate and emergent strategies (Quinn, Mintzberg)
- Levels and components of strategic management

1.2 Assess and evaluate models of the strategy process.   Study session 2
- Models of the strategy process
- The position, choice, action (PCA) model of strategic management (Johnson and Scholes)
- Rational planning models and strategic management
- The logical incremental model (Quinn) and strategic management
- Strategic management and deliberate and emergent strategies
- Strategic management in small businesses, multinational corporations, manufacturing, services and the public sector

1.3 Conduct a strategic analysis of the supply chain.   Study session 3
- Techniques for analysing the external environment: PESTLE analysis, Porter's Five Forces analysis
- Techniques for analysing the internal environment: SWOT analysis, resource audit, skills audit, knowledge audit, portfolio analysis
- Stakeholder mapping (internal and external)

1.4 Assess the importance of organisational structures, cultures, and   Study session 4
power to the development and implementation of corporate strategy.
- Characteristics of organisational structures: simple, functional, matrix, network, machine and professional bureaucracy
- Centralisation and decentralisation
- Nature of power in organisations: overt, covert and structural
- Sources and indicators of power in organisations
- Organisational culture and the cultural web
- The role and influence of stakeholders
- The importance of ethics and corporate social responsibility

1.5 Critically evaluate innovative strategies for organisational growth   Study session 5
and expansion.
- Generic strategies: price, differentiation and focus
- Directional strategies: consolidate or withdraw from a market, penetrate further into a market, product or market development, diversification
- Methods of developing strategies: internal development, mergers and acquisitions, joint ventures, strategic alliances

1.6 Analyse the means of managing and controlling resources to   Study session 6
support corporate strategy.
- The resource-based approach to corporate strategy
- Resources to support key corporate strategies: financial, human, intellectual, physical, informational

- Resource planning (forecasting, developing and allocating resources)
- Methods of controlling resources: planning systems, supervision, performance targets, social and cultural control, market mechanisms, self-control
- Management information as a key resource

1.7 Review and evaluate the corporate strategy process.   Study session 7
- Corporate strategy review and evaluation
- Methods of testing the suitability of corporate strategies
- Methods of testing acceptability of corporate strategies
- Methods of testing feasibility of corporate strategies
- Ways of improving corporate strategies
- Selection of appropriate corporate strategies

2.0 Converting strategy into action through effective alignment and implementation (Weighting 15%)

2.1 Analyse the methods of achieving commitment to corporate strategy across all functions and levels of the organisation.   Study session 8
- Purpose and value of corporate visions and mission statements
- Integration of functional and corporate plans
- Internal and external communications policy and processes
- Rewards and sanctions reinforcing commitment to corporate goals

2.2 Assess the need for alignment between strategy and structure.   Study session 8
- The 7S framework: strategy, structure, super-ordinate goals, staff, style, skills and systems
- Alignment of strategy and structure
- Alignment of strategy with super-ordinate goals, staff, style, skills and systems

2.3 Diagnose resistance to change and strategic drift, and identify how to address them through change management processes.   Study session 9
- Types of strategic change: incremental and transformational, managed and imposed
- Symptoms of strategic drift
- Forces blocking and facilitating change
- Change management styles through education, collaboration, intervention, direction, coercion
- Role of symbolic and political processes in managing change
- Strategic change roles: change agent, middle manager, other organisational member, stakeholder or outsider

3.0 The contribution of strategic supply chain management to corporate strategy (Weighting 15%)

3.1 Analyse the relationships between functional, business and corporate strategies, and the integration of supply chain strategies with corporate and business strategies.   Study session 10
- Relationships between functional, business and corporate strategies
- Integration of supply chain strategies with corporate and business strategies

- Formal and informal processes through which supply chain strategies may be integrated with corporate strategy: involvement in planning processes, role of main board, supportive chief executive

3.2 Assess the contribution of strategic supply chain management to corporate strategy.   Study session 10
- Contribution of strategic supply chain management to corporate strategy: cost reduction, quality, innovation, delivery
- Contribution of strategic make, do or buy decisions to corporate strategy
- Core competence analysis: core, complementary and residual competences
- Relational competence analysis (Cox)

3.3 Analyse and align organisational structures and processes, with supply chain strategies.   Study session 12
- Alignment of organisational structures and processes with strategic supply chain strategies
- Centralised, decentralised and mixed structures
- Future trends in purchasing organisation and processes (Carter and Narasimhan, Van Weele and Rozemeijer)
- Use of cross-functional teams to support supply chain strategies
- Use of inter-organisational networks to achieve strategic supply chain strategies

3.4 Propose innovative supply chain strategies to meet corporate and business targets.   Study session 11
- Benefits and difficulties in developing better supplier relationships
- Methods of cost reduction and cost improvement
- Strategies for quality improvement
- Strategies for repositioning the organisation on the supply or value chain

4.0 The nature of supply chains (Weighting 15%)

4.1 Assess the validity of the supply chain concept both in terms of the nature of supply and the chain metaphor.   Study session 13
- Concepts of supply and supply chain
- Assumptions about the nature of supply (Lamming and Cox 1997)
- Supply chain metaphors: chain, pipeline, network, channel
- Critiques of the supply chain concept (New and Ramsay 1997)
- Types of supply networks and supply chain models: internal supply chains, dyadic supply relationships, inter-business chains, inter-business networks (Harland 1996)
- Arguments and evidence for and against the application of supply chain management

4.2 Analyse internal and external supply chains and the flows across organisational boundaries upstream and downstream.   Study session 14
- Internal and external supply chains
- Interface and integrated models (Syson 1992)

- Roles of internal and external customers within supply chains
- Flows across organisational boundaries upstream and downstream
- Problems with forecasting demand accurately within supply chains

4.3 Compare and contrast the nature of supply chains in different sectors.   Study session 14
- Nature of supply chains in the manufacturing, retail and financial sectors
- Nature of supply chains in different public sector organisations: health and social care, defence, transportation

4.4 Diagnose drivers of change in global supply chains and propose strategies to address them.   Study session 15
- Nature and impact of globalisation
- Drivers of change in global supply markets: competition, cost reduction, technological advances, speed of new product
- Development, changing customer demand, environmental factors, collaborations and joint ventures, outsourcing
- Impact of drivers of change in global supply markets
- Strategies to address drivers of change in global supply chains

5.0 The role of strategic supply chain management in achieving competitive advantage (Weighting 15%)

5.1 Assess the validity of global sourcing as a means of achieving competitive advantage.   Study session 16
- The global supply market as a source of competitive advantage
- Arguments for and against local, regional, national and global sourcing
- Regulation of the global supply market by WTO, EU, NAFTA, ASEAN
- Obstacles to trade imposed by national or regional anti-competitive policies
- Cultural barriers to trade in global supply markets

5.2 Evaluate the concept of lean supply as a means of achieving competitive advantage.   Study session 17
- The concept of lean
- The seven types of waste
- Critique of the lean approach (New and Ramsay 1997)
- Alternatives to lean (agility) and hybrid approaches (leagility)

5.3 Critically evaluate the concepts of value, added value and value chain.   Study session 17
- Concepts of value and added value
- The value chain concept
- Porter's (1985) value chain model
- Critiques of Porter's model (Hines (1993)
- Strategies for adding value: repositioning on the value chain, value constellations

5.4 Analyse the sources, nature and role of power in supply chains.   Study session 18
   • Sources of power in supply chains
   • Nature and role of power in supply chains
   • Ways in which power may be exercised in supply chains: overt, covert and structural
   • Power relationships between large customers and small suppliers in supply chains

5.5 Evaluate the use of supply chains to deliver ethical and socio-economic outcomes alongside commercial goals.   Study session 18
   • Ethical considerations in supply chains
   • Types of socio-economic goals pursued through supply chains: environment, employment, equality, small and medium enterprises, prompt payment
   • Arguments for and against the use of supply chains to pursue non-commercial goals

6.0 Models of supply chain structures and relationships (Weighting 15%)

6.1 Assess the validity of the development of a 'best practice' strategic supply chain model.   Study session 19
   • Arguments for and against the existence of a 'best practice' strategic supply chain model
   • Contingent approach to strategic supply chain management (Cox and Lamming 1997)
   • Network sourcing as a 'best practice' strategic supply chain model (Rich and Hines 1997)

6.2 Compare the characteristics of adversarial and co-operative strategies and analyse their appropriateness in different circumstances.   Study session 19
   • Characteristics of adversarial and co-operative strategies
   • Partnership
   • Appropriateness of adversarial and co-operative strategies in different circumstances

6.3 Understand and apply competence-based approaches for determining supply chain structures and relationships.   Study session 20
   • Hamel and Prahalad's core competence model
   • Core, complementary and residual competences
   • The resource-based view, especially in relation to replicable and non-replicable competences

6.4 Assess the lean supply model as a prescription for supply relationships.   Study session 20
   • Partnership and lean supply
   • Trust in buyer–supplier relationships
   • Appropriateness of lean supply and partnership for different organisations

Study session 1
Concepts underlying strategy and strategic management

Introduction

The subject of strategy and strategic management are core themes of this study session. Strategies are all about the future and trying to achieve objectives, but they are not always written, formal plans developed in a rational and logical way. This session explores the concept of a strategy and the activities involved in strategic management in more depth.

Strategy! Sounds very grand and the sort of thing only a very senior manager does? Well, not quite. In fact, we all use and contribute to strategies every day.

Session learning objectives

After completing this session you should be able to:

1.1 Evaluate the concept of strategy.
1.2 Evaluate the concept of strategic planning.
1.3 Analyse rational and incremental approaches to formulating strategy.
1.4 Evaluate the concepts of deliberate and emergent strategies.
1.5 Evaluate the concept of strategic management.

Unit content coverage

This study session covers the following topics from the official CIPS unit content document:

Statement of practice

- Analyse the concept of strategy and the process of developing corporate strategy.

Learning objective

1.1 Evaluate the concepts of strategy, strategic planning, deliberate and emergent strategies and strategic management.
   - Definitions of strategy (Grant, Ohmae, Johnson and Scholes, Mintzberg)
   - Strategic planning models (Ansoff, Bryson, Mintzberg)
   - Rational and incremental approaches to formulating strategy
   - Deliberate and emergent strategies (Quinn, Mintzberg)
   - Levels and components of strategic management

Prior knowledge

No particular prior knowledge is assumed in this session, other than previous studies on the CIPS programme.

1

Resources

Access to Johnson, Scholes and Whittington (2007) chapter 1 is highly recommended for use throughout this session.

Timing

You should set aside about 5 hours to read and complete this session, including learning activities, self-assessment questions, the suggested further reading (if any) and the revision question.

1.1   What is a strategy?

In the UK alone, there are 57 books in print with the title Strategic Management. Most are weighty tomes, filled with charts, lists, axioms and plenty of valuable suggestions for the reader. Unfortunately, nearly all contain similar material and the same auspicious advice. Most of these books also sell for in excess of £25. So, if it is that easy, why do we need top managers? Here is the problem. A strategy is a bit like peering into the future and trying to predict what will happen; and then, trying to make it happen.

Strategy comes from the Greek word *strategos* meaning 'general', but its modern usage connotes a plan of how to get to a chosen position. As you might imagine, there are many definitions of strategy:

> 'Understanding where the business is at the moment. Having a clear view of where it wants to be in the future. Then, conducting a wide-scale debate about how it will reach its future destination.'

(Pascale, 1991)

> 'A strategy is a pattern of major objectives, purposes or goals and essential policies or plans for achieving those goals, stated in such a way as to define what business the company is in or is to be in and the kind of company it is or is to be.'

(Drucker, 1961)

> 'The pattern or plan that integrates an organisation's major goals, policies and action sequences into a cohesive whole…to help to marshal and allocate an organisation's resources into a unique and viable posture based upon its relative internal competences and shortcomings, anticipated changes in the environment and contingent moves by intelligent opponents.'

(Quinn, 1980)

> 'The direction and scope of an organisation over the long term, which achieves advantage in a changing environment through its configuration of resources and competences with the aim of fulfilling stakeholder expectations.'

(Johnson, Scholes and Whittington, 2007)

Henry Mintzberg (1997) offers a number of definitions using the five Ps:

- *Plan*: looking forward (being prescriptive).
- *Pattern*: looking back at consistency of behaviour (being descriptive).
- *Position*: looking at your products and markets.
- *Perspective*: looking at the fundamental way of doing things (the theory of your business).
- *Ploy*: a manoeuvre (to attack or defend).

From the various definitions, some common threads do emerge about the nature of a strategy. These are:

- It concerns an organisation and its environment.
- Strategies and strategic management are complex.
- A strategy will affect the overall welfare of an organisation.
- Strategies have content.
- Strategic management is a process.
- Strategies can exist at a number of levels (corporate, business and operational).
- Strategies involve different thought processes (conceptual and analytical).
- Strategies deal with the longer-term future.
- Strategies focus upon customers and markets, competitors and the company itself.
- Strategies are not necessarily deliberate.

Learning activity 1.1

Compare the validity of the various definitions of strategy in relation to your own experience.

Feedback on page 10

Now attempt the following question.

Self-assessment question 1.1

Develop your own definition of strategy, with an example of its practical application.

Feedback on page 11

1.2   What is strategic planning?

As mentioned earlier, strategic planning or strategic management is a process or an activity undertaken by an organisation (or more accurately, people in the organisation). This process can be visualised as having three elements:

1   Understanding the strategic position of an organisation.
2   Making strategic choices for the future.

1

3   Turning the strategy into action by implementing changes in the organisation.

These are, however, not separate phases or stages that can be understood totally in isolation. They are closely interlinked and overlapping issues that will 'inform' each other.

Figure 1.1: Elements of the strategy process

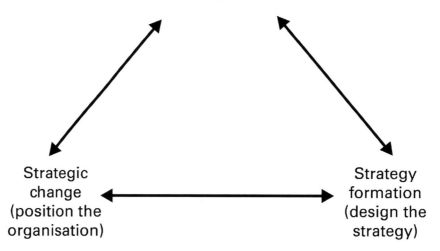

Strategic thinking and planning
(the strategist plans)

Strategic
change
(position the
organisation)

Strategy
formation
(design the
strategy)

Looking at figure 1.1, you would be forgiven for thinking that strategic management or strategic planning is a rational and logical activity – one that involves knowledge of the organisation's fit in its macro- and micro-environment, establishing the position of the organisation, setting objectives for where it would like to be in the future and creating a plan for delivering these objectives; a clear link between a deliberate process and profit-maximising outcomes.

This is the classical or corporate planning approach to strategy. It is one of the oldest and most influential planning methods witnessed in most textbooks and taught in business schools for the last 50 years. Associated with authorities such as Igor Ansoff (1965; 1991) and Michael Porter (1980; 1985), the classical approach gives textbook answers. Here, strategy is a rational approach of deliberate calculation and analysis, designed for maximum long-term advantage. If effort is taken to gather the information and apply the appropriate techniques, both the outside world and the organisation itself can be made predictable and shaped according to the careful plans of top management.

Unfortunately, strategic management, in this classical sense of future-oriented planning, is often irrelevant. The business environment is too unpredictable, dynamic and complex to anticipate and forecast effectively. The classical, planning approaches have subsequently been heavily criticised, with leading commentators arguing that the world is simply not that straightforward.

Henry Mintzberg (1987) suggests that the image of orderly thinking (a senior manager, or a group of them, sitting in an office formulating courses of action that everyone else will implement on schedule) is incorrect. Far better, he suggests, is the viewpoint of a strategy being crafted. Craft evokes traditional skill, dedication, and perfection through the mastery of detail. To a degree, thinking and reason are replaced with an intimacy and harmony with the materials at hand – a fluid process of learning, producing strategies that evolve. Mintzberg continues with the following points:

- Strategies are patterns of actions that can be planned and intended but also pursued and realised (or not realised).
- Some strategies that are intended are simply not realised.
- An organisation can have a realised strategy (a pattern) without knowing it, let alone making it explicit.
- Strategies can form as well as be formulated. A realised strategy can emerge in response to an evolving situation, or it can be brought about deliberately, through a process of formulation, followed by implementation.
- Effective strategies can develop in many ways. They can grow like weeds in a garden taking root wherever people have the capacity to learn (that is, are in touch with the situation).

Mintzberg (1994) also challenges the benefits of formal planning systems. In his view there are a number of salient points:

- Managers can confuse the process of planning with that of managing a strategy. This highlights the difference between intended and realised strategies.
- There is often confusion between budgetary processes and strategic planning processes. Planning gets reduced to financial forecasting and control.
- There can be an obsession with the one, and only one, right strategy, leading to inflexibility.
- Relying excessively upon a realised strategy can also lead to a blinkered vision that fails to recognise any strategic drift away from the real objectives.

Learning activity 1.2

Compare plans developed at work or in any other context with the models presented.

Feedback on page 11

Now try the following question.

Self-assessment question 1.2

Using bullet points, summarise and assess Mintzberg's critique of strategic planning in a memo to your manager.

Feedback on page 11

1.3 Approaches to strategy formulation

Hopefully, at this point it is becoming clear that strategies and strategic management processes are both complex and at times irrational. As early as the 1950s, Herbert Simon (1960) and Charles Lindblom (1959) were pointing out that rational decision-making models were unrealistic. Obtaining and processing the huge amounts of data necessary to understand the organisational environment makes such exhaustive analyses impossible. In addition, decision makers cannot always be relied upon to provide rational choices in predicting the future. As Simon pointed out, managers have a 'bounded rationality' that results in 'satisficing' rather than optimising. Cyert and March (1963) went further: they suggested that people are too different in their interests, too limited in their understanding, too wandering in their attention and too careless in their actions, to unite around and then carry through a perfectly calculated plan.

Learning activity 1.3

Identify the strategic goals of your own organisation or any organisation with which you are familiar and analyse the process by which they were established.

Feedback on page 11

The routes by which a strategy will develop can also be complex. As can be seen in figure 1.2, there are a number of possibilities:

Figure 1.2: Potential strategic development

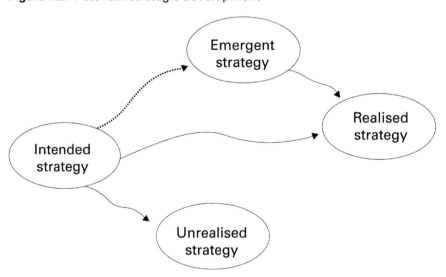

From this figure, it is evident that an intended strategy can become realised if the circumstances are right (both internally and externally). It may also become an unrealised (or partially unrealised) strategy for a number of reasons. It is also possible that the intended plan becomes realised, but in a different form as it emerges over time. Indeed, an emergent strategy may stem from the 'bottom up' in an organisation and replace both the intended and subsequently realised strategy.

The process by which intended strategies are developed will vary in each organisation. It is usually a step-by-step process involving senior managers, consultants and other stakeholders, determining various plans in formalised and iterative planning systems.

Emergent strategies, meanwhile, are less easy to plot. Quinn (1980) described this developmental process as 'logical incrementalism'. A number of characteristics led to this view:

- Managers tend to have a general view of the future of an organisation and they often 'inch' toward this position incrementally, leaving open the possibilities for experimentation.
- Uncertainty cannot be controlled or removed entirely. Far better to scan the environment and be sensitive to change by adapting in small steps.
- A strong, secure, yet flexible, core business allows tentative experimentation to test alternatives.
- This experimentation cannot be the sole responsibility of top management. Disparate groups of people across the firm will have a role to play in offering bottom-up learning and creativity.
- Top managers can utilise a mix of formal and informal (top-down and bottom-up) processes to arrive at an emerging pattern of strategies.

Quinn describes a process that bridges intention and emergence. Strategies are deliberate and intended but they rely on social processes in the organisation to sense the environment and experiment.

Self-assessment question 1.3

List the main elements of rational and incremental approaches to strategy formulation and develop a synthesis.

Feedback on page 11

1.4 Deliberate and emergent strategies

Intended strategic development is often equated with a formalised planning system. This may take the form of a step-by-step, chronological process involving different parts of the organisation. It is, however, likely to be a process that is top-down and originating with senior management. A formalised system of this type will have some advantages in helping to determine a strategy:

- It provides a structured method to think about complex issues.
- It offers a forum to question and challenge existing 'wisdom'.
- It helps to promote a long-term view (normally four to five years, but in some cases as many as 20).
- The formalised approach offers a means of coordination to bring together a number of strategic issues.

- The system will help to communicate strategic intentions to the rest of the organisation.
- It enables regular and agreed objectives and milestones that will measure performance.
- It offers a formalised, coordinating mechanism that will deploy existing resources.
- It involves people and creates a sense of ownership.
- The approach provides a sense of purpose and security.

The formalised and deliberate strategic process is likely to be undertaken by groups of managers and other stakeholders using specifically designated workshops and project groups. Consultants and other experts may also be called upon to advise and assist. There is also the possibility that such strategies are heavily influenced by external forces that can have a strong regulatory impact upon the choices available.

Studies have shown that the realised strategies of many organisations are probably better accounted for as emergent. Logical incrementalism describes a process by which there is a deliberate development of strategy by experimentation and learning from partial commitments. There are three other influences that may contribute to the emergent nature of strategies:

- Resource allocation routines: Every organisation will have various systems and routines used to undertake the operations of the business. These will include the regular decision-making processes used to acquire and allocate resources. Strategies can develop as a result of these routines (Burgelman, 1983). For example, what may begin as a relatively small project to explore a new product development and/or a new market niche, may, if successful, offer a future strategic opportunity.
- Cultural processes: Culture is an important, yet complex, element of organisation. At one level, it can be understood as shared basic assumptions and beliefs. At another, it includes certain taken-for-granted ways of doing things and structures. These elements guide and constrain how people view the organisation and its environment, as well as influencing their behaviour and assumptions. The outcome of this cultural process can result in an attempt by managers to resort to familiar patterns and past experience when dealing with ambiguity and change. The culture promotes, albeit sometimes in an unconscious manner, a strategic response based upon known and trusted historical assumptions about 'the way we do things'.
- Organisational politics: Closely linked to culture, the politics within an organisation will result in bargaining and negotiation among powerful internal and external stakeholder groups, such as executives. These various interests will have a strong influence upon the control of resources and the direction of any strategies.

Finally, whether deliberate or emergent, there will be a number of reasons why a strategy may fail or suddenly become no longer effective. Elaborate plans may not be workable in practice, people in the organisation may resist the new direction, or more likely, there will be changes in the environment. Such changes can be dramatic – for example, resources no longer being available, or competitor moves resulting in a product not being acceptable. These changes will force the organisation into a rapid strategic rethink. Just as likely, however, is the influence of strategic drift. Here, smaller incremental changes in the environment can steadily mount, often unnoticed, and the organisation slowly drifts off course.

Learning activity 1.4

Identify examples of deliberate and emergent strategies in your own organisation and/or from the literature.

Feedback on page 12

Now attempt the following question.

Self-assessment question 1.4

Explain in a memo to your manager why some of your organisation's intended strategies are not realised, and why different strategies may emerge.

Feedback on page 12

1.5 Evaluating the concept of strategic management

Strategies and strategic management are complex subjects. The rational and logical approach to corporate planning is probably now rather outmoded and most organisations will rely upon adaptation and a process similar to logical incrementalism, as strategies emerge as a result of environmental change. This understanding raises important points:

- There is probably no one right way to develop a strategy, just as there is no best way to manage. Different situations and environments will call for flexibility and alternative approaches.
- The process of strategic development will probably change over time and in different contexts. Turbulent environments call for rapid change and necessitate different strategic processes from steady-state situations, where change is slow and predictable.
- All of us have different perceptions that are formed by myriad cultural and social influences. As such, gaining agreement on an appropriate course of action is not always easy and will often depend upon the type of organisation and its environment.
- The strategic process is different in each organisation and will probably vary from one situation to another. Attempting to generalise or trying to rely upon what was successful in the past, although comforting and one way to understand complexity, may not always prove fruitful.

Viewing strategic development from three general perspectives will help to appreciate the complexity involved:

- As a design: A logical process that ensures the forces and constraints on the organisation are carefully balanced against its strengths and weaknesses, in order to achieve future competitive success.

1

- As an experience: Future strategies should be based upon the experience of managers and their ability to modify strategy to fit the current situation.
- As an idea: The importance of innovation, creativity, diversity and innovation cannot be overlooked. Here, the strategy is less top-down but emerges from people and change in the organisation.

Learning activity 1.5

Identify the various levels and components of strategic management as presented in cases from Johnson, Scholes and Whittington (2007) chapter 1.

Feedback on page 12

Now attempt the following question.

Self-assessment question 1.5

Analyse the nature of strategic management in any organisation with which you are familiar.

Feedback on page 12

Revision question

Now try the revision question for this session on page 257.

Summary

In this session we have looked at some of the core concepts associated with strategy and strategic planning, including:

- the rational and incremental approaches to strategy formulation
- the concepts of deliberate and emergent strategies
- the concept of strategic management.

Suggested further reading

Mintzberg and McHugh (1985) pp160–197.

Feedback on learning activities and self-assessment questions

Feedback on learning activity 1.1

You may have found this a difficult activity. Strategies are rather ephemeral and their exact nature is hard to pin down. This is frustrating, especially when a strategy clearly works but then a firm cannot replicate what it has done in the past. In some ways, a strategy is all about being in the right place at the right time. But it is also finding a way to think about the future and to link the strengths of the organisation to the opportunities in its environment. In addition, it is about appreciating that the organisation also has weaknesses and these are likely to be exposed by external threats.

Feedback on self-assessment question 1.1

It is likely that your definition was at an organisational level and considered its environment and its long-term aims and objectives. As such, the strategy looks at future opportunities for markets and customers. Strategies also need to encompass vital resources that a firm needs; consequently, many organisations develop partnerships and alliances with key suppliers and customers. These more detailed strategies are at an operational or functional level.

Feedback on learning activity 1.2

You may not have found written plans; plans in an organisation may exist only in the minds of senior managers. It is also likely that any strategies are in effect attempts to continue the patterns of the past (in the hope they will continue to be successful). Less evident will be the strategy that has grown, incrementally, from the bottom up.

Feedback on self-assessment question 1.2

The main points from Mintzberg's critique are:

- Successful strategies are not always rational and logical.
- Some strategies are incremental and grow organically from the bottom up.
- Many different people in an organisation can contribute to a strategy.
- Learning is an important element in developing a strategy.
- Not all strategies are realised; many can fall by the wayside.
- Planning is not the same as implementing a strategy.
- Strategic management is as much about flexibility as it is about a determination to achieve a pre-established goal. Failing to recognise that changes are taking place in the environment can spell disaster.

Feedback on learning activity 1.3

Identifying the process involved may not be easy in itself. If it was rational and logical, you may find that a distinct planning process exists. On the other hand, some successful strategies may have emerged without real structure. It is more likely that these two approaches were combined in a system similar to the logical incrementalism described in section 1.3.

Feedback on self-assessment question 1.3

Rational strategy:

- A step-by-step process.
- Involving senior managers, consultants and other stakeholders.

- Determining various plans in formalised and iterative planning systems.

Incrementalism:

- Managers tend to have a general view of the future for an organisation and they often 'inch' toward this position.
- A strong, secure, yet flexible, core business allows tentative experimentation to test alternatives.
- Disparate groups of people across the firm have a role to play in offering bottom-up learning and creativity.
- Top managers can utilise a mix of formal and informal (top-down and bottom-up) processes to arrive at an emerging pattern of strategies.

If you managed to list elements belonging to the two different approaches, you may have noticed that the main difference is the lack of formality involved in the latter. Indeed, if you were not able to list any elements all, it is likely that the process is incremental, organic, and proceeds in small adaptive steps.

Feedback on learning activity 1.4

Deliberate, intended strategies will have been easier to identify, as a particular strategic process or system may well be in place to develop, implement and monitor their progress. Emergent strategies are likely as a result of adaptations to the environment. For example, changes by competitors, market needs, resource availability and so on, that prompt adjustments in the direction of the organisation.

Feedback on self-assessment question 1.4

No matter how well designed, developed or crafted, a strategy will inevitably be subject to the changing influences of the environment that will be beyond the control of the organisation. These changes will not always be dramatic and may often be the result of incremental 'shifts'. Nevertheless, the speed of change and the sheer volume of information involved in monitoring environmental change make the strategic management task even harder. Often, strategies will emerge as a reactive attempt to keep pace with these changes and to avoid strategic drift.

Feedback on learning activity 1.5

The experience of Dell Computers illustrates the wide range of factors that has to be considered and assessed as part of strategic management. In the Electrolux example, meanwhile, there are different levels of strategy evident (corporate, business unit and functional).

Feedback on self-assessment question 1.5

Hopefully, you will have been able to identify a mixture of influences, from rational and logical to incremental and adaptive. If so, this shows that at any given time an organisation has to rely upon different approaches and ideas. The future is not always a continuation of the past!

Models of the strategy process

Introduction

This session examines models of the key processes for the *intended* (or *deliberate*) and *incremental* approaches to strategy development. In practice, these models are not used in independent or mutually exclusive ways, but in different combinations suited to situations and contexts that change over time. Three models and their suitability for a range of organisational contexts are discussed:

- position, choice and action (PCA)
- rational planning
- logical incremental.

'I believe the best test of a *model* is how well the modeller can answer the questions, "What do you know now that you did not know before?" and "How can you find out if it is true?"'
Jim Bower

Session learning objectives

After completing this session you should be able to:

2.1 Explain the nature and purpose of models of the strategy process.
2.2 Understand the position, choice and action (PCA) process model.
2.3 Choose between deliberate and emergent strategy process developments.
2.4 Compare the rational and emergent approaches to strategy development.
2.5 Determine the suitability and application of the rational planning model.
2.6 Determine the suitability and application of the logical incremental model.
2.7 Appreciate strategic management development in different organisational contexts.

Unit content coverage

This study session covers the following topics from the official CIPS unit content document:

Statement of practice

- Analyse the concept of strategy and the process of developing corporate strategy.

Learning objective

1.2 Assess and evaluate models of the strategy process.

- Models of the strategy process
- The position, choice, action (PCA) model of strategic management (Johnson and Scholes)
- Rational planning models and strategic management
- The logical incremental model (Quinn) and strategic management
- Strategic management and deliberate and emergent strategies
- Strategic management in small businesses, multinational corporations, manufacturing, services and the public sector

Prior knowledge

Study session 1.

Resources

Access to Johnson, Scholes and Whittington (2007) chapters 1 and 11 is highly recommended for use throughout this session.

Timing

You should set aside about 5.5 hours to read and complete this session, including learning activities, self-assessment questions, the suggested further reading (if any) and the revision question.

2.1 Nature and purpose of models of the strategy process

Strategy process is the method by which strategies are formulated. It consists of a series of elements that are interdependent, thereby forming a complex system. In turn, each element is made with subelements that are interdependent and form subsystems. If any part of the system is inadequate the performance of the whole system, and hence the formulated strategy itself, will reduce.

Distinction needs to be drawn between the *process*, *content* and *context* of the strategy formulation. They need to be used in a balanced way. Limited use of one will weaken the whole outcome – the formulated strategy.

- Process is a method by which strategies are developed. It is concerned with the *how, who* and *when* of the strategy.
- Content refers to the specific means and actions by which organisational and functional strategies are to be achieved. It is the product of the process and the *what* of the strategy.
- Context refers to the external and internal environments *where* an organisation exists and hence *where* process and content are determined.

Strategy processes are complex and large. They are often mapped, in summary form, as a conceptual model and presented in a simple graphical form, but they can take a descriptive form. Such models:

*   Provide a common approach by all contributors to the process.
*   Provide mechanisms for entering into focused low levels of detail and associated decision making, and reversing back to the conceptual model, that is the whole system.
*   Simplify the review and modification of the process, after a period of use.
*   Facilitate strategic thinking by easy access to the whole system of the conceptual model.
*   Can aid our understanding of each step, stage, action or subsystem (and possibly of the overall system). They may:
    (a) Describe their characteristics and qualities.
    (b) Explain by revealing more detail or relevant facts or ideas.
    (c) Predict by estimating or indicating what may happen in the future or be a consequence of something.
    (d) Prescribe and control, by stating particular courses of action.

Many organisations see the development of strategy of such great importance that they establish a strategy planning office staffed with senior line and functional managers and strategy analysts, economic and behavioural specialists, among others. Use of computer aids is common: to collect, store and analyse data; to model ranges of possible external and internal scenarios; and to model the attractiveness of strategic choices. However, senior line managers, the chairman, managing director and financial director are accountable for strategy formulation – it cannot be delegated.

Depending on the structure of the organisation, each department, or function, division or sub-business unit needs to develop its own strategy that becomes a subset of the organisation level strategy. Planning guidelines are provided in the form of mission, goals, objectives and process to be used. Development requires several iterations and extensive negotiation with organisation level managers.

The position, choices and action (PCA), rational planning and logical incremental models are considered in sections 2.2 to 2.4.

Learning activity 2.1

Critically evaluate an important process used in your organisation and test its usefulness in terms of process, content and context. Identify possible improvements.

Feedback on page 26

Now attempt the following question.

2

Discuss the usefulness, or otherwise, of models in order to understand and improve organisational activities.

Feedback on page 26

2.2 The position, choice and action (PCA) process model

The PCA strategic management process model (Johnson, Scholes and Whittington, 2007) is shown on page 16 of that textbook. The elements are not shown in a neat and tidy, sequential form; they are interlinked and inform each other – into and out of each element – and thus have access to all elements.

Strategic position is concerned with the impact on strategy of the external environment, an organisation's strategic capabilities (tangible and intangible resources, including competences) and the expectations and influence of stakeholders.

The external environment is complex, dynamic and hostile. Political, economic, social, technological, environmental, legal, competitor and stakeholder factors are constantly changing and reacting with each other. Organisations need to be aware of them and respond to them, preferably, in pre-emptive ways. The factors give rise to *opportunities* and *threats* to be considered in strategy development.

Tangible resources are physical assets that include buildings, equipment and processes such as manufacturing methods. Reputation, brand, image, employee knowledge, skills and experience are intangible assets. *Competences* are the activities and processes through which an organisation effectively deploys its resources. Core competences are those competences that are deployed in ways that give the organisation competitive advantage and are difficult for competitors to copy. Analysis of resources and competences identifies internal *strengths* and *weaknesses*, and their suitability for the external environment.

Expectations of stakeholders, shareholders, government, employees, and suppliers, among others, influence an organisation's mission, purposes, behaviour and objectives. Cultural influences, stakeholder beliefs and values are particularly powerful and constraining.

Strategic choices involve understanding the underlying base for future strategy and the option for developing strategy in terms of direction and methods of development. The bases of competition must be known. They arise from an understanding of strategic capability, markets, customers and competitors.

Strategy may develop in different directions in terms of products, markets and market territories. Methods of development include internal development, such as developing a new range of products, joint ventures and acquisition of another organisation.

Strategy into action is concerned with ensuring that strategies are working in practice.

Appropriate structuring, support strategies and the management of change are prerequisites for successful implementation actions. Structuring involves appropriate organisational structures, processes, internal and external relationships and their interactions. For success, enablement strategies include making available information, finance, technology, knowledge, skills and experience. Managing change considers the roles and styles of different people and the application of particular change processes. As with all models, it depends on the cognitive ability of the individual using it or else information overload may impact upon decision making. The PCA model is different from some in that it provides a clear, sequential but linked process. Elements are not separate and therefore can influence each other. This develops a more rounded and realistic way of thinking.

Learning activity 2.2

Write a memo to your manager describing the major elements of the PCA model, and explaining the nature and importance of the linkage mechanism.

Feedback on page 26

Now attempt the following question.

Self-assessment question 2.2

Roughly sketch the PCA model, initially from memory, and then complete it by referring to the original in Johnson, Scholes and Whittington (2007).

Feedback on page 26

2.3   Deliberate/intended and emergent strategy development

This section develops ideas covered in study session 1.

Deliberate, or intended, strategy is an expression of the desired future state and direction of the organisation deliberately formulated or planned by managers. Processes include rational planning, strategy workshops, strategy consultants and externally imposed strategies.

Emergent strategy comes about through everyday routines, activities and processes in the organisation. Processes include resource allocation, cultural and political routines.

Realised strategy is the strategy actually being followed by and achieved by an organisation. It may be the deliberate strategy, or a form of incremental strategy.

There are four challenges for managing strategy development:

1   Strategic drift occurs where strategies progressively fail to address the strategic position of the organisation and performance deteriorates. Frequent reviews and recovery actions of performance and content, context and process of strategy may halt the drift.

2   A learning organisation is capable of continual regeneration from the variety of knowledge, experience and skills of individuals, within a culture that encourages mutual questioning and challenge around a shared purpose or mission. Individuals learn from successes and failures, particularly where failure is tolerated.

3   In uncertain, complex, dynamic and hostile environments, the challenge is to create conditions necessary to encourage managers and staff to be forward-thinking, intuitive, imaginative and risk-taking.

4   Organisations will have to manage different combinations of the strategy development process and tools of analysis. Multiple processes and tools are likely to be needed if organisations wish to create a learning and creative internal environment and cope with the external environments. This will require considerable financial investment and time, involving a wider range of the workforce.

Selection of the approach depends on:

•   Dynamics, complexity and hostility of the external environment: Highly dynamic environments feature uncertainties that require continuous scanning for identification of evolving threats and opportunities.

•   Size and structure of the organisation: Large complex organisations with diverse product or service ranges and diverse geographic coverage require some form of planning and control processes, particularly if control is highly centralised. Imposition of strategy is common.

•   Management style: Autocratic managers are likely to impose a top-down approach and use the deliberate or intended approach coupled with imposed goals, objectives and processes. Democratic managers use a wide range of consultative and participative processes that require much time, but result in enriched strategy formulation.

•   Cognitive capabilities and biases: Managers, as human beings, have limited information processing, sensing and storage capabilities that constrain their ability to reason correctly. They are 'boundedly rational' thinkers who bring into play personal and professional biases, general 'rules of thumb' developed over many years, and fixed views of their worlds, despite evidence to the contrary.

•   Levels of strategic thinking available: Strategic thinking is a creative process that attempts to see beyond the present and near-term. It involves flexible thinking, avoiding wrongly-focused precision, keeping details in perspective, focusing on suitability of distinctive competences of the organisation and taking a holistic, or systems, view of the internal and external environments and their likely developments.

- The information available and associated systems in use in the organisation.
- The abilities of individuals who hold planning positions.
- Availability and suitability of key internal resources.
- Levels of power and interest of all stakeholders.
- The type of sector or industry. For example, the public sector favours a very rational approach, the computer industry needs to be more emergent to deal with rapid change, and entrepreneurs tend to be freewheeling opportunists taking opportunities as they arise.

Learning activity 2.3

Discuss, with evidence, how your organisation or department responds to the four challenges for managing strategy development. What are the consequences where your organisation is not responding to the challenges?

Feedback on page 26

Now attempt the following question.

Self-assessment question 2.3

Assume that your organisation or department is not responding to the four challenges. Propose actions to remedy the situation.

Feedback on page 27

2.4 Rational planning model

Rational, intended processes, implying proactive rational and unemotional thinking and decision making, involve the development of strategy through formally documented, linear planning processes. They are based on objective analysis, achieved by a consistent application of logic, and assume that the future can be accurately forecast. Further, it can be considered as a scientific style of management that relies on availability and analysis of data, information, facts and historical records. The realised strategy that arises from this approach can be justified at a later stage. Outcome of the process is a series of company-level formal strategies and tactics in the form of imposed, prescribed plans that are managed in a top-down way. For each business unit in large organisations, and each department or function, a strategic plan can be produced that is an interdependent part of the company-level strategies and tactics. Advocates of this approach argue that the use of imagination, emotions, intuition and judgement are inappropriate.

Figure 2.1: Model of the rational strategic management process]

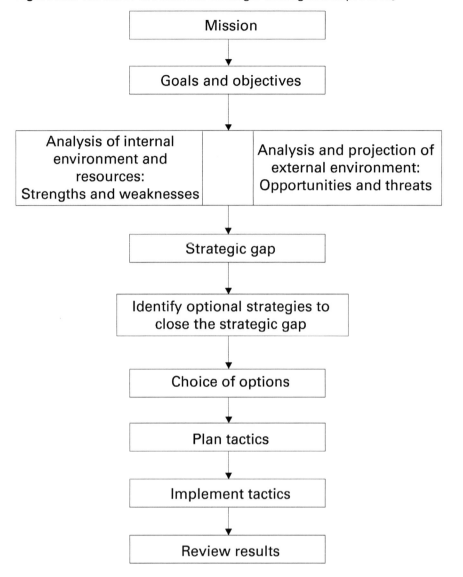

Figure 2.1 illustrates the rational model as a group of discrete elements that are carried out in sequence, in a linear fashion, with an outcome matched to the mission, goals and objectives. In practice, its use involves backward and forward iterations until the desired outcome is achieved. The associated formal plans of strategies and tactics tend to be fixed for long periods of time. Again, in practice, the outcomes are reviewed by senior managers and interventions made to bring actual performance into line with planned goals and objectives. For example, decisions may be made to delay major investments and cut costs, and to get back to the planned strategy. Meanwhile, prudent strategists should continue to track the internal and external environments and review the underlying assumptions, mission, goals and objectives.

The benefits of formal rational planning are:

- Provides a discipline, making managers periodically look ahead.
- Provide staff with authoritative statements about goals, objectives, strategic issues and resource allocation priority. This will improve motivation levels and encourage goal-congruent behaviour.

- Gives bases for evaluating and integrating short-term plans.
- Creates a psychological backdrop and information framework for the future against which managers can take short-term decisions and help to implement strategic changes.
- Empirical evidence suggests that strategic planning might give some benefit.

There are also problems associated with rational models:

- Setting objectives often descends into the formulation of empty platitudes and irrational desires that offer little positive and realistic direction for managers. Contradictory objectives are implied by the organisation's long-term strategy and the conflicting interests of stakeholders. Shareholders may seek maximum short-term profits that necessitate downsizing and restructuring.
- Forecasting the future external environment is difficult; indeed, a common view is that it cannot be forecast with any usable accuracy.
- Short-term pressure for acceptable results makes managers prone to changing long-term strategy frequently and spending their time on operational matters. Preparation of the organisation for the medium- to long-term is neglected.
- Rigidity: managers are held prisoner by the rigidity of planning processes, because plans have to be set out in detail long before the period to which they apply.
- If adherence to the strategy becomes all-important, it stifles flair, initiative and creativity.
- Cognitive limitations of managers: managers may find it difficult to collect and process the information needed in order to review and then select appropriate strategic options.
- The top-down nature of the rational planning process may lack input from lower-level staff.
- Changes in the environment may cause strategic drift due to the fixed nature of the plan.

Learning activity 2.4

Why might the use of the rational model in your organisation not result in innovative strategies? How could this result be avoided?

Feedback on page 27

Now attempt the following self-assessment question.

Self-assessment question 2.4

Identify five main strengths and weaknesses of the rational process. Justify your choices.

Feedback on page 27

2.5 Comparing the rational and emergent approaches

The emergent approach is an alternative to the rational approach. It is an informal, bottom-up and responsive way of working. It can be useful in rapidly changing environments but also may result in a lack of general focus and direction. Unlike the rational approach, where there is clear and logical planning, here strategies emerge through day-to-day operations and are implemented informally.

Learning activity 2.5

Evaluate the rational and emergent models for strategy development.

Feedback on page 27

Advantages of the emergent approach:

- Opportunities and threats can be dealt with when they arise.
- It is flexible, speedy and adaptable, without recourse to documented analysis and plans.
- It can encourage flexible, creative attitudes among managers.

Disadvantages of the emergent approach:

- It fails to provide a coordinating framework for the organisation as a whole. The organisation may become fragmented.
- It cannot guarantee that all threats and opportunities are identified.

Other organisational processes that might account for emergent strategy development include:

- Resource allocation routines: Individual managers, other than top managers, compete for scarce resources (for example, finance and specialist knowledge) by submitting proposals that contain financial yardsticks and benchmarks. Approval is given depending on the quality of fit with the organisation strategy.
- Cultural processes: The dominant values, beliefs and 'the way we do things around here' are powerful determinants of strategic decision making. Culture constrains what is seen as appropriate behaviour and activities and defines situations in terms of that which is familiar, whether appropriate or not.
- Organisational politics: Bargaining and negotiating among powerful internal and external interest groups, or stakeholders, often determines the content of strategy. Stakeholders try to position themselves such that their views prevail or they can control key resources.

2.6 Logical incrementalism and other approaches

Johnson, Scholes and Whittington (2007) define logical incrementalism as: 'the deliberate development of strategy by experimentation and learning from partial commitments.'

Quinn (1980) visualises logical incrementalism as a proactive process of evolution and emergence suited to uncertain or unknowable environments;

it moves strategy from broad concepts to specific commitments, making the latter concrete as late as possible to narrow the bands of uncertainty and the unknown.

This practical process is related to the rational process model and is quite top-down, but tends to be less formal. Senior managers work towards a picture of where they want to go, even before they can describe it. They move their people towards the goal, but will shift targets along the way, experimenting, learning, holding off irrevocable decisions until more information is available. Also, they get like-minded people around them and seek support for new ideas, and can progressively define an increasingly precise strategy. By the time the strategy begins to crystallise, pieces of it are already being implemented. This approach builds up a momentum and psychological commitment to the strategy, which cause it to flow toward flexible implementation.

Other related models:

*   Incrementalism: A proactive process where an organisation plans and implements strategy in a piecemeal way by using fine-tuning strategies which, although relatively small and incremental in nature, collectively represent considerable change to the organisation's strategic position over a long time. It avoids major errors and is likely to be acceptable because consultation, compromise and accommodation are built into the process.
*   'Free-wheeling opportunism': This process is reactive to threats and opportunities as and when they arise, judged on their individual merits and not within a rigid structure of an organisational level plan. It is widely used in small and medium-sized organisations, particularly those inclined to entrepreneurship.
*   Imposed strategy: This may occur as a result of a recession forcing action. In the public sector, the government may privatise state industries or impose legislation.

Learning activity 2.6

Discuss the implications of logical incrementalism for the design of organisation structure.

Feedback on page 27

Now attempt the following question.

Self-assessment question 2.5

Explain the circumstances in which you would recommend an organisation to adopt the logical incremental model.

Feedback on page 27

2.7 Strategic management in different organisational contexts

How strategies develop will be seen differently by different managers in different types of organisation. Senior managers tend to be concerned with mission, precise goals and objectives, detailed planning, analysis of the environment and evaluation of strategic options – strategy development tends towards being intended, logical and rational. Middle level managers tend to be concerned with cultural and political processes that influence selection of tactics and methods of implementation.

Different organisational contexts

Small businesses, with fewer than 50 employees, that offer a limited range of products or services to a single or small number of markets; geographic coverage is often limited. They are usually managed by the founder or owner/manager, perhaps with members of the family. Strategy development is greatly influenced by their values, expectation, limited levels of experience and knowledge, and available resources and competences. Development is likely to be simple in form. Strategic concerns are: making the business secure for the future, development of bases of competition, raising finance and, usually, growing the business on emerging opportunities. Some 60 per cent of small businesses fail within four years of start-up, despite the imposition of business planning processes by funding bodies. Often strategy is not in written form but resides in the mind of the owner/manager.

Manufacturing organisations that make physical products available to customers, in selected market places. Attractive products and associated customer support services are central to competitive strategy. Products are often seen as being similar. To differentiate between competing products intangible features such as brand, reputation for reliability and investment in new technologies and products are important. Such organisations can range from very small to very large in size and can have local to global geographic coverage.

Service organisations where there is no physical product, that provide, for example, car insurance, management consultancy, training and professional services. Customers often determine the attractiveness of the service by intangible features – such as, the attitude of staff, soundness of advice given and confidence in the organisation. Such organisations can range from very small to very large in size and have local to global geographic coverage.

Public sector organisations, for example, central government, regional government, local government, police authorities and national health authorities, that have near monopoly of provision to citizens. Funding is from direct and indirect taxation imposed on the citizens rather than paying customers. Political ideology, of elected central and local governments, provides the driving force for strategy development that provides a range of universal services. Missions, goals and objectives, for each service, are determined by the governmental providers of funds rather than the users of the services. Strategic objectives tend to be short to medium-term due to the time-limited tenure of office of elected officials. Arising from the political ideologies of ruling parties and the scarcity of funds, political bargaining, negotiation and compromise dominate what are dynamic and complex strategy developments. Governments, at national and local levels, are increasingly seeking 'better value' for expenditure and are using business philosophies and methods. Typically, a plethora of priorities and objectives are imposed on service areas.

Multinational/global organisations, likely to have diverse products or services produced and marketed in many countries. Structure and control may take the form of subsidiary companies or divisions that call for sophisticated and costly methods of coordination and control by the 'parent' company. Key issues include the management of diverse external environments, diverse product or service portfolios, prioritising allocation of scarce financial and human resources and the extent of centralised control required.

Voluntary and not-for-profit organisations, for example, charities, religious bodies, political bodies and private schools. Their underlying beliefs, values and ideologies, hence goals and objectives, are major determinants of strategy development. Generation of profit for disbursement to those involved is not allowed, by statute. Financial accounts are rigorously scrutinised by statutory bodies. However, generation of surpluses are permitted for later use. In the great majority of cases, providers of funds are unlikely to be direct beneficiaries of the services provided. Sources of funds include street collections, grants, endowments and media appeals. Much of their operation depends on voluntary workers, though a number of paid employees may be required to organise activities and represent the organisations. Strategic issues include sources of funding, in a fiercely competitive environment, political lobbying, the need for centralised decision making and control.

Learning activity 2.7

Identify those elements and subelements of the PCA model that apply to all organisational contexts. Justify your selection.

Feedback on page 27

Now attempt the following question.

Self-assessment question 2.6

Prepare an organisational context for your organisation or an organisation with which you are familiar.

Feedback on page 28

Revision question

Now try the revision question for this session on page 257.

2

Summary

This session examined the nature of process models and the key processes for the *intended (or deliberate)* and *incremental* approaches to strategy development. It was shown that they are not used in independent or mutually exclusive ways, but in different combinations suited to situations and contexts that change over time. The position. choice and action (PCA), rational planning and logical incremental models and their suitability for a range of organisation contexts were discussed.

Suggested further reading

You could read the relevant sections of De Witt and Meyer (1999).

Feedback on learning activities and self-assessment questions

Feedback on learning activity 2.1

Test it for suitability of process, content and context. Is it easy to understand and comply with? Is it descriptive and/or in the form of a flow chart? To what extent is it computer-aided? Does it achieve what is intended? If you have identified possible improvements, justify them.

Feedback on self-assessment question 2.1

Process models attempt to standardise activities in the interest of efficiency and consistency across organisations. They answer the questions: how, who, when, what and where in organisational activities. In application, they have powers to describe, explain, predict, prescribe and control activities.

Feedback on learning activity 2.2

Use the three major elements of the PCA model as a structure for your answer. Don't forget to explain that the components aren't a logical series of tasks, but rather a complex collection of interrelated components.

Feedback on self-assessment question 2.2

See Johnson, Scholes and Whittington (2007) for the answer. It is worthwhile trying the question several times, over time, because of its great importance and to increase your familiarity with management terminology. Much of the unit content is based on the PCA model.

Feedback on learning activity 2.3

Responses to the challenges are dependent on the current and likely future situations of your organisation and department. You may assess the likely impact on performance and preparedness for, perhaps, an uncertain future.

Feedback on self-assessment question 2.3

Specific actions depend on the particular circumstances, but could include:

- Strategic drift: A range of cost and investment reduction actions, coupled with a vigorous, autocratic leadership style.
- Learning organisation: Open and frank reflection and discussions on good and bad experiences such that they inform future decisions and behaviour. Managers take on roles as tutors and providers of support and encouragement.
- Uncertain, complex environments: Use of small, progressive experiments, coupled with more political and cultural routines.
- Process and analytical tools: The process in use may be unsuitable for the external environment; better strategic thinking or development of a strategic plan may be needed.

Feedback on learning activity 2.4

Consider the attempted suppression of intuition, imagination and judgement, management style and organisation culture.

Feedback on self-assessment question 2.4

Your answer should be based on the benefits and problems listed in section 2.3.

Feedback on learning activity 2.5

Here it is important not to just compare and contrast the different models but also to look at the pros and cons of each to develop a full evaluation.

Feedback on learning activity 2.6

Strategy development and organisation structure need to be consistent with each other – a concept of strategic fit. As the strategy emerges, procedures, content of jobs and formal and informal structures must be simultaneously and continuously adapted and coupled with learning, political and cultural processes. They need to be open and fluid to facilitate the incremental movements. It may be necessary to let the structure emerge as the strategy emerges over time. In parallel, attention must be given to recruitment and training, reward systems and information systems and processes.

Feedback on self-assessment question 2.5

Circumstances might include: uncertainties about the external environment, for example possible deterioration of the economic climate; incomplete knowledge, where new technology is slowly evolving; transformational change, where significant political, cultural and learning processes are involved, and where limited planning and financial resources are available.

Feedback on learning activity 2.7

You are likely to find that the position and action elements and their subelements are common to all contexts but that some of the choice

2

subelements are not applicable. These are comments on organisation structure and size, and product/service and geographic diversity.

Feedback on self-assessment question 2.6

The descriptions of organisational contexts in section 2.7, coupled with the contents of the PCA model, should inform your answer.

Importance of position to corporate strategy

Introduction

In this session we look at the external and internal environments of an organisation, and how they affect the strategy process. All organisations are 'open systems' and, as such, must adapt to their changing environment or accept the consequences. We also look at the concept of 'stakeholders', and whether we should modify our plans to take into account their views. This leads us to the point where we can carry out a thorough strategic analysis of our organisation.

Managing an organisation while ignoring the outside world is like driving a car while wearing a blindfold. I think you can work out the rest for yourself...

Session learning objectives

After completing this session you should be able to:

3.1 Analyse the external environment using appropriate techniques.
3.2 Identify key features of supply chains and value chains.
3.3 Identify the key resources of your organisation.
3.4 Assess the role and importance of internal and external stakeholders.
3.5 Formulate an overall strategic analysis of your organisation.

Unit content coverage

This study session covers the following topics from the official CIPS unit content document:

Statement of practice

- Analyse the concept of strategy and the process of developing corporate strategy.

Learning objective

1.3 Conduct a strategic analysis of the supply chain.
 - Techniques for analysing the external environment: PESTLE analysis, Porter's Five Forces analysis
 - Techniques for analysing the internal environment: SWOT analysis, resource audit, skills audit, knowledge audit, portfolio analysis
 - Stakeholder mapping (internal and external)

Resources

Access to Johnson, Scholes and Whittington (2007) chapters 2–4 and cases is required for use throughout this session.

3

Timing

You should set aside about 7 hours to read and complete this session, including learning activities, self-assessment questions, the suggested further reading (if any) and the revision question.

3.1   The external environment

Why is it so important to begin our strategic analysis by looking at the business environment? What is it about the business environment that makes it such a key driver of the strategy process?

For many years, strategic planners in many large organisations believed that a 'rational' approach to strategy was appropriate, as the environments of their organisations changed only slowly. They therefore built their strategic plans on long-term views of the environment and steady changes in the organisation's operations.

In a situation where environments are relatively simple and static, a rational approach may well remain appropriate, as a key role of strategy is to ensure that the organisation adapts at the same pace as the environment. However, there are very few relatively simple and static environments left in business. Even previously 'safe' organisations, such as those in the public sector, now have dynamic and complex environments. They are subject to a barrage of new legislation, and may even be privatised, or become merger or takeover targets.

As we will see later, opportunities and threats to the organisation normally originate in the environment. If we agree that the business environment of most organisations is complex and dynamic, and that a key role of strategy is to ensure that the organisation achieves 'a good fit' with its environment, then our strategic planning process must focus on understanding, and adapting to, the changing environment. We might even try to predict changes in our environment, so we can be the first to exploit such changes to our advantage.

Figure 3.1: The business environment

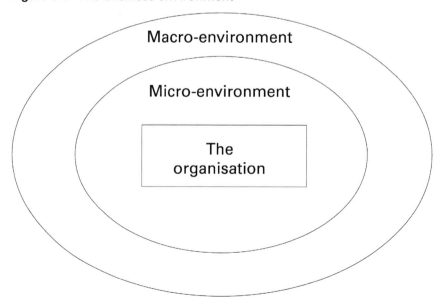

Business environments are often seen as multi-layered (figure 3.1) and planners often differentiate between two of these layers:

- The 'global', 'general', or *macro*-environment, consisting of very general factors that affect many different industries.
- The 'local', 'task' or *micro*-environment, consisting of an organisation's industry or sector.

Different tools are available to analyse these two different layers, and we are going to concentrate on two: *PESTLE* analysis for the macro-environment, and the *Five Forces* model for the micro-environment.

PESTLE analysis categorises environmental variables under six headings: political, economic, social, technological, legal and environmental. Examples of factors that might be relevant to an organisation are as follows:

- *Political*: taxation policy, political stability, grants or subsidies.
- *Economic*: disposable income levels, economic growth, interest rates.
- *Social*: buying behaviour, fashion, demographics.
- *Technological*: new production techniques, the internet, spending on research.
- *Legal*: employment, competition or product safety law.
- *Environmental*: waste, energy supply, 'green' pressure groups.

Although PESTLE analysis is commonly used, it has its drawbacks. Many of the factors that affect organisations transcend the rigid 'six box' framework of PESTLE. If you consider, for example, the growth of the internet, it clearly began as a technological change. However, the consequences of this development soon became social (buying patterns), economic (the development of online banking and secure transactions), political or legal (the need for legislation to allow or prevent online trading). Thus, the environment may be better regarded as a series of themes that affect the organisation, with each theme impacting on one or more of the PESTLE categories.

Learning activity 3.1

Carry out a PESTLE (political, economic, social, technological, legal and environmental) analysis of your organisation.

Feedback on page 39

One specific aspect of the business environment that does not easily fit into one or other categories of the PESTLE model is *competition*. While many of the effects of competition are economic (such as reduced profits) it may affect the organisation in many other ways. A key tool for the analysis of competition within an industry or sector is the *Five Forces* model (Johnson, Scholes and Whittington, 2007: 80), developed by Professor Michael Porter of the Harvard Business School in the late 1970s.

Managers tend to be too blinkered in their view of competition, looking only at competitive rivalry (the 'middle' force in the model). Porter argues that competition is any activity in an industry that affects margins, so an organisation 'competes' with its customers and suppliers, as well as other organisations looking to 'steal' market share.

The model identifies five sources of competitive force acting on an organisation:

1 the threat of new entrants
2 the threat of substitutes
3 the bargaining power of buyers (or customers)
4 the bargaining power of suppliers
5 competitive rivalry.

Each of these forces is examined in more detail below.

The threat of new entrants

The threat of new entrants into an industry is that they will be determined to achieve a significant market share in a short period of time. This will necessarily require the entrant to steal customers from the incumbent organisations, normally by providing higher quality, or initiating a price war, or both. The level of the threat is, to a great extent, determined by the existence and effectiveness of barriers to entry, of which Porter identifies eight types:

- *Economies of scale*, that allow an established organisation to earn higher margins than a new entrant.
- *Upfront capital requirements*, such as plant and machinery, or advertising spend.
- *Control of supply or distribution channels*, such as retail networks or logistics firms.
- *Customer or supplier loyalty*, having formed good relationships throughout the supply chain.
- *Experience*, or other cost advantages, that do not depend on the scale of the organisation.
- A track record of *hostile reaction* to new entrants from the incumbent organisations.
- *Legislation* or government intervention, to prevent or deter entry.
- *Differentiation* of the products or services being provided by incumbent organisations, such that customer loyalty can be assured and switching is unlikely.

The threat of substitutes

The threat of substitutes is that they will render the products or services of an industry or sector completely obsolete. Substitutes may take a number of different forms:

- *Product-for-product* substitutes, such as margarine and butter, or CDs and records.

- *Need* substitutes, where the new product satisfies the same need as the old, but is very different in form, such as home computing replacing secretarial or printing services.
- *Generic* substitutes, where the alternative products compete for the same disposable income, such as cinema and books.

The bargaining power of buyers

Buyer power is likely to be high where some or all of the following are true:

- There is a concentration of buyers, or they are far less numerous than their suppliers.
- Buyers are large in comparison to their suppliers.
- They are buying a relatively unimportant input or component part.
- The cost of switching supplier is low.
- The product or service being bought is generic, rather than specialised.
- The buyer threatens backward integration, either by acquiring a supplier or by starting up business in direct competition.

The bargaining power of suppliers

Supplier power is likely to be high where some or all of the following are true:

- There is a concentration of suppliers, or they are far less numerous than their buyers.
- Suppliers are large in comparison to their buyers.
- They are selling a relatively important input or component part.
- The cost of switching supplier is high.
- The product or service being bought is specialised, rather than generic.
- The supplier threatens forward integration, either by acquiring a customer or by starting up business in direct competition.

Competitive rivalry

Rivals are organisations with similar products or services, which try to sell to the same customers. While competitive rivalry is better understood than the others, as it corresponds with the 'traditional' definition of competition, it is still important to consider in detail. The degree of competitive rivalry in an industry is affected by the following factors:

- The extent to which the rivals are of equal size or market share. If one or two rivals are very large, they will tend to dominate and there will be less rivalry.
- Industry growth rates may affect rivalry. Growing industries tend to suffer less rivalry, as rivals can grow without stealing customers from each other.
- High fixed costs tend to lead to a higher degree of rivalry, as rivals fight to remain viable.
- Where there are high exit barriers, an industry will tend to experience more rivalry as rivals are trapped in the industry.
- Where products or services are undifferentiated, there tends to be a high degree of rivalry as firms try to persuade customers to switch.

Self-assessment question 3.1

Draw a diagram of Porter's Five Forces model, and briefly explain its meaning.

Feedback on page 39

3.2 Supply chain and value chains

Supply chains are discussed in more detail in section 13.1. They are made up from the people, activities, information and resources that are involved in moving materials as they flow from their source to the end customer.

Value chains are discussed in more detail in section 17.5. They explore how activities performed by the organisation add or do not add value from the point of the customer. They are split into primary activities and secondary (or support) activities.

Learning activity 3.2

Consider the make up of the supply chain of your own organisation or an organisation with which you are familiar.

Feedback on page 39

Self-assessment question 3.2

Consider the value chain of a company with which you are familiar. How is it composed, and what do you see as its core competences?

Feedback on page 39

3.3 Unique resources and core competences

The resources of an organisation can be classified as either tangible or intangible:

- *Tangible* resources are physical assets of the organisation, such as materials or employees.
- *Intangible* resources are non-physical, such as knowledge or reputation.

Alternatively, resources can be classified into four categories:

- *Physical* resources, such as machines or buildings.
- *Financial* resources, such as cash.
- *Human* resources, such as employees and contractors.
- *Intellectual* resources, such as know-how and patents.

For these resources to become strategically significant, they need to be *unique resources*, access to which is not available to the organisation's rivals. They also need to underpin some aspect of the organisation's competitive advantage. Although it is possible for organisations to have resources that are, in themselves, sources of competitive advantage, this is more likely to be gained as a result of the way the organisation *uses* those resources.

A *competence* is an activity or process through which an organisation deploys or utilises its resources. It is, as mentioned earlier, something the organisation *does*, rather than something it *has*.

Strategic competences can be classified as follows:

- *Threshold* competence is the level of competence necessary for an organisation to compete and survive in a given industry and market. For example, an online bookseller must have a logistics system that allows books to be delivered as promised, to the customers who have bought them.
- A *core* competence is something the organisation does that underpins a source of competitive advantage. For example, if an online bookseller is able to deliver books a day or two earlier than its rivals, this represents a core competence.

It should be clear from these explanations that there is often a direct link between a unique resource and a core competence. For example, the online bookseller with the shorter delivery times might have that core competence as a result of unique human or technological resources in its logistics function.

A key tool for identifying core competences is Porter's Value Chain. This is covered by study session 17.

Learning activity 3.3

List, in order of importance, your organisation's core competences, and how they give you a competitive advantage.

Feedback on page 40

Now attempt the following question.

Self-assessment question 3.3

Write a memo to your manager outlining:

1   your organisation's key resources, and
2   resource areas in which the organisation is weak.

Feedback on page 40

3

3.4 Stakeholder analysis and stakeholder mapping

Stakeholders are those individuals or groups who depend on the organisation to fulfil their own goals and on whom, in turn, the organisation depends.

Learning activity 3.4

Think about your own organisation or one with which you are familiar. Identify the major internal and external stakeholders.

Feedback on page 40

Stakeholders fall into two categories, as follows:

- *External* stakeholders, such as shareholders, financial institutions, customers, suppliers, trades unions and the local community.
- *Internal* stakeholders, such as employees, managers and subcontractors.

Since the expectations of stakeholder groups differ, it is normal for conflict to exist between (as well as within) the various stakeholder groups. The organisation must understand the expectations of each stakeholder group in respect of each aspect of its strategy, and must decide whether to satisfy one or more stakeholder, compromise between them or ignore them.

While it is tempting to see strategy formulation as an exercise in compromise between stakeholders, this is far from the truth. The various stakeholders may expect to be treated as equals but, in reality, every organisation will rank its stakeholders into a hierarchy and favour some over the others. Part of the art of strategy formulation is to identify, for each strategic decision, the 'dominant coalition' of stakeholders. These are the individuals and groups who must be satisfied if that decision is to be successfully implemented.

The importance of stakeholders to the strategic decision-making process can be assessed by means of 'stakeholder mapping' (Johnson, Scholes and Whittington, 2007). This model assesses two variables for each stakeholder group:

- The extent of the stakeholder group's *interest* in the strategic decision. That is, the degree to which that decision impacts on the group.
- The amount of *power* that group has over the decision-making process. That is, the extent to which the group can bring their influence to bear on the decision makers or interfere with the implementation of the strategy.

These two variables are plotted on the axes of a 2×2 matrix, as shown in Johnson, Scholes and Whittington (2007), and each stakeholder put into the appropriate quadrant of the matrix. Each stakeholder is then classified as '+' if they are likely to support the decision, '-' if they are likely to oppose it, and '0' if they are likely to be indifferent. Depending on their position

3

in the matrix, four strategies are available to the organisation with regard to each stakeholder:

- *Key players.* These are the really important stakeholders in respect of this decision. Either we have to make the decision the way they want us to, or we have to work really hard to get them to buy into our decision. If these stakeholders are thought to support our decision, we can use them to influence other stakeholder groups.
- *Keep satisfied.* These are important stakeholders and we need to persuade them to accept our decision, if they are likely to oppose it.
- *Keep informed.* We need to ensure that these stakeholders are kept up to date about progress in the decision and implementation of the strategy.
- *Minimal effort.* These stakeholders are not very important in the context of this strategy.

While stakeholder mapping can be a useful aid to strategic decision making, it has some shortcomings:

- Stakeholder groups usually consist of a number of subgroups or individuals, each with their own expectations. It can therefore be the case that one stakeholder group appears in more than one quadrant of the stakeholder map.
- Stakeholder expectations change over time, or in response to the views of other stakeholders, so a stakeholder may 'move round' the matrix.
- Some stakeholder groups are represented by powerful individuals, such as union leaders or a company chief executive. Their position on the matrix may change if a different individual is appointed to the lead role.
- Stakeholders adopt a different position depending on the strategic decision being made. While conducting a 'generic' stakeholder analysis may be of some value, the exercise should really be conducted for each major strategic decision.

Self-assessment question 3.4

Explain what is meant by a stakeholder map, and how an organisation might develop one.

Feedback on page 40

3.5 SWOT analysis

The purpose of analysing the external environment of an organisation is so that we can identify, or even predict, changes in that environment that are likely to affect the way we determine the strategy of the organisation. We tend to classify such changes as either opportunities or threats:

- An *opportunity* is a situation or change in the external environment that the organisation could exploit to its advantage.
- A *threat* is a situation or change in the external environment of an organisation that the organisation should defend itself against.

3

Whether an environmental factor is classified as an opportunity or a threat really depends on the perception of those doing the analysis. Often the same factor presents both an opportunity and a threat: for example, a customer experiencing reduced levels of profitability might present an opportunity for potential acquisition and a threat in terms of a risk of reduced prices.

In order to fully appreciate the potential impact of external opportunities and threats, we have to look at the ability of the organisation to deal with them. The process of analysing the internal factors affecting an organisation's strategy is sometimes referred to as 'position analysis' or 'internal environment analysis'. We looked at two specific aspects of such analysis earlier in this session: core competences and key resources. We should now recognise that organisations have strengths and weaknesses that will impact on their ability to deal with opportunities and threats:

- A *strength* is something that an organisation does well, or a resource that is not available to its rivals.
- A *weakness* is something that an organisation does badly, or does not do, or a resource to which it does not have access.

SWOT analysis, sometimes known as corporate appraisal, looks at the strengths, weaknesses, opportunities and threats of an organisation. The results of SWOT analysis are often shown in a cruciform (cross-shaped) diagram, as shown in figure 3.2. This allows the relationships between the factors to be seen.

Figure 3.2: SWOT analysis

Strengths	Weaknesses
Opportunities	Threats

Learning activity 3.5

Carry out a SWOT analysis of your organisation.

Feedback on page 41

Now attempt the following question.

Self-assessment question 3.5

Produce an action plan, based on your SWOT analysis, summarising the key issues, in order of importance, that need to be addressed in your organisation.

Feedback on page 41

Revision question

Now try the revision question for this session on page 257.

Summary

This session has looked at the major strategic analysis tasks of the planning process: environment, position and stakeholder analyses. It has also introduced the concept of SWOT analysis (or corporate appraisal).

Suggested further reading

If you look at a few lengthy articles in the business section of a decent daily newspaper, it should be possible to perform a stakeholder or PESTLE analysis for a real organisation.

Feedback on learning activities and self-assessment questions

Feedback on learning activity 3.1

Although this should have been a straightforward activity, you may have found some environmental factors that did not fit neatly into one or other category. Do not be afraid to duplicate points in different areas of a PESTLE analysis, or to cross-reference points.

Feedback on self-assessment question 3.1

Your answer should be based on the diagram in Johnson, Scholes and Whittington (2007), and the explanation in section 3.1.

Feedback on learning activity 3.2

Remember to extend your thinking beyond the internal parts to also consider suppliers and customers.

Feedback on self-assessment question 3.2

You need to be able to identify the value chain and core competence areas and explain why and how they might help develop competitive advantage. Also think about what areas you might consider outsourcing and why.

3

Feedback on learning activity 3.3

If you work in a large or famous organisation, it might be lucky enough to have a long list of core competences. If, however, you work for a much smaller organisation it might have only one or two. If you failed to identify any core competences in your organisation, either you need to try harder or it's time to look for a new job!

Feedback on self-assessment question 3.3

The easiest way to do the first part of this task is to work backwards from the core competences in order to identify the resources supporting them. The second part of the task is more difficult, but could simply be all areas in which the organisation fails to meet threshold competence levels.

Feedback on learning activity 3.4

Don't just use the lists given in section 3.4. Think whether your organisation has any stakeholders that are different from 'the norm'.

Feedback on self-assessment question 3.4

Stakeholder mapping is a model used to assess the importance of stakeholders to the strategic decision-making process. This model assesses two variables for each stakeholder group:

- The extent of the stakeholder group's *interest* in the strategic decision. That is, the degree to which that decision impacts on the group.
- The amount of *power* that group has over the decision-making process. That is, the extent to which the group can bring their influence to bear on the decision makers or interfere with the implementation of the strategy.

These two variables are plotted on the axes of a 2×2 matrix and each stakeholder put into the appropriate quadrant of the matrix. Each stakeholder is then classified as '+' if they are likely to support the decision, '-' if they are likely to oppose it, and '0' if they are likely to be indifferent. Depending on their position in the matrix, four strategies are available to the organisation with regard to each stakeholder:

- *Key players.* These are the really important stakeholders in respect of this decision. Either we have to make the decision the way they want us to, or we have to work really hard to get them to buy into our decision. If these stakeholders are thought to support our decision, we can use them to influence other stakeholder groups.
- *Keep satisfied.* These are important stakeholders and we need to persuade them to accept our decision, if they are likely to oppose it.
- *Keep informed.* We need to ensure that these stakeholders are kept up to date about progress in the decision and implementation of the strategy.
- *Minimal effort.* These stakeholders are not very important in the context of this strategy.

Feedback on learning activity 3.5

Carrying out a SWOT analysis is not difficult, but making it really valuable to the strategy process is. The problem with SWOT is that the points on it tend to be superficial, and really need a great deal of further analysis before their strategic consequences can be seen. Also, SWOT simply summarises facts and opinions. To really add value to the strategy process, we need to take the SWOT analysis and look at how the strengths and weaknesses match up with the opportunities and threats. Only by doing this can we produce a prioritised action plan to be covered by our strategy.

Feedback on self-assessment question 3.5

The better your SWOT analysis, the better your action plan. Notice how the actions can be linked back to a combination of one or more strength or weaknesses with one or more opportunities or threats.

3

Importance of structures, cultures, and power to the corporate strategy

Introduction

One of the big debates in strategic planning is whether the structure and culture of an organisation are determinants of its strategy, or implementation tools. In this session we look at the relationship between strategy and structure, power and culture.

A strategy is just 'words on a page'. Unless you change the way the organisation is, what it does, or how it does it, all you'll be left with are those words (and a vague feeling that strategy formulation was a bit of a waste of time).

Session learning objectives

After completing this session you should be able to:

4.1 Identify various organisational structures.
4.2 Analyse an organisation's structural configuration.
4.3 Describe the nature, sources and indicators of power in organisations.
4.4 Explain the nature and components of organisational culture.
4.5 Analyse the culture of an organisation.
4.6 Explain the role and influence of stakeholders.
4.7 Explain the importance of ethics and corporate social responsibility.

Unit content coverage

This study session covers the following topics from the official CIPS unit content document:

Statement of practice

- Analyse the concept of strategy and the process of developing corporate strategy.

Learning objective

1.4 Assess the importance of organisational structures, cultures, and power to the development and implementation of corporate strategy.
  - Characteristics of organisational structures: simple, functional, matrix, network, machine and professional bureaucracy
  - Centralisation and decentralisation
  - Nature of power in organisations: overt, covert and structural
  - Sources and indicators of power in organisations
  - Organisational culture and the cultural web
  - The role and influence of stakeholders
  - The importance of ethics and corporate social responsibility

Resources

Access to Johnson, Scholes and Whittington (2007) chapters 4 and 12 is required for use throughout this session.

Timing

You should set aside about 6–7 hours to read and complete this session, including learning activities, self-assessment questions, the suggested further reading (if any) and the revision question.

4.1 Organisational structure

The structure of an organisation refers to the way it is divided into divisions, departments or functions. We often record the structure of organisations by means of an organisation chart. The most common basic structures are as follows:

- entrepreneurial or 'small firm'
- functional
- divisional
- matrix.

Each of these is described in detail below. There are also other complex structures, such as project or multinational organisations, and these are summarised below.

Figure 4.1: Entrepreneurial, or 'small firm' structure

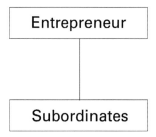

An *entrepreneurial*, or small firm, structure is very informal (see figure 4.1) and the organisation often does not have an organisation chart. The 'boss' simply asks or tells subordinates what to do, and they do it. Entrepreneurial organisations also tend to have very few formal procedures, no written job descriptions, and no rigid hierarchy.

As small firms grow, they often find that they need to formalise their structure. The most logical first formal structure, for most growing organisations, is a *functional* structure (see figure 4.2).

Figure 4.2: Functional structure

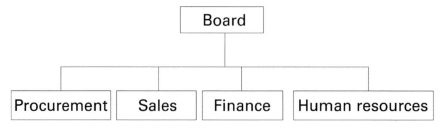

Functional structures organise resources into departments according to the functions that they perform. For example, all the staff and assets that are involved with marketing are allocated to the marketing function, and so on. Each department has a functional head, and those at a senior level often make up the board of directors.

Learning activity 4.1

Ask someone who has worked for your organisation for a long time to explain how its structure has changed. See if you can find any evidence of the origins of the organisation, and its structure in the early years of its existence.

Feedback on page 55

As an organisation increases in complexity, it often finds that its business has developed several distinctive 'parts'. These parts might be, for example, different product groupings, different customer segments, or different geographical regions. In these circumstances, many organisations develop a *divisional* structure (see figure 4.3), where the divisions are whatever is appropriate to the nature of the business (for example, regions or product groups).

Figure 4.3: Divisional structure

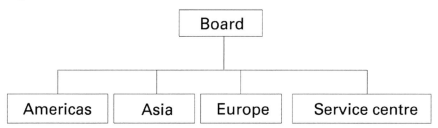

Divisional structures often split the 'primary' functions of business (logistics, production, sales) between the divisions, but retain the 'support' functions (marketing, finance, human resources, research and development) in a central service centre.

Table 4.1 Analysis of organisation structures

	Small firm	Functional	Divisional
Controllability	**	***	*
Flexibility	***	*	**
Knowledge sharing	**	***	*
Efficiency	***	**	*
Manager motivation	*	**	***
Service levels	**	*	***

If we analyse the strengths and weaknesses of these three 'basic' organisation structures (see table 4.1) we see that they are each applicable in very different situations. This has led to the development of a number of specialised or complex structures, which attempt to combine the strengths of two or more of the basic structures.

Figure 4.4: Matrix structure

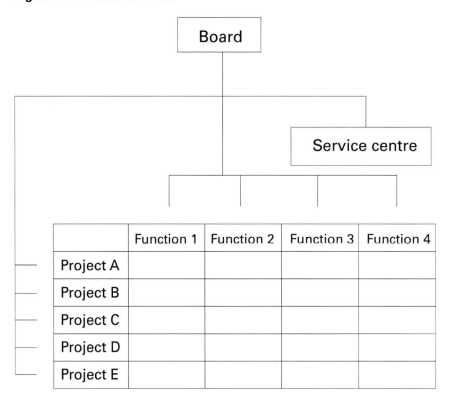

The most common of these 'specialised' forms is the *matrix* structure (see figure 4.4), which attempts to combine the controllability and knowledge sharing of the functional structure, with the flexibility and service levels of the divisional form. It does this by organising all of the organisation's resources into functional departments, so as to exploit the control and knowledge-sharing strengths of this structure. A number of project divisions are then established, each with the responsibility for a product group, customer group, region or major project. This allows the divisional heads to be 'close to the customer' and to be responsible for service levels and product delivery – very motivational. The divisions 'buy' their resources from the appropriate functions and are recharged with their cost. This allows the organisation to have the optimal level of resources, which can be reallocated from division to division in line with their needs.

As was the case with divisional structures, it is common in a matrix organisation for the shared service functions (often finance, human resources and research and development) to remain as part of a service centre, rather than being made part of the matrix.

If we assess the matrix structure using the criteria from table 4.1 it scores highly on all aspects except controllability. The reason for this is that, as all the resources effectively have two reporting lines, there is a tendency for functional heads to blame divisional managers for any problems, and vice versa.

While many organisations choose one or other of these simple organisation structures, larger organisations often need to adopt a more complex form in order to fit the nature of their business. In large organisations it is common to see *mixed* structures, with some parts being organised functionally, others divisionally, and maybe even the occasional matrix. This is perfectly acceptable, as long as each different structure is chosen to fit the local needs of that part of the organisation. Other organisations adopt a very fluid, team- or project-based structure, where new parts of the organisation are formed in accordance with business needs, and others are closed down when no longer needed.

In order to select the most appropriate structure for the organisation, Goold and Campbell (2002) devised a series of nine structural design tests, as shown below:

1   *The market advantage test.* This is a basic test of 'fit' with the market strategy. For example, if implementation of the strategy requires close communication between two parts of the organisation, they should be placed in the same unit.

2   *The parenting advantage test.* The structure chosen should suit the role being taken by the corporate centre. For example, if the corporate centre decides that it wishes to increase innovation, the structure chosen should encourage entrepreneurism.

3   *The people test.* The design chosen must fit with the human resources available to staff it. For example, there must be sufficient managers (with the required skills) to cover the number of divisions or functions in the structure.

4   *The feasibility test.* The structure must fit with constraints such as legislation and stakeholder needs. For example, accounting firms tend to separate audit and consultancy functions, in the wake of such corporate scandals as Enron.

5   *The specialised cultures test.* Whatever structure is chosen must keep any specialised cultures, such as that which often exists between design and production, intact.

6   *The difficult links test.* This test checks whether other aspects such as policy or procedure compensate for any links that are likely to be strained by the chosen structure. For example, if operating divisions are separated from the financial control function by long distances or time zones, does the organisation have a sophisticated information system to compensate?

7   *The redundant hierarchy test.* Any structure should not have, for example, too many layers of management.

8   *The accountability test.* There should be clear reporting paths through the organisation. For example, matrix structures are often criticised for failing this test.

9   *The flexibility test.* To what extent will it be possible to adapt the structure to any changes in strategy? For example, divisions should be defined in such a way as to make it clear how far managers are allowed to 'expand' their domains through innovation.

Self-assessment question 4.1

Produce a report to the director of logistics of a divisionalised organisation, which evaluates the advantages and disadvantages of all procurement staff

(continued on next page)

4.2 Structural configurations

Henry Mintzberg (1979) suggested that the structure of organisations was related to the relationships and processes within them. He suggested that a simple diagram of the organisation's hierarchy could not convey the way the organisation worked, and proposed six structural configurations, each suitable for a different mix of organisational characteristics:

- *The simple form.* This may have no formal structure, and is similar to the entrepreneurial structure discussed in section 4.1. This is suitable for small, entrepreneurial organisations.
- *The machine bureaucracy.* This is typically structured around functional departments, but tends towards centralisation. Strict planning systems lead to a high degree of standardisation. This is suitable for organisations providing repetitive, cost-focused products or services.
- *The professional bureaucracy.* This is still bureaucratic in that it has standardised procedures, but is less centralised than the machine bureaucracy. Cultural controls maintain consistency, while enough flexibility exists to allow services or products to be tailored to customer needs. This structure is suitable when a service or product requires limited modification.
- *The divisionalised form.* Divisions are normally controlled through target setting, and market processes can be used to regulate the relationship between divisions that operate as customer and supplier. This form is most suitable to large, complex organisations.
- *The 'adhocracy'.* This form of organisation tends to use project structures, and many relationships exist within and outside the organisation. Adhocracies are particularly good at flexibility and responsiveness, and rely on cultural factors to maintain control. This form is often found in the creative area of consultancy organisations.
- *The missionary.* These organisations often lack any formal structure and few control systems. They operate almost entirely through cultural controls and are common in the voluntary and charitable sectors.

Although few organisations fit neatly into one of these forms, they are useful to help us decide what combination of structure (see section 4.1) and culture (see section 4.5) might be appropriate.

Johnson, Scholes and Whittington (2007) summarise the characteristics and situations of the six configurations.

So, does structure follow strategy? It's fairly obvious that, in an ideal world, the structure of an organisation should be used as an implementation tool for its strategy. However, not all strategies are radical or 'big' enough to justify major changes to the organisation's structure. In many cases, the current structure of an organisation just makes it easier or more difficult to implement particular strategies, so structure can sometimes act as a constraint on the strategies available to the organisation.

4

Self-assessment question 4.2

What are the six structural configurations proposed by Mintzberg?

Feedback on page 55

4.3 Power in organisations

We often refer to people as powerful without really knowing exactly what we mean. Furthermore, we think that people have power, but we're often not sure where they get it from or why they have it. This section will address these questions.

Power is the ability of an individual or group to exert an influence on others, to persuade them into following a particular course of action. Power comes from a number of sources, as we will see, and only some of them are anything to do with the individual's position in the organisation.

A concept that is closely related to power is authority. Unlike power, this is a right, rather than an ability. *Authority* is the right, possessed as a result of a person's status in the organisation, to obedience from subordinates.

Learning activity 4.3

Look around your organisation, or one with which you are familiar. Can you find examples of individuals with the following?

- power but no authority
- authority but no power.

Feedback on page 55

According to French and Raven (1959), there are five sources of power:

1   *Legitimate power* – the authority that comes with the position a person holds, sometimes called position power.

2   *Reward power* – based on ability to reward a follower for compliance, or control over the remuneration or bonus system.
3   *Coercive power* – the power to punish (the opposite of reward power).
4   *Expert power* – possessing special knowledge or skill that is highly valued and in short supply. People with expert power can use their knowledge as a bargaining tool and are often owed favours.
5   *Referent power* – based on desire of followers to identify with, and be accepted by, the individual. They will tend to emulate that person and to be very compliant.

Legitimate, reward, and coercive power generally operate in conjunction with a prescribed position and are therefore closely related to authority. However, fear of rejection can operate interpersonally without formal authority. Expert and referent power, however, are personal qualities which are generally possessed as a result of the individual's personality, rather than their position.

Johnson, Scholes and Whittington (2007) suggest a slightly different set of sources of power. They suggest a range of sources for both internal and external stakeholders. This framework is very useful when doing a stakeholder mapping exercise (see section 3.3). They also suggest that there are a number of indicators of power:

- The status of the individual or group.
- The claim on resources (such as the size of their budget).
- The representation of the individual or group in powerful positions.
- Symbols of power, such as a large office or a powerful-sounding title.

Self-assessment question 4.3

What are the five sources of power suggested by French and Raven?

Feedback on page 55

4.4   Organisational culture

Schein (1997) defines *organisational culture* as the 'basic assumptions and beliefs that are shared by members of an organisation'. Thus, the culture of the organisation represents the informal aspects of the organisation, while its structure, policies and procedures represent its formal aspects.

The culture of organisations is important for a number of reasons:

- It is often an ability to 'fit in' with the corporate culture that differentiates successful employees from those that are less successful.
- In situations where the structure, strategy or policy of an organisation conflicts with its culture, the culture often overrides the formal aspects. Employees will behave as they have always done, rather than accept the new formal direction.

- In implementing change, changing the culture of the organisation will always be more difficult than changing the formal aspects of structure. Successfully changing the culture is often a critical success factor for change implementation.

Although we often talk of the organisational culture as if it is a single, easily identified concept, the different parts of an organisation may have completely different cultures. Individual departments, functions or work teams may have developed their own unique cultures which have become deeply embedded. This may lead to conflict between different parts of the organisation and may also make the implementation of change much more complex.

4

Learning activity 4.4

Identify instances where the culture of your organisation overrides the formal aspects of its structure (such as hierarchy, policy or strategy).

Feedback on page 56

According to Johnson, Scholes and Whittington (2007), the *paradigm* is at the core of an organisation's culture. The paradigm is the set of assumptions held in common and taken for granted in an organisation. For an organisation to function effectively there has to be such a set of assumptions. The cultural web (Johnson, and Whittington, 2007) is a diagrammatic representation of these assumptions and it consists of seven components, as follows:

- The *routines and rituals* of an organisation are those practices that make up the detail of the organisation's behaviour patterns. They are not just 'what' the organisation does, but 'how' they do those things – for example; recruitment procedures or Friday lunchtime drinks in the pub.
- *Symbols* include logos and trademarks, as well as the language and terminology used within the organisation. There might be other symbols, such as the use of job titles rather than names in correspondence.
- *Power structures* (see section 4.3) can also influence culture. The powerful individuals are often able to impose their own personal cultures on the organisation.
- The *control systems* of the organisation are such things as target setting, measurement and reward. Does the organisation, for example, rely on its IT system to monitor performance, or is the appraisal process more important?
- The *organisational structure* is not part of the culture in itself, but instead reflects what is important to the organisation. Which functions are represented on the main board? Are all the directors perceived to be equal, or are there a 'chosen few'?
- The *stories* told in an organisation, about its formation, history or crises, can provide a clear insight into its culture. Are the stories about particular heroes from the organisation's past? Or are they about solving problems in a certain way?

- The *paradigm* of the organisation summarises its core beliefs and values. It reinforces the other elements. For example, is the whole organisation driven by a desire not to disappoint customers? Or perhaps the organisation focuses on quality?

4

Self-assessment question 4.4

Identify the components of the cultural web.

Feedback on page 56

4.5 Classifying corporate cultures

Harrison (1992) suggested that corporate cultures could be classified into one of four categories:

- *Role* cultures put the emphasis on the job done by the individual, rather than on the individual themselves. They have a rigid and clearly defined hierarchy and can tend towards bureaucracy.
- *Task* cultures tend to associate individuals to the task they perform or the product or project they work on. There is a lot of collaborative working and very little bureaucracy.
- *Power* cultures tend to be dominated by a single, charismatic individual. All decisions are taken by reference to that individual and there is little delegation.
- *Person* cultures allow individuals to behave as such and recognise that those individuals are key to success. Such organisations tend to contain a large number of charismatic staff, each with their own personal suborganisation.

Learning activity 4.5

Look around your own industry and try to identify individual organisations with the different cultures described in the above classification.

Feedback on page 56

A number of research studies have shown that cultures differ between countries, and even regions within countries. Such differences might include the following:

- Attitudes to work and the balance between working and family life.
- Attitudes to authority and prevailing management styles.
- Attitudes to equality and career potential for males and females.
- Working hours and attendance levels.
- The degree of bureaucracy that is seen as normal or desirable.

- Whether decisions are rational and analytical or instinctive and 'gut feel'.

Self-assessment question 4.5

What type of culture (according to Harrison) is most likely to prevail in the following organisations?

1   an advertising agency
2   a hospital
3   a taxi firm.

Feedback on page 56

4.6   The role and influence of stakeholders

There are many different types of internal and external stakeholders who can play very different roles. Some are selling/providing products or services; others will be inside communities who are receiving/using products or services. There may be specialists or people with local knowledge. Some may have particular roles, such as the government. If these stakeholders are considered and involved in business they can potentially provide useful insight. On the other hand, they can also block progress if not managed appropriately.

Stakeholders can bring with them knowledge and understanding of particular services and processes and their delivery and impact. This can help shape and maximise future strategies. Therefore, it means stakeholders can exert a great deal of influence. It is important to identify who stakeholders are through careful use of tools such as those identified in section 3.3.

Learning activity 4.6

Consider the role and influence of stakeholders in your own organisation.

Feedback on page 56

Self-assessment question 4.6

Compare and contrast the role and influence of stakeholders in the private and public sectors.

Feedback on page 56

4

4.7 The importance of ethics and corporate social responsibility

In the public sector there is a need to behave 'appropriately' as custodians of the government's and tax payers' money. This requires transparency and accountability in actions and behaviours. There is also a real drive for corporate social responsibility (CSR) and sustainability. This means, for example, purchasing wood from suppliers that use sustainable methods.

In the private sector consumer awareness is helping to drive many changes in practice. Firms need to be active in making sure they source their products appropriately and that they do not use child labour and processes that impact upon the environment. This awareness has also been seen as an opportunity by some to develop differentiation by focusing on the ethical and environmental angle.

Legislation drives both sectors, and global initiatives also encourage countries to take steps to help preserve the environment. The consequences of not taking steps towards CSR policies can be put bluntly as loss of business and credibility, and potential harm to individuals and the environment. See section 18.4 for more content.

Learning activity 4.7

Consider the importance of ethics and corporate social responsibility in business today and the implications of not adopting these policies.

Feedback on page 57

Self-assessment question 4.7

Identify the drivers for businesses increasingly adopting ethical and corporate social responsibility policies.

Feedback on page 57

Revision question

Now try the revision question for this session on page 257.

Summary

We have seen how structure, power and culture should all be implementation tools for strategy, but may instead be constraints on strategy selection. You should analyse the structure and culture of a range of organisations, in order to prepare yourself for the examination.

Suggested further reading

Look at the advertising or recruitment materials of a range of organisations.

Feedback on learning activities and self-assessment questions

Feedback on learning activity 4.1

Although it is often difficult to find documentary records relating to the early history of organisations, there is sometimes an 'elder statesman' working within the organisation who remembers such days. Not all organisations start life as small, entrepreneurial structures. Many are formed as a result of mergers between other, mature organisations. Others start life as the division of a much larger organisation, and are de-merged.

Feedback on self-assessment question 4.1

This is an example of how Goold and Campbell's tests are also in constant tension with one another. In this case, the arguments for procurement staff being centralised will often be based on the 'specialised cultures' or 'people' tests, whereas the arguments for separating procurement staff over the divisions might include the 'market advantage' test.

Feedback on learning activity 4.2

You probably found that your own organisation did not fit neatly into one of Mintzberg's configurations. This is normal, but you should have found that your organisation bore some similarity to one or two. Is your organisation in the sort of business for which Mintzberg suggested that one (or more) particular configuration might be appropriate? Look at other organisations in your industry. Do they all tend to have the same configuration?

Feedback on self-assessment question 4.2

- the simple form
- the machine bureaucracy
- the professional bureaucracy
- the divisionalised form
- the 'adhocracy'
- the missionary.

Feedback on learning activity 4.3

Charismatic individuals often have power without authority. They are able to persuade people through force of personality. Any weak manager may have authority without power.

Feedback on self-assessment question 4.3

1 legitimate power
2 reward power

4

3   coercive power
4   expert power
5   referent power.

Feedback on learning activity 4.4

This is actually a very common phenomenon in business. In many situations, for example, personal relationships can be used to 'sidestep' the formal hierarchy and influence the decision-making process.

Feedback on self-assessment question 4.4

The cultural web consists of seven components, as follows:

- routines and rituals
- symbols
- power structures
- control systems
- organisational structure
- stories
- paradigm.

Feedback on learning activity 4.5

If you are unable to identify the culture of rival organisations, try looking around your own. In larger organisations, it is common for each department or function to have its own culture. This is even more common in divisional or multinational organisations, due to the lower levels of centralisation and the wider variety of 'local' conditions.

Feedback on self-assessment question 4.5

1   person culture
2   role culture
3   task culture.

Feedback on learning activity 4.6

Make sure you can map who they are on a stakeholder 2 x 2 matrix (see sections 7.2 and 3.3). Consider the impact of each of the groups on organisational policies and strategies.

Feedback on self-assessment question 4.6

You need to consider who the stakeholders are and their impact. Areas for discussion may include:
- Shareholders and tax payers
- Government policy and steers
- Political and legislative influences
- Sources of funding
- Need for accountability for actions and spending.
- Shareholders and tax payers
- Government policy and steers

- Political and legislative influences
- Sources of funding
- Need for accountability for actions and spending.

Feedback on learning activity 4.7

Think of organisations that have had publicity due to poor ethics and the impact of this on their business. Also consider companies that are now using ethics and corporate social responsibility to develop customer loyalty.

Feedback on self-assessment question 4.7

Examples may include:
- EU and national government legislation.
- Customer awareness driving buying decisions.
- Using the policies as a means of differentiation.
- Public sector legal requirements.
- Poor publicity and loss of business.
- A desire to trade appropriately with overseas suppliers.

4

Strategies for business growth

Introduction

It's very common for organisations to have 'to grow' as one of their strategic objectives but, if that's where they want to get to, which way should they go? The choice of strategic direction is at the core of strategic choice. In this session we look at two frameworks for strategic choice: Porter's generic strategies and Ansoff's product–market matrix.

'"Would you tell me, please, which way I ought to go from here?" "That depends a good deal on where you want to get to," said the Cat. "I don't much care where," said Alice. "Then it doesn't matter which way you go," said the Cat.'

Lewis Carroll

Session learning objectives

After completing this session you should be able to:

5.1 Explain generic strategies such as cost leadership, differentiation and focus.
5.2 Assess strategies based upon the direction in which the business may move.
5.3 Analyse methods by which strategies may be developed.

Unit content coverage

This study session covers the following topics from the official CIPS unit content document:

Statement of practice

* Analyse the concept of strategy and the process of developing corporate strategy.

Learning objective

1.5 Critically evaluate innovative strategies for organisational growth and expansion.
    * Generic strategies: price, differentiation and focus
    * Directional strategies: consolidate or withdraw from a market, penetrate further into a market, product or market development, diversification
    * Methods of developing strategies: internal development, mergers and acquisitions, joint ventures, strategic alliances

Resources

Access to Johnson, Scholes and Whittington (2007) chapters 6 and 9 and cases is *essential* if you wish to obtain maximum value from this session.

Timing

You should set aside about 3–4 hours to read and complete this session, including learning activities, self-assessment questions, the suggested further reading (if any) and the revision question.

5.1 The generic strategies model

In study session 3, we were introduced to the concept of competitive forces. Developed by Michael Porter in the late 1970s, that model and the others associated with it became, over the following decade, some of the most commonly used strategy tools. You should bear in mind that these tools are designed to help us craft strategy at the product or strategic business unit (SBU) level. The tools were not designed to be used in corporate strategy formulation, so do not work for complex organisations.

The *generic strategies* model is the tool that Porter proposed for strategic choice. The underlying assumption of the model is that there are three 'key themes' that run through most of the competitive forces, and that these themes can become the core of an organisation's strategic direction. These themes are known as 'generic' strategies, for two reasons:

- One of the three themes is applicable to any organisation, in any situation.
- Each of the themes is very general, and must be developed into a detailed strategy that fits the specific situation of the organisation concerned.

The three generic strategies proposed by Porter are:

- *Cost leadership.* This is the situation where, by manipulating the competitive forces acting on it, an organisation achieves the lowest unit cost of production in the industry.
- *Differentiation.* In this case, the customers of an organisation perceive its products or services to be better, different or unique.
- *Focus.* The organisation produces a product (or products) that is tailored to meet the specific needs of a particular target market. That market might be geographic, or demographic.

Learning activity 5.1

Identify examples of strategies in your own organisation, or one with which you are familiar, that appear to support one of the generic strategies.

Feedback on page 65

Despite its popularity, this model is not without its problems. The main criticisms are as follows:

- There are really four generic strategies, not three (see below).

- The 'strategies' are really 'objectives', as they are statements of what the firm aims to achieve, or where it wants to get to, rather than how it intends to do that.
- Porter cautions against being 'stuck in the middle', but it is now seen as perfectly acceptable to pursue, for example, cost reduction *and* differentiation (see below).

With regard to whether there are three generic strategies or four, this is really a matter of practicalities. Most academics, when they reviewed Porter's original model, and many practitioners who used it, felt that 'focus' was really a secondary strategy. The key themes of cost reduction and differentiation were understood and accepted, but few could see how a focus strategy could achieve a competitive advantage without being combined with either low cost or some form of differentiation. Thus Porter's original framework of three generic strategies has now 'matured' into a 2×2 matrix with cost leadership and differentiation 'across the top', and high and low focus 'down the side'.

The four strategies are as follows:

- *Overall cost leadership.* This strategy is sometimes referred to as 'high volume, low cost'. Cost reductions may be based on economies of scale, for example, or be the result of experience curve effects.
- *Unfocused differentiation.* In this strategy, the organisation has an attribute, such as high product quality or sophisticated features, for example, that is associated with a range of products or the whole product portfolio.
- *Cost focus.* This strategy combines cost reduction with a focus on one target market, often that with the lowest disposable income levels. In this strategy, prices may be lowered in line with cost, but this is not essential.
- *Differentiation focus.* This is what other authors call 'niche' strategy. The organisation finds a fairly small target market and positions the product to satisfy perfectly the needs of that market.

Many people believe that 'cost leadership' necessarily means 'low price'. This is not so, as Porter makes it clear that firms with a low unit cost should try to avoid reducing price. The whole point of having the lowest unit costs in an industry is to deter price wars. That way, you get to earn the highest margins. If you cut cost and engage in price wars you will probably win, but at what cost?

Also, it is important to recognise that the essential nature of the two strategic themes differ. Cost reduction is *real* – to be a cost leader it is necessary to actually have the lowest unit cost. Differentiation, on the other hand, is *perceived* – what is important is what the customers believe, not what is actual fact. If you have a product that is high quality, but the customers don't realise, it is not differentiated. If you have a product that is no better than its rivals, but the customers believe it to be of higher quality, it is differentiated.

When it comes to Porter's advice to avoid being 'stuck in the middle' the criticisms may be a little unfair. He really meant that organisations should be clear, for each of its SBUs, which one of the generic strategies it is trying to pursue. We can all see the difficulties, from the perspectives of control and motivation, with trying simultaneously to reduce cost (a 'cost leadership' strategy) and improve quality (a 'differentiation' strategy). However, such a conflict is surely one of the accepted facts of life of modern business, so can it really be used as an argument to invalidate Porter's model? Porter would probably argue that a firm should decide which of the two strategies (cost reduction or differentiation) is more relevant, and put the emphasis on that strategy, while not totally ignoring the other.

Self-assessment question 5.1

Apply the four generic strategies matrix to the car industry.

Feedback on page 65

5.2 Directions for growth

Whereas Porter's generic strategies model is designed for business strategy, Igor Ansoff's product–market strategy matrix (Johnson, Scholes and Whittington, 2007) is definitely for corporate strategy choice.

Commonly used and widely recognised, the matrix classifies strategies by looking at the various combinations of existing or new products and markets. This gives four categories of strategy, as follows:

- *Market penetration strategies*. These involve the use of a product or products from the existing portfolio, being offered for sale to a market that the organisation currently serves.
- *Product development strategies*. These strategies concern the identification and provision of new products to existing markets.
- *Market development strategies*. These are strategies that involve identifying and servicing new markets for the existing products of the organisation.
- *Diversification strategies*. These are strategies that simultaneously involve the development of new products for sale to new markets.

Non-growth strategies such as 'consolidate' or 'withdraw' are often put in the 'market penetration' quadrant, as they look at the existing product/ market mix of the organisation. They are not, of course, growth strategies.

Learning activity 5.2

Identify examples of strategies in your own organisation, or one with which you are familiar, that appear to fit one of the quadrants of the Ansoff matrix.

Feedback on page 66

There isn't much more to say about Ansoff's matrix. In fact, it is so simplistic that many practitioners and authors feel that it is of little use. While the matrix provides a useful aide-memoire to the strategic options available to an organisation, it has been widely criticised, on the following grounds:

- As mentioned, the matrix is very simplistic. The four strategies identified are not really strategies, but categories of strategy. To really find strategies that are capable of implementation we need to look at a more detailed level.
- Once again, the categories are really objectives, rather than strategies. 'Market penetration' is what we want to achieve, not how we intend to get it, isn't it?
- What exactly are 'existing' and 'new' products and markets? If X plc sells books in the UK and CDs in the US, into which category do we put a strategy that involves selling books in the US? And when is a derivative of an existing product a 'new' product?
- 'Diversification' means something very specific in the matrix – a strategy that combines new product and market development. In normal usage, companies are often said to diversify into any new market or new product (as in 'we've recently diversified into Europe,' which is probably 'market development' in the Ansoff matrix, rather than diversification).

Despite these apparent shortcomings, Ansoff's matrix is much used (and hence very examinable). The terminology of the matrix is in very common usage, so make sure that you understand it.

In a separate but related work, Ansoff (1965) outlined a number of 'directions' for growth:

- *Horizontal integration.* This is the situation where an organisation acquires another business in the same industry that is at the same stage in the supply chain as itself (in other words, its rival).
- *Forward vertical integration.* In this strategy, the organisation moves (either by acquisition or by organic growth – see section 5.3) into areas previously occupied by its customers.
- *Backward vertical integration.* In this strategy, the organisation moves (either by acquisition or by organic growth) into areas previously occupied by its suppliers.
- *Conglomerate integration.* This is where an organisation moves (either by acquisition or by organic growth) into areas unrelated to its current supply chain.

These are often cited as different types of diversification – although that isn't strictly true, as horizontal integration is really a market penetration strategy. The others are types of diversification, but it isn't as simple as this being a set of subdivisions of diversification.

Returning to the Ansoff matrix, a number of writers have pointed out the relationship between the four strategy categories and the nature of business risk. Because market penetration involves the organisation in two aspects (product and market) with which it is already familiar, it is perceived as the lowest risk option. Diversification, however, with its two 'unknowns', is the highest risk option. The other strategies (market development and product development) are 'moderate' risk.

Self-assessment question 5.2

Briefly explain the quadrants of the Ansoff matrix, and the various types of diversification available to an organisation.

Feedback on page 66

5.3 Methods of achieving growth

As we mentioned earlier, when talking about the directions for growth, there are different methods of pursuing any of the strategies in the Ansoff matrix. These are:

- *Organic growth.* This is where the organisation pursues its strategy as an independent entity, without acquiring another organisation (or organisations).
- *Mergers and acquisitions.* This is where the organisation pursues its growth by taking over, or merging with, an existing and established business (or businesses).

Learning activity 5.3

Identify examples of strategies in your own organisation, or one with which you are familiar, of the different methods of achieving growth.

Feedback on page 66

The relative merits of the two approaches to growth are shown in table 5.1.

Table 5.1 Organic growth and acquisitions

	Organic growth	Acquisition
Timescale	Slow	Quick (in theory) but may drag on if bid is hostile
Risk	May not succeed	May not get what you expect
Controllability	Good – we do it	Poor – they've done it
Overcoming entry barriers	Poor	Good
Cost	Difficult to budget for	Certain, but may be higher or lower
Financing required	Spread over a period	All at once (normally)

There are, of course, other methods in between these two extremes. Pursuing joint ventures, or forming strategic alliances, are often seen as alternatives. However, they are really just versions of the organic growth option as any growth is internally generated. While joint ventures were popular in the 1980s and 1990s, they tend to become very bureaucratic and often dissolve into a protracted legal argument between the partners. As the only people who normally benefit from a joint venture are the lawyers, less formal strategic alliances have become a more popular form of collaborative strategy. Many strategic alliances are formed within supply chains, so we will be looking in detail at them later in this unit.

Self-assessment question 5.3

List the circumstances under which each method of development may be appropriate.

Feedback on page 67

5

Revision question

Now try the revision question for this session on page 257.

Summary

In this session we have looked at two models of strategic choice: Porter's generic strategies and Ansoff's product–market matrix. We have also considered the methods of achieving growth – by organic growth or mergers and acquisitions.

Suggested further reading

Look on the internet for articles about the growth of the big 1980s conglomerates such as Hanson or ABB. Try to find the arguments that were put forward to justify their acquisitions, and any excuses they made when they were unsuccessful.

Feedback on learning activities and self-assessment questions

Feedback on learning activity 5.1

In order to find evidence of the generic strategies, you really need to look at individual products. Unless your organisation has a relatively narrow product mix, or only produces one product, it is unlikely to apply the same generic strategy to all its products. You may also have found instances where the organisation seems to be pursuing cost leadership *and* differentiation. This contradicts Porter's model, as we will see, but may not be such a bad thing.

Feedback on self-assessment question 5.1

This is an interesting question! If we had done this exercise ten years ago, it would have been much easier. A rather simplistic, and some would say obsolete, analysis might categorise car manufacturers as follows:

- *Overall cost leadership*: Ford, GM.
- *Unfocused differentiation*: Volvo (safety), Mercedes (quality), Subaru (4-wheel drive).

- *Cost focus*: Seat, Lada, Skoda.
- *Differentiation focus*: Maserati, Land Rover.

The problem is that the last decade has seen the convergence of motor company brands, and the growth of many strategic alliances such as that between Porsche, VW and Skoda. This has blurred the boundaries between the generic strategies of the various companies. Perhaps it might be better to apply the model to individual car models, rather than to brands? Possibly, but that might require a far greater understanding of the car industry than we have. If you are asked to apply this model in the exam, the scenario of the case study will be written in a fairly simplistic way. Exam questions are seldom as complex as real life!

Feedback on learning activity 5.2

You shouldn't have too much trouble with this task, as the matrix is very easy to understand and most strategies are easy to classify. Did the strategies that you identified all fit into one or other of the Ansoff categories or is there little pattern to the strategies?

Feedback on self-assessment question 5.2

The four quadrants of the Ansoff matrix are:

- *Market penetration strategies*. These involve the use of a product or products from the existing portfolio, being offered for sale to a market that the organisation currently serves.
- *Product development strategies*. These strategies concern the identification and provision of new products to existing markets.
- *Market development strategies*. These are strategies that involve identifying and servicing new markets for the existing products of the organisation.
- *Diversification strategies*. These are strategies that simultaneously involve the development of new products for sale to new markets.

The types of diversification available to organisations are as follows:

- *Forward vertical integration*. In this strategy, the organisation moves (either by acquisition or by organic growth) into areas previously occupied by its customers.
- *Backward vertical integration*. In this strategy, the organisation moves (either by acquisition or by organic growth) into areas previously occupied by its suppliers.
- *Conglomerate integration*. This is where an organisation moves (either by acquisition or by organic growth) into areas unrelated to its current supply chain.

Feedback on learning activity 5.3

You might find that all your organisation's growth has been achieved by organic means. If this is the case, have a look through the newspapers for examples of acquisitions.

Feedback on self-assessment question 5.3

Your answer should be similar to table 5.1.

5

Resources to support corporate strategy

Introduction

In this session we take another look at the idea that resources must support strategy. This time, we look in detail at what those resources might be.

Session learning objectives

After completing this session you should be able to:

6.1 Explain the resource-based approach to corporate strategy.
6.2 Identify resources to support corporate and business strategies.
6.3 Evaluate people as key resources.
6.4 Evaluate information as a key resource.
6.5 Evaluate finance as a key resource.
6.6 Evaluate technology as a key resource.

Unit content coverage

This study session covers the following topics from the official CIPS unit content document:

Statement of practice

- Analyse the concept of strategy and the process of developing corporate strategy.

Learning objective

1.6 Analyse the means of managing and controlling resources to support corporate strategy.
  - The resource-based approach to corporate strategy
  - Resources to support key corporate strategies: financial, human, intellectual, physical, informational
  - Resource planning (forecasting, developing and allocating resources)
  - Methods of controlling resources: planning systems, supervision, performance targets, social and cultural control, market mechanisms, self-control
  - Management information as a key resource

Resources

Access to Johnson, Scholes and Whittington (2007) is highly recommended for use throughout this session.

'The more specific and measurable your goal, the more quickly you will be able to identify, locate, create, and implement the use of the necessary resources for its achievement.'
Charles J. Givens

6

Timing

You should set aside about 4.5–5.5 hours to read and complete this session, including learning activities, self-assessment questions, the suggested further reading (if any) and the revision question.

6.1 The resource-based approach to corporate strategy

Strategy theorists disagree on how organisations gain a competitive advantage. Until the 1990s, most writers took a positioning view; however, more recently, a resource-based approach has become popular.

The two views may be explained as follows:

- *Positioning view.* Competitive advantage stems from the organisation's position in relation to its competitors, customers or stakeholders. It is sometimes called an 'outside-in' view because it is concerned with adapting the organisation to fit its environment. Michael Porter clearly adopts this approach.
- *Resource-based view.* Competitive advantage stems from some unique asset or competence possessed by the organisation. This is an 'inside-out' view of strategy because the organisation must go in search of environments that enable it to harness its internal competences. Writers such as Kay (see later in this section) subscribe to this view.

Learning activity 6.1

Look at the way your organisation, or one with which you are familiar, does its strategic planning. Does it appear to be taking a position-based approach, or a resource-based approach? Why is that?

Feedback on page 81

Resource-based theorists make the following criticisms of the positioning view:

- *Competitive advantage based on positioning is not sustainable.* These advantages are too easily copied in the long run. Therefore, superior long-run profitability cannot be explained or assured by possession of a differentiated product, a dominant market position or low-cost position. According to resource-based approach (RBA) writers (such as Barney, 1991), superior profitability instead depends on the organisation's possession of unique resources or abilities that cannot easily be duplicated by rivals.
- *Environments are too dynamic to enable positioning to be effective.* Positioning depends on the customer group, suppliers, buyers, rivals (and so on) to remain the same long enough for the organisation to formulate and implement strategy. However, shorter product life cycles,

the impact of IT and global competition make this impossible. RBA writers (for example, Stalk et al, 1992) argue that superior competitive performance depends on developing business processes and structures that allow the organisation to respond quickly to changes in customer demand.

- *It is easier to change the environment than the organisation.* Some RBA writers (Hamel and Prahalad, 1994; Kay, 1997) are suspicious of the positioning school's belief that organisations are infinitely flexible. They argue that such continual organisational change is likely to destroy the complex structures on which the organisation's competitive advantage depends.

Stalk et al (1992) suggest four principles of competence-based competition:

1 The building blocks of corporate strategy are *business processes* not products and markets.
2 Competitive success depends on the ability to *transform these processes* into strategic capabilities able to provide superior value to the customer.
3 Creating these capabilities requires *group-wide investments* that transcend traditional functional or business unit boundaries.
4 Therefore the champion of capabilities-based strategy is the *chief executive officer* (CEO).

Superior competitive performance will result from the organisation using these competences to outperform rivals on five dimensions:

1 *Speed*: more able to incorporate new ideas and technologies into its products.
2 *Consistency*: all its innovations satisfy the customer.
3 *Acuity*: able to see its environment clearly and forecast changing needs.
4 *Agility*: able to adapt on many fronts simultaneously.
5 *Innovativeness*: able to generate and combine business ideas in novel ways.

Kay (1997) writes of 'distinctive capabilities' arising from four sources:

1 *Competitive architecture.* These are the relationships that make up the organisation. These can be divided into:
   (a) internal architecture: relations with employees
   (b) external architecture: relations with suppliers and customers
   (c) network architecture: relations between a group of collaborating organisations.
2 *Reputation.* This is the high esteem that the public has for the organisation. Among customers it is a reason to buy the product and to remain loyal, while for investors, suppliers and potential employees it is a reason to become involved and give exceptional levels of support to the organisation.
3 *Innovative ability.* This is the ability to develop new products, services or solutions. These stave off competitors and enable the organisation to enjoy the high margins of early life cycle markets.
4 *Ownership of strategic assets.* This is close to the barriers to entry discussed in traditional economic theories of monopoly. The

organisation may have a unique source of materials or possess exclusive legal rights to a market or invention.

Prahalad and Hamel (1990) propose three tests to identify a core competence:

- It must provide access to a wide variety of markets. This is sometimes called the 'extendability' condition.
- It must provide a significant contribution to the perceived customer benefits of the final product.
- It must be difficult for competitors to imitate.

6

Self-assessment question 6.1

Describe and explain the common criticisms levelled at the positioning view by theorists from the resource-based school.

Feedback on page 81

6.2 Strategic resources and levels of strategy

You will remember from study session 3 that, to support a competitive advantage, the organisation needs: unique resources or core competences.

According to Johnson, Scholes and Whittington (2007), in order for a strategy to be implemented successfully, strategic resources must be used as enabling tools to support the strategy. They suggest that such resources may be of four types:

1 people
2 information
3 finance
4 technology.

These are dealt with in detail in the following sections.

Learning activity 6.2

In study session 3 you identified your organisation's key resources. Classify those resources under the four headings. Does any pattern emerge or are the resources fairly evenly distributed?

Feedback on page 81

Strategy exists at several levels in the organisation (see figure 6.1).

Figure 6.1: Three levels of strategy

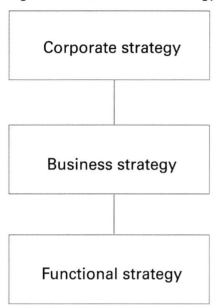

A textbook written 20 years ago would have assumed that all strategy was formulated at corporate level and then implemented in a 'top-down' manner by instructions to the business divisions. *Corporate strategy* today typically restricts itself to determining the overall purpose and scope of the organisation. Common issues at this level include:

- Decisions on acquisitions, mergers and sell-offs or closure of business units.
- Conduct of relations with key external stakeholders such as investors, the government and regulatory bodies.
- Decisions to enter new markets or embrace new technologies.
- Development of corporate policies on issues such as public image, employment practices or information systems.

A strategic business unit (SBU) is a part of the organisation that has some degree of autonomy in crafting its own strategy. SBUs are most often product groupings or divisions. Management of the SBU will be responsible for winning customers and beating rivals in its particular market. Consequently it is at this level that *business* (or *competitive*) *strategy* is usually formulated. The considerations at this level will include:

- Marketing issues such as product development, pricing, promotion and distribution.
- Decisions on production technology.
- Staffing decisions.

A business strategy should be formulated within the broad framework of objectives laid down by the corporate centre to ensure that each SBU plays its part. The extent to which the management of the SBU is free to make strategy decisions varies from corporation to corporation and reflects the degree of centralisation in the management culture of the organisation.

The *functional* (or sometimes called operational) level of the organisation refers to main business functions such as sales, production, purchasing, human resources and finance. Functional strategies are the long-term management policies of these functional areas. They are intended to ensure that the functional area plays its part in helping the SBUs achieve the goals of their business strategies. It is at this level that the enabling resources are planned for and managed.

Self-assessment question 6.2

Identify the four types of resource that Johnson, Scholes and Whittington suggest may enable business strategy.

Feedback on page 81

6.3 People as a key resource

The management of people as a strategic resource is a fairly recent phenomenon. Until the 1970s or 1980s, people were seen as a relatively basic factor of production, to be bought and used in much the same way as materials or machines. The development of enlightened human resource management practices in the latter decades of the twentieth century changed this view, at least in the textbooks if not in all organisations.

Human resources are now seen as key to the way organisations are able to compete. People perform tasks, but they also have ideas and carry around knowledge and expertise.

Learning activity 6.3

Talk to colleagues who have been in your organisation for a long time. Ask if they have seen the organisation's attitude to human resources change significantly. Look around your industry. Do the rivals appear to all treat their staff the same, or do some seem to value their human resources more highly than others?

Feedback on page 81

The management of human resources can be viewed as a 'life cycle': a series of steps or stages. In most of these stages, the organisation can consider the way that its human resources support the strategy. The strategic aspects of each of the main stages in the human resource management (HRM) cycle are as follows:

- *Planning.* Planning to ensure that the organisation has the right people, with the right skills, at the right time is a core component of the organisation's strategic planning processes. Whereas HR planning used to be simply a numbers exercise – making sure the organisation had the right number of staff – it is now much more. HR planning looks at the development and training of staff, and ensures that the individuals attain their own goals as well as supporting the organisation in the achievement of its goals.

- *Recruitment.* The recruitment and selection process gives the organisation access to new human resources. Matching the competences of the individual to any gaps identified in the organisation's competences is a key task in the recruitment process.
- *Induction.* The purpose of induction is to align the values of the individual with those of the organisation. It is at this stage that the organisation can make its expectations clear, and ensure that new staff members are aware of the organisation's strategy and their role in its implementation.
- *Appraisal.* This control system gives the organisation the opportunity to communicate, to the individual, any changes to the strategy or the individual's role in its implementation.
- *Reward.* If the reward system is correctly structured, it should ensure goal congruence between the individual and the organisation. Any bonus schemes should ensure that employees receive financial rewards only if their achievements support the strategy of the organisation.
- *Training and development.* During training and development processes, staff should be acquiring the skills and competences required to support and implement the organisation's strategy.
- *Exit.* If there are staff in the organisation who have skills that are not required to support the organisation's strategy, their exit from the organisation should be made as painless as possible. Rationalising head count is often a key component of any strategy aimed at improving efficiency. The organisation must, however, be careful not to lose any resource with core competences.

Self-assessment question 6.3

Explain to your manager how the organisation can manage its people as a 'strategic resource'.

Feedback on page 82

6.4 Information as a key resource

In this section we look at the role of information as a key strategic resource, and also that of information technology (IT). A later section looks at technology in general terms, but IT is considered here because it is often difficult to distinguish between the roles of information itself, and IT as the enabling tool for its delivery.

Learning activity 6.4

Identify some ways in which information or IT are contributing to the strategy of your organisation, or one with which you are familiar. You may find it beneficial to talk to an IT expert within the organisation.

Feedback on page 82

Johnson, Scholes and Whittington (2007) identify seven ways in which the enhanced capabilities of IT have increased the threshold competences of many industries:

1   *Lower prices,* through reduced costs, especially where the product is informational.
2   *Improved pre-purchase information*, through website browsing.
3   *Easier and faster purchasing* through e-commerce.
4   *Shorter development times* for new features and products.
5   *Improvements in product or service reliability* and diagnostics.
6   *Personalised products and services* being offered, as IT is used to gather personal needs and instruct production systems.
7   *Improved after-sales service* provision by better information systems.

Rather than just having a general list of the influences of IT, we could set them within the framework of the strategy models we considered in earlier sessions. If we look at the possible role of IT in the competitive forces model, we can see the following:

- Investments in IT can be a *barrier to entry*. If, for example, an organisation were deciding whether to become an online bookseller, it might see the need for a sophisticated e-commerce system to rival that of Amazon as a deterrent. However, IT quickly becomes less significant as a barrier to entry, as the cost falls and performance levels increase.
- IT can be used to affect the relative *bargaining power* in the customer/supplier relationship. It may be possible to 'lock in' trading partners through the use of integrated logistics systems, thus creating an effective switching cost.
- It may also be possible to differentiate products or services by providing better, IT-enabled, service levels. This would help to overcome *rivalry*, but IT-based advantages are often short-lived as they are easily copied.
- IT may be the source of *substitute* products or services. It is only necessary to look at the impact of the internet on the markets for books or CDs to see that an advance in IT can make a whole way of doing business completely obsolete. This has also been the case in banking and household insurances.

We could also look at the role of IT in generic strategy. In a previous session we saw that there are three concepts in the generic strategies model (whether there are three strategies or four):

- IT can be used as a tool to significantly reduce the cost of producing and delivering both products and services. Thus it can form the core of a *cost leadership* strategy.
- It is possible to use IT to *differentiate* a product or service, for example by using it to improve product quality. However, it is more likely that information itself will be the source of any sustainable differentiation. Modern products come with an associated 'information package' that consists of advice on what to buy, how to use the product and any after-sales service. If these pieces of information can be provided better, or faster, a competitive advantage may be achieved.
- In order to *focus* on the needs of an individual customer, or a small group, we need to know what they need. This is where the information

system of the organisation can really add value, as we may have access to large volumes of data about past purchases or buyer behaviour. Using tools such as data mining (see below), or simply by keeping more or better information than our rivals, we may be able to satisfy customer needs more fully by using the data to forecast sales behaviour and stock.

As organisations recognise the value of their information databases, more and more are exploiting the power of new technologies such as 'data warehousing'. This uses sophisticated database structures and query tools to achieve significant improvements in the way that information can be stored and retrieved. However, the huge growth in data volumes within the organisation can lead to problems. It is no longer possible for an individual to search an organisational database effectively, in order to identify trends or relationships between data items. Instead, 'data mining' software can be used. Such software packages can search huge volumes of data, and can also work without direct control from the operator, effectively searching a corporate database 'in the background', while the user gets on with other work.

Organisations can monitor and control their information resources by carrying out a periodic 'information audit'. This would typically consist of the following four steps:

1 *Analyse the decisions* being made in the organisation. This would establish the objectives of the information system.
2 *Identify the information required* to allow those decisions to be made. This establishes the desired outputs from the information system.
3 *Identify the information being provided* by the information system. This will allow the auditor to determine whether the information needs of managers are being satisfied.
4 *Produce a gap analysis.* This would identify any instances in which the information needs of managers were not being met.

Self-assessment question 6.4

Evaluate the ways that IT might be used, in the context of the Five Forces model, to attain or protect a competitive advantage.

Feedback on page 82

6.5   Finance as a key resource

The availability and management of finance is often a critical success factor in strategy implementation. The financial managers of the organisation have a number of key decisions to make:

- *Financing* decisions relate to the amount and mix of finance to raise or repay, in order to ensure that the organisation remains liquid and has sufficient funds to meet its commitments and invest in strategy.
- *Investment* decisions relate to the choice of projects in which to invest. Managers should be on the lookout for projects that yield a return

6

in excess of the cost of capital, without exposing the organisation to excessive risk.

- *Dividend* decisions, in organisations financed by shares, relate to the amount and timing of dividend payments.

In commercial organisations, sources of finance can be broken down into debt and equity.

- *Debt finance* consists of loans made to the organisation by individuals, organisations or financial institutions. The cost of such finance is normally the payment of interest on the amount of finance, at either a fixed rate or variable rate (normally expressed as a margin 'over base'). The payment of interest is normally mandatory. Debt finance is normally provided for a fixed period, at the end of which it is repayable.
- *Equity finance* consists of funds raised from the issue of shares (called 'stock' in the US). The cost of such finance is normally in the form of a periodic (once or twice a year) dividend payment, expressed as an amount per share. The payment of dividends is normally discretionary. Equity finance is normally provided for an indefinite period.

Learning activity 6.5

Identify the different sources of finance available to, and used by, your organisation or one with which you are familiar.

Feedback on page 82

The main strategic issues in financing decisions are:

- Ensuring that the amount of finance raised is sufficient to cover the obligations of the organisation and to enable it to pursue its strategies. Raising too much finance can expose the organisation to a higher than necessary cost and can also dilute the earnings per share of the organisation – a key performance indicator for investors and analysts.
- Getting the right mix of debt and equity. This is called the 'gearing' level of the organisation, and is normally expressed as a ratio of debt to (debt plus equity). So, if an organisation is described as 40% geared, that means that 40% of its finance is debt (and, we assume, the remaining 60% is equity). Gearing is an issue, as the cost of debt is often lower than the cost of equity (due to tax being paid after deduction of interest), but interest is mandatory. Thus, any liability for interest payments must be settled, with any remaining profit (less tax) being available to pay dividends (and be included in earnings per share calculations). This means that, the more debt an organisation has, the higher the risk that a downturn in profitability might lead to the organisation being unable to maintain its dividend. Shareholders therefore see high levels of gearing as increasing the risk of their investment and they often require higher dividends as compensation, thus increasing the cost of capital of the organisation.

The main tool used to monitor and control the organisation's finances is budgeting. This allows the company to forecast its income and expenditure and can have a crucial role in the success of project and investment management. You should be familiar with the basics of budgeting from your earlier studies. If you have not studied this topic for some time, it may be worth looking back at your course notes or downloading a couple of relevant articles from the internet.

Self-assessment question 6.5

What are the main differences between debt and equity, as sources of finance?

Feedback on page 82

6

6.6 Technology as a key resource

Johnson, Scholes and Whittington (2007) suggest four 'technological paths' which have different strategic implications:

- *Supplier-dominated developments*. Seeking to capitalise on such developments provides a producer with the challenge of rapid learning on how these technologies may affect business processes. An example of this is the impact of IT on many industries (as discussed in section 6.4).
- *Scale-intensive developments*. Advantage is gained when new technologies are developed as a result of economies of scale or learning. The challenge is to achieve continuous improvement and to diffuse the developments throughout the organisation. An example is large car manufacturers.
- *Information-intensive developments*. Where the exploitation of the IS is the central issue.
- *Science-based developments*. Here the challenges are controlling academic research and monitoring risk. An example is the pharmaceutical industry.

Learning activity 6.6

Identify how technology is used to support the strategy of your organisation, or one with which you are familiar.

Feedback on page 83

Technology can have a significant impact on the five forces operating within an industry. We have already looked at the impact of IT, but there are other types of technology to consider:

- *Barriers to entry* can be created or overcome by means of technology. An example would be the use of automated production methods in manufacturing.
- Technology can enable *substitution*, for example different forms of transportation.

6

- Technology can change relative *bargaining power*, for example by improving quality, or providing an alternative raw material or component.
- Technology can affect the level of *rivalry*, as some organisations can patent technological advances.

In study session 4 we saw that there were different methods of achieving growth. These same methods can be used to develop technology:

- Technology can be developed in-house, particularly if the organisation is keen on developing a core competence and wishes to exploit first-mover advantage.
- Organisations may enter into strategic alliances, particularly when they wish to develop threshold competences. Exchanging technologies would allow both organisations to save the cost of developing such technologies themselves.
- Alternatively, an organisation might acquire a rival, or buy the rights to technology. This can accelerate the adoption of technology, and also provides a way of developing technologies when the organisation lacks in-house ability.

Decisions must be made regarding whether to have a research and development (R&D) function, how much investment to make in it and whether to centralise or decentralise the R&D function. In some cases, organisations might even outsource R&D. However, it is far less likely that any competitive advantage could be derived in such a situation.

Technology can be used to support corporate strategy. For example, the use of enterprise resource planning (ERP), materials requirements planning (MRP), point-of-sale mechanisms, electronic data interchange (EDI), e-catalogues and websites may streamline the process to the customer and market the company's offerings more effectively.

Technology may be monitored and controlled by means of a combination of budgeting and environmental scanning. To enable the latter, a manager should be given responsibility for reading technical articles and keeping in touch with what the competition is doing.

Self-assessment question 6.6

Discuss the advantages of developing technology in-house, compared with acquiring it by buying a licence.

Feedback on page 83

Learning activity 6.7

How can you plan to maximise the use of resources by forecasting, developing and allocating them?

Feedback on page 83

Revision question

Now try the revision question for this session on page 258.

Summary

In order to support a strategy, the appropriate resources must be developed. They must also be 'integrated'; in other words, they must work together to ensure successful implementation of the strategy. It is the role of the managers of the organisation to ensure that this happens.

Suggested further reading

Find a few case studies of successful strategy implementations, in the recommended text or elsewhere (perhaps from the internet or business journals), and identify the resources used to support the strategies.

Feedback on learning activities and self-assessment questions

Feedback on learning activity 6.1

Could you find the information you needed, in order to be able to decide? The problem with this decision is that real organisations, as opposed to academics, just don't make the distinction. Most real organisations use both approaches simultaneously. This whole debate is really about academics arguing with one another, rather than real life!

Feedback on self-assessment question 6.1

1   Competitive advantage based on positioning is not sustainable.
2   Environments are too dynamic to enable positioning to be effective.
3   It is easier to change the environment than the organisation.

Feedback on learning activity 6.2

Having all or most of your key resources under one heading is dangerous, as it shows the organisation to be vulnerable to attack from rivals. If, for example, all your key resources are human, the organisation might be at risk from rivals headhunting key staff.

Feedback on self-assessment question 6.2

1   people
2   information
3   finance
4   technology.

Feedback on learning activity 6.3

It is very common to find different human resource management (HR) practices among rivals within an industry. The *Sunday Times* has an annual survey of the '100 Best Companies to Work For'. You can check it out online, by searching for that phrase. The survey results will tell you something about the HRM practices of the winners. Whether that has an impact on competitiveness, will be discussed later in the section.

Feedback on self-assessment question 6.3

You should base your response on the HRM cycle, as described in section 6.3:

- planning
- recruitment
- induction
- appraisal
- reward
- training and development
- exit.

Feedback on learning activity 6.4

It is rare to find an organisation that does not use its information system as a strategic weapon. Even if it is just a case of 'keeping up' with the threshold competence level of the industry, IT is close to the heart of most organisations' strategies.

Feedback on self-assessment question 6.4

This question can be answered in line with the points listed in section 6.4:

1   Investments in IT can be a *barrier to entry*.
2   IT can be used to affect the relative *bargaining power* in the customer/ supplier relationship.
3   It may also be possible to differentiate products or services by providing better, IT-enabled, service levels. This would help overcome *rivalry*.
4   IT may be the source of *substitute* products or services.

Feedback on learning activity 6.5

You will probably need to see the published financial statements of your organisation. Unless you are looking at a public sector organisation, you should find headings such as 'debt', 'loans', share capital' or 'equity' on the organisation's balance sheet. If you have problems finding this information, ask a colleague from the finance department.

Feedback on self-assessment question 6.5

You can answer this question by reference to the points in section 6.5:

- *Debt finance* consists of loans made to the organisation by individuals, organisations or financial institutions. The cost of such finance is normally the payment of interest on the amount of finance, at either a fixed rate or variable rate (normally expressed as a margin 'over base'). The payment of interest is normally mandatory. Debt finance is normally provided for a fixed period, at the end of which it is repayable.

- *Equity finance* consists of funds raised from the issue of shares (called 'stock' in the US). The cost of such finance is normally in the form of a periodic (once or twice a year) dividend payment, expressed as an amount per share. The payment of dividends is normally discretionary. Equity finance is normally provided for an indefinite period.

Feedback on learning activity 6.6

You may need to talk to someone involved with R&D to answer this. Don't assume that technology is 'nothing to do with us' just because, for example, you are a service business. Think about IT as a supplier-dominated development.

Feedback on self-assessment question 6.6

The answer to this question can be based on table 5.1. In table 6.1, the 'advantages' of each approach are in italics:

Table 6.1 Advantages of developing technology in-house

	Organic growth	**Acquisition**
Timescale	Slow	*Quick* (in theory) but may drag on if bid is hostile
Risk	May not succeed	May not get what you expect
Controllability	*Good* – we do it.	Poor – they've done it
Overcoming entry barriers	Poor	Good
Cost	Difficult to budget for	*Certain*, but may be higher or lower
Financing required	*Spread over a period*	All at once (normally)

Feedback on learning activity 6.7

First, make sure you can identify people, information, financial and technological resources. Then consider what methods are available to maximise each resource.

6

Study session 7
Review the corporate strategy process

Introduction

At some point we need to be able to decide whether the organisation's strategy processes are right and whether the organisation is pursuing the right strategies. Of course, there's really no such thing as 'right' in either of these cases, but we should at least be able to decide whether what the organisation is doing seems reasonable and appropriate.

This session looks at two aspects of strategic evaluation: assessing the strategy process, and assessing each available strategy.

Session learning objectives

After completing this session you should be able to:

7.1 Review the corporate strategy process and propose changes to improve corporate performance.
7.2 Evaluate the suitability of corporate strategies.
7.3 Evaluate the acceptability of corporate strategies.
7.4 Evaluate the feasibility of corporate strategies.

Unit content coverage

This study session covers the following topics from the official CIPS unit content document:

Statement of practice

• Analyse the concept of strategy and the process of developing corporate strategy.

Learning objective

1.7 Review and evaluate the corporate strategy process.
   • Corporate strategy review and evaluation
   • Methods of testing the suitability of corporate strategies
   • Methods of testing acceptability of corporate strategies
   • Methods of testing feasibility of corporate strategies
   • Ways of improving corporate strategies
   • Selection of corporate strategies

7

Resources

Access to Johnson, Scholes and Whittington (2007) chapters 1, 9 and 11 is highly recommended for use throughout this session.

Timing

You should set aside about 3 hours to read and complete this session, including learning activities, self-assessment questions, the suggested further reading (if any) and the revision question.

7.1 Reviewing the corporate strategy process

In order to review the strategic planning processes of an organisation, it is important to take a contingency approach. There is nothing inherently wrong with any of the various approaches discussed in study session 2, but each may be more or less appropriate to the context in which they are used (see table 7.1). That context has two components: the organisation's position and its environment.

Table 7.1 Strategy development in context

	Internal context	External context
Rational planning	• Mature business model • Large organisation	Fairly static environment
Logical incrementalism	• Many types of organisation • Flexible structure • Innovation culture	Dynamic environment
Emergent strategy	• Small organisations • Entrepreneurial culture	Chaotic environment

In this case, any evaluation of the strategy process of an organisation will involve testing to see whether the process is *suitable for the context*. If the process seems inappropriate, it should be changed to one more relevant to the context.

Learning activity 7.1

Reread the descriptions and explanations of the various approaches to strategy formulation outlined in study session 2. Think (and make a few brief notes) about how each approach relates to the relevant context suggested in table 7.1. Do you agree with the summary in the table?

Feedback on page 92

Another way to evaluate the strategy development process is to see how well the various *tasks* within it are performed. Most strategy processes, regardless of which approach they adopt, tend to consist of a series of tasks, each of which has *tools* associated with it (see table 7.2). Each of these tools may be used appropriately or inappropriately, and applied well or badly (or, perhaps, not at all).

Table 7.2 Tasks and tools of the strategy process

Task	Tools
Analysis of the environment	• PEST (or PESTLE) • Porter's Five Forces
Analysis of position	• The value chain • Financial ratio analysis • Resource audit
Analysis of stakeholders	• Stakeholder mapping
Summarising strategic analysis	• SWOT • Gap analysis
Identification of strategy options	• Ansoff matrix • Generic strategies
Evaluation of strategy options	• Suitability, feasibility, acceptability
Implementation and control of strategy	• Budgeting • Change management • Organisation structure • Organisation culture • Control systems.

A further way to assess the strategy development process is to look at the culture of the organisation, as it relates to the process. Goold and Campbell (1987) suggest that there are three general approaches to strategy development and review, often known as 'strategy styles':

- *Strategic planning style.* This does not relate to the processes themselves, but to the relationship between the centre and the SBUs during those processes. The centre is the master planner, prescribing parameters and assumptions (and often the plan itself) to the SBUs, whose role is the delivery of the plan. While this style is perhaps more common in large organisations, it achieves goal congruence at the expense of motivation levels and innovation.
- *Financial control style.* In this style the centre adopts the role of shareholder and banker to the SBUs. Each SBU is allowed to determine its own strategy, and the centre simply sets and monitors against performance targets. The centre will only intervene in the operation of the SBU in the case of significant failure, and then most likely to replace the SBU manager.
- *Strategic control style.* This is a compromise between the extremes of the other two styles. The centre acts as strategic shaper to influence the behaviour of the SBUs. It also assesses performance and intervenes if performance is poor. This intervention might involve influencing and directing SBU strategy, rather than replacing a manager.

The specific strategies of the organisation can be assessed by using three tests:

1   *Suitability* tests whether the strategy is appropriate to the position and environment of the organisation.

2   *Acceptability* tests whether a strategy might be acceptable to the stakeholders of the organisation.

3   *Feasibility* tests whether the strategy is an efficient use of the resources available to the organisation.

These tests are covered in detail in sections 7.2 to 7.4.

7

Self-assessment question 7.1

Identify at which stage of the strategic planning process each of the following tools is used:

1   SWOT
2   the value chain
3   PEST (or PESTLE)
4   control systems
5   budgeting
6   Porter's Five Forces
7   financial ratio analysis
8   organisation structure
9   stakeholder mapping
10 gap analysis
11 generic strategies
12 suitability, feasibility, acceptability
13 change management
14 resource audit
15 organisation culture
16 Ansoff matrix.

Feedback on page 93

7.2   Strategy evaluation – suitability

Suitability looks at whether the strategy is appropriate to the position and environment of the organisation. Suitability may therefore be thought of as the rationale behind the strategy, and whether it makes sense.

You must recognise that, if the strategy generation tools such as the Ansoff matrix have been used correctly during the planning process, all of the strategies under consideration should be suitable. However, some will be more suitable than others.

Learning activity 7.2

How would you assess the suitability of strategic options? Think about the tools you have studied in earlier sessions. Which ones could be used to assess suitability?

Feedback on page 93

The major tools used to assess suitability are, necessarily, the same ones that are used to analyse the environment and position of the organisation.

Analysis of the organisation's environment is most often carried out by means of PEST (or PESTLE) analysis or the Five Forces model. When using these to test for suitability, we are looking for the degree of fit between the proposed strategy and the various environmental factors. In particular, we are looking at whether the strategy exploits opportunities or defends against threats.

When carrying out an analysis of an organisation's strategic position, we are most likely to use the *value chain*, perform a *financial appraisal* using ratio analysis, or carry out a *resource audit*. We are particularly looking at whether a strategy exploits the strengths of an organisation, or corrects it weaknesses.

We can thus see that possibly the most appropriate single tool to use in the assessment of suitability is SWOT analysis. This is sometimes used (see figure 7.1) in the form of a 'TOWS matrix' ('TOWS' is SWOT backwards, of course).

Figure 7.1: TOWS matrix

	Strengths • Shares only owned by directors. • •	Weaknesses • • • •
Opportunities • • • •	S/O strategies • • • •	W/O strategies • • • •
Threats • • Major rivals have been making acquisitions.	S/T strategies • Defend against hostile takeover by ensuring director loyalty.	W/T strategies •

The TOWS matrix is drawn by putting the content of the SWOT analysis around the outside of the matrix, then by looking for strategies that, for example, utilise a strength of the organisation to overcome a threat in the environment (an 'S/T strategy', as shown in figure 7.1).

The TOWS matrix can be very useful, as it can be used to prioritise (to some extent) the strategies in which an organisation might invest. Normally, the organisation would first invest in weakness/threat strategies, followed by strength/threat and weakness/opportunity strategies, with strength/opportunity strategies being the lowest priority.

Self-assessment question 7.2

What tools can be used to analyse the position and environment of an organisation, and how can these help us to assess the suitability of strategies?

Feedback on page 93

7.3 Strategy evaluation – acceptability

Acceptability tests whether a strategy is likely to be seen as reasonable by the stakeholders of the organisation.

Learning activity 7.3

Identify what, in your opinion, are the two most powerful stakeholder groups in relation to your organisation, or one with which you are familiar. List what you believe to be their main needs.

Feedback on page 93

In section 3.3 we were introduced to stakeholder mapping. This tool allows us to identify the stakeholder groups that are likely to have high power over, and/or interest in, any strategic decision. An example of a stakeholder map is shown in figure 7.2. This shows how stakeholders are likely to react to a decision by Arco, a large chemical company, to expand its production capacity at a site near a major city.

Figure 7.2: Stakeholder map for Arco factory expansion

		Interest	
		Low	High
Power	Low	Suppliers (+) Customers (+)	Community (-) Employees (+) Conservation lobby (-)
	High	Managers (0)	Shareholders (+) Planning authority (?)

Arco would have to make a key decision – should it seek to reach compromise between the competing aims of the different stakeholder groups, or should it recognise that a 'dominant coalition' exists. This is a combination of stakeholder groups that have a right to be treated as more important than the rest. In this case, such a coalition is likely to include the shareholders and the local planners, as the former is the de facto owner of the company and provider of its capital, and the latter is the representative of the government and the local community.

In the case of Arco's decision, much would depend on the attitude of the planning authorities, as they may hold the only power of veto over the planned expansion. In constructing a case to present to the planning authorities, Arco must try to determine what the authorities need and further decide to what extent their needs might reasonably be satisfied. For example, the authorities might need safety equipment to be installed at the site. There may be a range of safety products available, at vastly differing costs. Arco must decide what level of expenditure to commit, bearing in mind that such cost will reduce the return to shareholders from the project.

7

Self-assessment question 7.3

Xanda plc is a large insurance company. It is considering whether to relocate its head office from the city centre to an out-of-town business park. This relocation would be very expensive and Xanda feels that a stakeholder analysis will help with the decision. Produce a stakeholder map for this decision.

Feedback on page 94

7.4 Strategy evaluation – feasibility

Feasibility is concerned with whether the organisation has the resources and competences to enable it to implement a strategy.

There are various types of feasibility, as follows:

- *Financial.* Can we afford to pursue the strategy? Will it provide us with a good enough return, at an acceptable risk level?
- *Practical.* Do we have the resources that we need? Do we have enough staff, materials or tools to do the job?
- *Social.* Is the culture of the organisation such that we could pursue this strategy? Are people likely to 'buy in' to the strategy?
- *Technical.* Do we have access to the sort of technology that we need to allow us to pursue this strategy?

Learning activity 7.4

How would you assess the financial feasibility of a strategic option?

Feedback on page 94

There are a number of common tools for assessing financial feasibility:

- *Breakeven analysis.* This looks at the time taken to recover the initial investment in the strategy, plus any subsequent cash outflows.
- *Net present value.* This discounts the cash inflows and outflows associated with the strategy back to present values, and calculates the surplus (a positive net present value) or deficit (negative) resulting from the strategy.
- *Ratio analysis.* This looks at the likely effect of the strategy on key financial ratios such as return on capital employed (ROCE) or the price/earnings (P/E) ratio.
- *Risk analysis.* This looks at the degree of risk associated with the strategy, and the impact of the strategy on the overall risk profile of the organisation.

These tools are covered fully in Level 6, Finance for Purchasers.

Practical and technical feasibility are covered by the resource analysis section of study session 6. Social feasibility is addressed in study session 9 on the management of change.

Self-assessment question 7.4

What are the different types of feasibility?

Feedback on page 94

Revision question

Now try the revision question for this session on page 258.

Summary

This session has looked at two aspects of strategy evaluation – whether the strategy processes of the organisation are appropriate, and whether the individual strategies under consideration should be pursued.

Suggested further reading

Try the questions based on the Tesco case example in Johnson, Scholes and Whittington (2007).

Feedback on learning activities and self-assessment questions

Feedback on learning activity 7.1

It's fine to disagree. Table 7.1 is only a summary, and no two organisations are the same. Also, the three approaches are only examples of how strategy might be formulated. Indeed, they are really 'groupings' of large numbers of slightly different approaches. In any given situation, in the exam, you might be required to describe an appropriate approach for an organisation described in a scenario. Pick the most useful components of whichever seems the relevant approach.

Feedback on self-assessment question 7.1

1   summarising strategic analysis
2   analysis of position
3   analysis of the environment
4   implementation and control of strategy
5   implementation and control of strategy
6   analysis of the environment
7   analysis of position
8   implementation and control of strategy
9   analysis of stakeholders
10 summarising strategic analysis
11 identification of strategy options
12 evaluation of strategy options
13 implementation and control of strategy
14 analysis of position
15 implementation and control of strategy
16 identification of strategy options.

Feedback on learning activity 7.2

See the continuation of section 7.2.

Feedback on self-assessment question 7.2

Analysis of the organisation's environment is most often carried out by means of PEST (or PESTLE) analysis or the Five Forces model. When using these to test for suitability, we are looking for the degree of fit between the proposed strategy and the various environmental factors. In particular, we are looking at whether the strategy exploits opportunities or defends against threats.

When carrying out an analysis of an organisation's strategic position, we are most likely to use the value chain, perform a financial appraisal using ratio analysis, or carry out a resource audit. We are particularly looking at whether a strategy exploits the strengths of an organisation, or corrects it weaknesses.

Feedback on learning activity 7.3

If you work for an organisation with shareholders, they are probably 'top two'. They are likely to need a certain level of return on their investment, either in the form of dividend or capital growth, and a risk level that is seen as 'not excessive'. In public sector organisations, the government (either directly or via a minister or department) is normally stakeholder number one. They generally need value-for-money service provision, however that may be defined.

7

Feedback on self-assessment question 7.3

The real benefit of this exercise is going through the process of identifying the stakeholders and considering how much power and interest each is likely to have. There is no right answer, as we have very little information about the organisation. As a plc, Xanda should expect its major shareholders to have both high power and high interest, but smaller shareholders to have far less power and possibly less interest. The staff of Xanda is likely to be very interested and may also have quite high power as staff might refuse to relocate, leaving the organisation short-staffed.

Feedback on learning activity 7.4

The basic financial assessment tools are outlined in the continuation of section 7.4. You should be familiar with them from your earlier studies. If you need a reminder of how they work, check your course notes or search on the internet.

Feedback on self-assessment question 7.4

There are four types of feasibility (as detailed in section 7.4):

- financial
- practical
- social
- technical.

Develop commitment to, and alignment with, corporate strategy

Introduction

In this session we look at various ways in which the organisation can ensure that the strategy is translated into action and results.

'Certainly, a leader needs a clear vision of the organisation and where it is going, but a vision is of little value unless it is shared in a way so as to generate enthusiasm and commitment. Leadership and communication are inseparable.'

Claude Taylor

8

Session learning objectives

After completing this session you should be able to:

8.1 Explain the purpose and value of corporate visions and mission statements.
8.2 Assess the effectiveness of an organisation's internal and external communications policy and processes.
8.3 Identify and assess incentive structures within an organisation.
8.4 Analyse the alignment of strategy with structure, shared values, staff, style, skills and systems.

Unit content coverage

This study session covers the following topics from the official CIPS unit content document:

Statement of practice

- Analyse the concept of strategy and the process of developing corporate strategy.

Learning objectives

2.1 Analyse the methods of achieving commitment to corporate strategy across all functions and levels of the organisation.
  - Purpose and value of corporate visions and mission statements
  - Integration of functional and corporate plans
  - Internal and external communications policy and processes
  - Rewards and sanctions reinforcing commitment to corporate goals
2.2 Assess the need for alignment between strategy and structure.
  - The 7S framework: strategy, structure, super-ordinate goals, staff, style, skills and systems
  - Alignment of strategy and structure
  - Alignment of strategy with super-ordinate goals, staff, style, skills and systems

Resources

Access to Johnson, Scholes and Whittington (2007) chapters 4 and 12 is highly recommended for use throughout this session.

Timing

You should set aside about 3–4 hours to read and complete this session, including learning activities, self-assessment questions, the suggested further reading (if any) and the revision question.

8.1   A hierarchy of objectives

At some point in its strategic planning process, the organisation must set objectives for itself, its functions or divisions, and the individuals within it. As these objectives relate to different levels, they are often referred to as a 'hierarchy' of objectives. A typical hierarchy is shown in figure 8.1, though different strategy authors each have their own terminology. Some suggest that the hierarchy might consist of 'mission, goals and targets', while others use the terms 'mission, goals and objectives'. The principle of the hierarchy is really more important than the precise terminology, so do not let yourself be confused by minor differences in wording.

Figure 8.1: Hierarchy of objectives

The terms 'vision' and 'mission' are often used interchangeably, though some textbooks consider them to be different. Here we are going to stick to mission, as it seems to encapsulate the intangible, long-term nature that we are looking for.

The mission of an organisation is a general expression of its overall purpose. It may be referred to as: 'What business are we in?'.

While many American writers use the term 'vision' in this context, most European writers seem to agree that an organisational vision is much more an aspiration for what the organisation will look and feel like. Also, a vision is often a view expressed by an individual (the CEO or a strategist, for example) whereas the mission is really agreed by all involved with the strategy process.

It is important to differentiate between the organisation's mission and its 'mission statement'. While the former is its underlying general objective, or purpose, the latter is a communication tool. In many organisations, the mission statement does not 'match up' with the actual mission of the organisation, as the mission statement is published widely. The true mission of the organisation might contain aspects that are felt to be confidential, or may even be felt to be inappropriate for publication. For example, an organisation that has a mission containing the phrase 'most profitable' might choose to find a different phrase for its mission statement, to avoid offending or demotivating suppliers and staff.

Learning activity 8.1

Find out whether your organisation has a mission, and collect examples of its mission statement.

Feedback on page 102

8

The purpose of a hierarchy of objectives is to enable the organisation to translate its necessarily vague mission into a series of objectives that can be used to target the organisation's efforts, and measure its performance. Viewing the objectives of the organisation collectively will allow us to ensure that behaviour throughout the organisation is 'goal congruent'. In other words, that the activity and effort throughout the organisation are focused on helping the organisation to achieve its mission. A failure to achieve this consistency will lead to dysfunctional behaviour, where each part of the organisation pursues its own individual objectives, which may conflict with one another and with the mission.

Critical success factors (CSFs) are objectives that are expressed in such a form that achievement of them is seen as necessary for the organisation to achieve its mission. Some authors see the CSFs of the organisation as relating to those aspects of the business where it might be able to achieve a sustainable competitive advantage. CSFs are a lot more specific than the mission, and it is common for organisations to have one or more CSFs relating to each aspect of the organisation. Thus, the CSFs help functional or divisional managers to understand what aspects of their business are the most important, so they can focus their attention and make decisions when priorities appear to conflict.

Though CSFs are more specific than missions, they may still be in a form that is too vague, or too general, for performance to be assessed against them. It is commonly felt that, to be suitable for performance assessment, objectives should have the following characteristics:

- *Specific.* The objective should be clearly defined and described, so it cannot be misinterpreted or manipulated by managers.

- *Measurable.* The objective should be quantifiable, and be expressed in such a way that the actual achievement and target level can be compared.
- *Achievable.* Those whose performance is going to be assessed against it should perceive the objective as achievable.
- *Relevant.* Those whose performance is going to be assessed against it should perceive the objective as being within their control.
- *Time-constrained.* Part of the definition of the objective should be a clear statement as to the date or time by which that level of achievement should be attained.

This model is often known as the 'SMART' model.

Objectives that conform to this model, and support one or other of the CSFs of the organisation, are called key performance indicators (KPIs). These KPIs will be embedded in the budgeting and performance appraisal systems of the organisation. Achievement of the KPIs will necessarily lead to achievement of the CSFs and, in turn, the mission.

Self-assessment question 8.1

Explain how having a suitable hierarchy of objectives can encourage goal congruence within an organisation.

Feedback on page 103

8.2 Communications policy and processes

Having designed an appropriate structure of objectives, these must be communicated effectively to those responsible for achieving them. The organisation also needs to communicate the objectives to others who might be interested in them. The shareholders, for example, might wish to know what the stated objectives are, despite not being involved in their achievement.

While the organisation may have several formal communications channels, much of the activity of the organisation is necessarily directed by less formal means, such as conversations. These communication channels are far more difficult to control and the organisation must try to ensure that the formal and informal channels do not contradict one-another.

Learning activity 8.2

Collect some examples of corporate communications media within your organisation, or one with which you are familiar. Look at the characteristics of each medium (speed, level of detail, user-friendliness and so on) and think about which media seem most appropriate for which type of message.

Feedback on page 103

The following are examples of common, formal communication media:

- press release
- corporate brochure
- website
- intranet
- staff briefing (by letter or email)
- notice board
- meeting
- video or multimedia presentation
- policies and procedures
- operating manual
- the strategic plan.

Each of these media has different strengths and weaknesses, depending on the context of the communication. In choosing a medium, you should think about criteria such as:

- Who is the intended target of the communication? The medium needs to be one to which they will pay attention and, if necessary, respond.
- How urgent is the communication? Some of the media (such as a website) are passive, in that they require the recipient to take action to receive the communication. Other media, such as email, are active.
- How much detail should the communication contain? Some media (such as email) are more suited to brief communication, rather than others (such as a brochure) that contain a lot of detail.
- Is it possible to cover all the issues? Written media (such as a procedure) tend to become very long, so recipients may not read them. Verbal media (such as a meeting) allow the recipient to ask questions or ask for clarification.
- Is there a need for evidence? If the recipient is likely to query the content at a later date, it might be wise to use written communication where an 'audit trail' can be kept.
- How many recipients do we want to reach? Written or electronic media are easily duplicated, and this can be done very cheaply. Verbal communication can be expensive and is not easily duplicated.

8

Self-assessment question 8.2

Discuss which communications media might be appropriate for informing suppliers about a change to tendering processes.

Feedback on page 103

8.3 Incentives and remuneration

One of the ways to encourage goal congruence is to allow individuals within the organisation to share in the wealth generated. This is done through the design of the reward system, consisting of salaries, bonus schemes and other financial and non-financial rewards.

You will be familiar, from your studies of management theory, with the arguments surrounding the role of remuneration as a motivator. If it is a while since you studied management, you might benefit from a quick review of your course notes on motivation theories.

Learning activity 8.3

Talk to someone from the HR function about the rationale of your organisation's remuneration policy.

Feedback on page 103

There are lots of issues surrounding the design of remuneration structures, such as motivation, comparative salary levels and increases in the cost of living. In this session we are only really interested in how the remuneration system can be used as a way of implementing strategy, and encouraging goal-congruent behaviour in the organisation.

Salary structures can be designed in such a way as to attract staff with the skills and competences that the organisation wishes to develop. If, for example, the organisation wishes to increase the focus on quality, it may increase the remuneration levels attached to any vacancies in the quality assurance function. This will allow the organisation to recruit better staff, and also give a clear signal to the organisation and the market that quality is seen as important.

Bonus schemes are often used to encourage goal-congruent behaviour. Linking all or part of an employee's financial reward to some measure of performance is very likely to lead to that employee seeking to achieve the relevant objective. Performance targets must, of course, conform to the SMART model discussed in section 8.1.

The first major step in designing performance-related bonus schemes is to decide what level of performance to link the bonus to. Bonuses might be linked to one or more of the following:

- *Personal performance*, such as achievement of a target for sales secured, calls made or savings secured.
- *Group performance*, such as the cost savings made by a department, or the achievement of delivery times by a project team.
- *Company performance*, such as the achievement of a profit or share price target.

The decision here often depends on the answer to two questions:

1   Does the individual primarily work on his or her own, as part of a team, or as a 'cog in the machinery' of the organisation?
2   Does the organisation wish to specifically encourage team building or corporate identity? In this case, schemes are more likely to be linked to group or organisational performance.

Another key issue relating to the design of remuneration schemes is how much of the individual's salary should be 'basic pay' and how much should be performance-related bonus? The general view is that the proportion of an individual's reward that is performance related should depend on the extent to which the individual is in control of their own performance level. Thus, sales staff, who can directly influence the level of sales they make or the number of orders they win, are often able to earn very high levels of bonus. Even in this situation, however, staff often complain that their performance level is directly affected by factors outside their control, for example macroeconomic factors. Or do they only make this complaint when their bonus is low?

Self-assessment question 8.3

Discuss whether reward schemes for procurement staff should be based, in part, on corporate, functional or personal performance.

Feedback on page 103

8

8.4   Alignment with strategy

In study session 4 we saw how important it is that the structure and culture of the organisation support the strategy being implemented. Although structure and culture are, to some extent, constraints, determinants or influences on the strategy process, they should really be outcomes from it. In this way the organisation will be able to develop more innovative and challenging strategies. You might find it beneficial to reread your notes on study session 4 before attempting the following activity.

Learning activity 8.4

Look around your organisation. What aspects of the organisation, other than structure and culture, do you feel should be 'aligned' with the strategy?

Feedback on page 103

McKinsey, a large US management consultancy, produced a framework for understanding organisations (the McKinsey 7-S framework) similar to one used by Koontz since 1955. The 7-S name is clearly intended to stick in the memory rather than arising strictly from empirical data, but it was this framework that Peters and Waterman (1982) used to identify their 'excellent' companies. The seven factors referred to are:

- systems
- structure
- style

- strategy
- staff
- skills
- shared values.

This model has several similarities to the 'cultural web' that we studied in study session 4. However, some of the elements in this model are 'hard' (such as structure and staff) rather than being 'soft' cultural aspects.

When McKinsey designed the model, 'shared values' was shown as the central factor, with all the others supporting it. We can, however, make 'strategy' the central factor and use the other 6 S-factors as the aspects of the organisation that must be aligned to its strategy. Although this is not the way McKinsey intended the model to be used, it is only a memory aid. The fact that all seven factors begin with the same letter simply serves to make it more memorable.

8

Self-assessment question 8.4

Explain how an organisation might ensure that other aspects of its operation are aligned with a new strategy of 'identifying and partnering sole suppliers for key inputs'.

Feedback on page 104

Revision question

Now try the revision question for this session on page 258.

Summary

In this session we have looked at various aspects of strategy implementation. In particular, we have concentrated on aspects of the organisation's operations that can (and should) be 'aligned' with any new strategy.

Suggested further reading

Look through the communication documents that you collected during this session. See if you can identify any consistent messages that appear to support the implementation of a specific strategy.

Feedback on learning activities and self-assessment questions

Feedback on learning activity 8.1

Strictly speaking, if you don't know whether your organisation has a mission, then there's not much point looking. Isn't the whole point of having a mission to ensure that people buy into it? It's very difficult to do that if you don't know what the mission is!

Feedback on self-assessment question 8.1

The purpose of a hierarchy of objectives is to enable the organisation to translate its necessarily vague mission into a series of objectives that can be used to target the organisation's efforts, and measure its performance. Viewing the objectives of the organisation collectively will allow us to ensure that behaviour throughout the organisation is 'goal congruent'. In other words, that the activity and effort throughout the organisation are focused on helping the organisation to achieve its mission. A failure to achieve this consistency will lead to dysfunctional behaviour, where each part of the organisation pursues its own individual objectives, which may conflict with one another and with the mission.

Feedback on learning activity 8.2

Don't forget that some of the communications might be external. You need to consider the full range of stakeholders. Think about how the organisation communicates with customers and suppliers, for example.

Feedback on self-assessment question 8.2

In this situation, a combination of written and verbal communication might be sensible. Although it is important to document the changes and the detail of the new process (for example, in a new procedures document) it might also be necessary to allow the supplier(s) to raise questions. Subject to the number of suppliers being manageable, it might be preferable to follow up the new procedure with a series of meetings. It might not be a good idea to hold one presentation for all suppliers.

Feedback on learning activity 8.3

Don't just think about bonus schemes, if indeed your organisation has one. Ask about salary levels, and other non-financial benefits such as pensions and company cars. How does the organisation decide on the structure of its reward scheme, and what is it trying to achieve?

Feedback on self-assessment question 8.3

To answer this question you need to take the arguments outlined in section 8.3 and think about how they relate to the procurement function. In this case, it might be more appropriate to base performance bonuses on personal performance.

Feedback on learning activity 8.4

Look at the suggestions of McKinsey in the continuation of section 8.4.

8

Feedback on self-assessment question 8.4

If you use the 7-S framework, you can produce a diverse answer to this question. Think abut how the other six aspects in the framework might be changed to support the strategy described in the question. For example:

- Systems: new procedures and control systems will be needed.
- Structure: it might be sensible to identify a key procurement manager for each major supplier.
- Style: this strategy might need the whole function to be more 'friendly' and less 'confrontational'.
- Staff: additional staff may need to be recruited.
- Skills: staff may need to be trained.
- Shared values: the function must buy in to the new strategy, and accept that it will benefit the organisation.

Change management

Introduction

In this session we look at types of strategic change and discuss how to manage it.

'In a time of drastic change it is the learners who inherit the future. The learned usually find themselves equipped to live in a world that no longer exists.'
Eric Hoffer

Session learning objectives

After completing this session you should be able to:

9.1 Distinguish types of strategic change.
9.2 Discuss the context of, and attitudes to, change.
9.3 Manage strategic change processes.
9.4 Distinguish strategic change roles.

9

Unit content coverage

This study session covers the following topics from the official CIPS unit content document:

Statement of practice

• Identify how strategy is converted into action through effective alignment and implementation.

Learning objective

2.3 Diagnose resistance to change and strategic drift, and identify how to address them through change management processes.
   • Types of strategic change: incremental and transformational, managed and imposed
   • Symptoms of strategic drift
   • Forces blocking and facilitating change
   • Change management styles through education, collaboration, intervention, direction, coercion
   • Role of symbolic and political processes in managing change
   • Strategic change roles: change agent, middle manager, other organisational member, stakeholder or outsider

Resources

Access to Johnson, Scholes and Whittington (2007) chapters 1 and 11 is highly recommended for use throughout this session.

Timing

You should set aside about 3–4 hours to read and complete this session, including learning activities, self-assessment questions, the suggested further reading (if any) and the revision question.

9.1 Types of strategic change

Strategic change is necessary for a number of reasons:

- Because the environment has changed, or is predicted to change, so the organisation must adapt to gain a competitive advantage, or to remain competitive.
- Because the competences of the organisation are no longer sufficient to give it a competitive advantage, so new competences (or increased levels) need to be developed.
- Because the stakeholders of the organisation have changed their expectations.

These issues have been explained in detail in the previous sessions.

We need to distinguish between *planned strategic change* and a concept known as 'strategic drift'. While the former is obviously an example of 'deliberate' strategy, the latter is due to a combination of inertia and resistance to change. Strategic drift is the situation where successive strategies fail to address the strategic issues of the organisation and performance progressively deteriorates. It is a symptom of poor change management, and there are a number of causes of it:

- The organisation may fail to keep pace with changes in the environment. If the rate of environmental change exceeds the pace of incremental change in the organisation's strategy, the organisation's performance will worsen.
- The organisation may simply be reactive to changes in the environment, rather than trying to innovate. This will lead to complacency and a worsening of performance.
- 'Taken for granted' assumptions may become embedded in the organisation's culture, and it may be incapable of changing at the rate, or to the extent, necessary.

Learning activity 9.1

Identify examples of strategic drift and planned strategic change in your own organisation, or one with which you are familiar.

Feedback on page 111

According to Balogun and Hope Bailey (1999), there are two dimensions to change:

1   Change is either *incremental* or *big bang*: the former consists of a series of minor changes, whereas in the latter the change comes all at once.

2   Change is either about *realignment* or *transformation*: the former is about changing the strategic direction of the organisation, whereas the latter is about a radical shift in its position.

Combining these two factors, we have four types of change:

- *Adaptation.* This is incremental realignment. It is often evidenced by a series of gradual changes to strategy, without fundamentally affecting the business model. This is probably the most common form of change encountered in business. It is also the form most likely to be confused with strategic drift.
- *Evolution.* This is incremental transformation. This is a strategy that requires a fundamental change to the business model, but such a change is allowed to take place over a period of time. Think, for example, about an organisation gradually withdrawing from production of a good, by subcontracting its operations, and concentrating on 'badging' the product and marketing it.
- *Reconstruction.* This is big-bang realignment. It is a fast process, but does not fundamentally change the business model. Many organisations attempt this when there is a need for radical cost cutting.
- *Revolution.* This is big-bang transformation. It is often a response to some sort of crisis, such as a change in legislation or a hostile takeover bid. It might also be undertaken in order to exploit a new technology.

9

Self-assessment question 9.1

Identify the different types of strategic change, and give examples relevant to an organisation with which you are familiar.

Feedback on page 112

9.2   Change: attitudes and context

There is no right way to manage change. Success or failure often depends on two variables: the *attitudes* of the individuals affected by that change, and the *context* within which the change takes place.

Learning activity 9.2

Look at the people that you work with. Do they appear to like or dislike change? Why do people resist change?

Feedback on page 112

In general terms, there are four attitudes to change:

- *Inactivists* want nothing to do with change and prefer to leave it to other people. They may be persuaded to become reactivists.

- *Reactivists* dislike change, and will try to reverse it by forcing the organisation back to its pre-change state. They are dangerous, as they can persuade others to support them.
- *Proactivists* like change, and are fully in favour of it, but are happy to allow others to lead the change process. They see change as inevitable and tend to be very compliant.
- *Interactivists* love change. Not only do they see it as a natural and inevitable aspect of business, they also want to become actively involved. Interactivists, of course, make the best change leaders.

There are a number of aspects to the context within which change takes place. According to Johnson, Scholes and Whittington (2007), they are:

- *Time*: how quickly is change required?
- *Scope*: what degree of change is required?
- *Preserved*: what organisational characteristics need to be prepared?
- *Diversity*: how similar or different are the individuals and groups affected?
- *Capability*: how able are the management and organisation to implement change?
- *Capacity*: what resources are available to support the change?
- *Readiness*: how ready for change is the workforce (see section 9.3)?
- *Power*: is the change leader able to impose change?

The cultural web (see section 4.4) can also be used to assess the change context of an organisation. The elements of the web are those aspects that need attention if the likelihood of successful change implementation is to be increased.

Self-assessment question 9.2

Explain how the cultural web can be used to assess the context in which change takes place.

Feedback on page 112

9.3 Managing change

If we are to manage change successfully, we must first be able to analyse the 'starting position'. We can do this by using force field analysis, where we analyse those *forces promoting or supporting change* (such as, for example, proactivists and interactivists) and those *forces opposing change* (such as inactivists and reactivists). Having identified the various forces, we must try to use the forces supporting change to help us overcome the forces opposing change.

According to Lewin (1943), there are three steps to any successful change programme:

1 *Unfreeze* the context, to create an environment that is conducive to change.
2 *Implement* the required changes.

3 *Refreeze* the context, to 'cement' the change in place and prevent the reactivists from undoing all our good work.

However, other writers such as Peters (1987) have suggested that refreezing the context just leads to an organisation that lacks flexibility. Instead, change should become part of the culture of the organisation, so there is no need to refreeze.

Learning activity 9.3

Try conducting a force field analysis for any planned change programme that you are familiar with.

Feedback on page 112

Having analysed the context in which the change is to take place, we must decide how best to overcome any resistance we might encounter from individuals and groups within the organisation. According to Johnson, Scholes and Whittington (2007), there are five strategies for overcoming resistance to change:

1 *Education and communication.* This involves explaining the reasons why change is necessary, and the benefits to arise from it.
2 *Collaboration or participation.* Getting people who resist change involved in the process is difficult, but can be very effective. The danger in this approach, however, is that the individual might hijack the change process to meet his or her own aims.
3 *Intervention.* This is where a change agent controls the change process, but delegates responsibility for elements of it. This is a version of collaboration, but has a lower risk of the change process being hijacked.
4 *Direction.* This is an essentially top-down change process, where the change agent or senior manager uses his or her own personal authority to establish a strategy.
5 *Coercion.* This is an extreme form of direction, where the manager imposes the change and threatens some sort of penalty for failure to comply.

As well as changing people's behaviour, it is also important to change the organisation's routines. These are the behaviour patterns that, over time, become firmly embedded in the organisation's culture. There is a risk that, rather than being core competences, these routines can become core rigidities that are impossible to change.

Finally, it is also important to change any symbols in the organisation. These are objects, events, people or activities that bring more than just their intrinsic value to the organisation. They also, to some extent, define what the organisation is or what it stands for. Many of these symbols are also components of the cultural web, and examples of symbols include:

- *Rituals.* The things that individuals in the organisation like to do, that bind them into a cohesive whole. Examples include parties, early finish times, or 'dress-down' days.

9

- *Systems and processes.* These are organisational routines, as mentioned earlier.
- *Physical aspects.* These aspects include such things as the location of the organisation's offices or their layout.
- *Behaviour of change agents.* The people driving change can give clear signals about the need for change and the benefits of it. Top management buy-in is almost always a critical success factor for change implementation.
- *Language.* Change agents need to be careful that the way they speak about change reinforces the process and objectives that the organisation desires.
- *Stories.* New rumours and anecdotes can be developed that support the desired state.

Self-assessment question 9.3

Distinguish between 'collaboration' and 'intervention' as change management styles.

Feedback on page 112

9

9.4 Change roles

It has been impossible to avoid using the term *change agent* in earlier sections. This is the individual whose role it is to lead and drive the change. They may or may not be the designer of the strategy, and they may or may not come from within the organisation.

Strategic leadership takes many forms, but most writers agree that there are two main styles of change leadership:

- *Charismatic* leaders tend to enthuse and energise people to strive towards their vision.
- *Instrumental* or *transactional* leaders focus on designing systems that will control the organisation's processes.

While charismatic styles are best suited to radical transformational change, transactional styles suit incremental change.

Learning activity 9.4

Assess your own role in any change process with which you have been involved.

Feedback on page 112

Senior managers are the most likely to find themselves in the role of change agent. As well as being responsible for the formulation of strategy, the senior managers are also responsible for its implementation. As mentioned before, it is essential that senior managers be seen to buy into the change process and the new strategy.

According to Floyd and Wooldridge (1994), middle managers have an active role (or roles) to play in the management of change:

- They are responsible for *implementation and control* of the change process.
- They are responsible for *translating* an often vague strategy into something capable of being implemented.
- They are likely to be involved in the *adjustment of strategy*, as events unfold, as they are involved day to day with its implementation.
- They form a *relevance bridge* to lower level staff, and become translators of strategy into terms that are easily understood by junior staff.
- They are likely to be *advisors to senior management*, particularly in relation to what might reasonably be achieved, or how best to approach implementation.

Outsiders such as consultants are often brought in to assist with the implementation of change, and sometimes adopt the role of change agent. This may be good, as such individuals may be skilled at change management. However, there is a danger that outsiders can provoke an instinctive mistrust of the new strategy.

9

Self-assessment question 9.4

Explain the different types of leader that might be found in organisations, and identify how each type might manage change.

Feedback on page 113

Revision question

Now try the revision question for this session on page 259.

Summary

In this session we have looked at various issues surrounding the management of change in organisations. Successful change management is often a critical success factor for strategy implementation.

Suggested further reading

Try a biography of a successful charismatic leader, such as Richard Branson.

Feedback on learning activities and self-assessment questions

Feedback on learning activity 9.1

This is a tricky one, as strategic drift is often justified after the event, and becomes part of an organisation's emergent strategy. You really need to find evidence that pre-dates the change, in order to prove that it was 'planned'.

Feedback on self-assessment question 9.1

The four types are often shown in a matrix, as shown in Johnson, Scholes and Whittington (2007).

Feedback on learning activity 9.2

There are lots of reasons to resist change. Common ones include lack of understanding, laziness, being risk-averse or wanting to preserve traditions.

Feedback on self-assessment question 9.2

The cultural web consists of seven components:

- The *routines and rituals* of an organisation are those practices that make up the detail of the organisation's behaviour patterns.
- *Symbols* include logos and trademarks, and also the language and terminology used within the organisation.
- *Power structures* can also influence culture.
- The *control systems* of the organisation are such things as target setting, measurement and reward.
- The *organisational structure* is not part of the culture in itself, but instead reflects what is important to the organisation.
- The *stories* told in an organisation, about its formation, history or crises, can provide a clear insight into its culture.
- The *paradigm* of the organisation summarises its core beliefs and values. It reinforces the other elements.

In order to successfully implement change, all of these aspects must be changed to support the 'desired state' of the organisation.

Feedback on learning activity 9.3

Don't just look for individuals to include in the analysis. Think about the various aspects of the cultural web, and how they might promote or resist change.

Feedback on self-assessment question 9.3

Collaboration (or participation) is where reluctant individuals are persuaded to get involved in the change process. There is a risk that either the change will not happen or it may be 'hijacked' and the goals of the individuals achieved at the expense of those of the organisation.

Intervention is where a change agent controls the change process, but delegates responsibility for elements of it. This is a version of collaboration, but has a lower risk of the change process being hijacked.

Feedback on learning activity 9.4

Look at your general attitude to change (proactivist, interactivist, and so on) and whether you tend to be a change agent. If so, would you say your style was charismatic, or instrumental? If you are struggling to find a workplace example, think about how you organise a holiday or social event.

Feedback on self-assessment question 9.4

- *Charismatic* leaders tend to enthuse and energise people to strive towards their vision.
- *Instrumental* or *transactional* leaders focus on designing systems that will control the organisation's processes.

While charismatic styles are best suited to radical transformational change, transactional styles suit incremental change.

9

9

Integration of supply chain strategies with corporate and business strategies

Introduction

This session looks at the way an organisation's supply chain strategy can support, and integrate with, the corporate strategy of the organisation.

Session learning objectives

After completing this session you should be able to:

10.1 Explain the contribution of strategic supply chain management to corporate strategy.
10.2 Analyse the integration of supply chain strategies with corporate and business strategies.
10.3 Explain the contribution of strategic 'make/do or buy' decisions to corporate strategy.

Unit content coverage

This study session covers the following topics from the official CIPS unit content document:

Statement of practice

• Explain the contribution of strategic supply chain management to corporate strategy.

Learning objectives

3.1 Analyse the relationships between functional, business and corporate strategies, and the integration of supply chain strategies with corporate and business strategies.
• Relationships between functional, business and corporate strategies
• Integration of supply chain strategies with corporate and business strategies
• Formal and informal processes through which supply chain strategies may be integrated with corporate strategy: involvement in planning processes, role of main board, supportive chief executive
3.2 Assess the contribution of strategic supply chain management to corporate strategy.
• Contribution of strategic supply chain management to corporate strategy: cost reduction, quality, innovation, delivery
• Contribution of strategic make, do or buy decisions to corporate strategy

'There are no short cuts to business success, and firms will only prosper if they adopt a flexible and open approach to their internal and external resource management strategies.'
Andrew Cox

10

- Core competence analysis: core, complementary and residual competences
- Relational competence analysis (Cox)

Resources

Access to Johnson, Scholes and Whittington (2007) chapters 4 and 12 is highly recommended for use throughout this session.

Timing

You should set aside about 3 hours to read and complete this session, including learning activities, self-assessment questions, the suggested further reading (if any) and the revision question.

10.1 Supply chain strategy as a 'functional strategy'

You should remember, from section 6.2, that strategy exists at several levels in the organisation (see figure 10.1).

Figure 10.1: Three levels of strategy

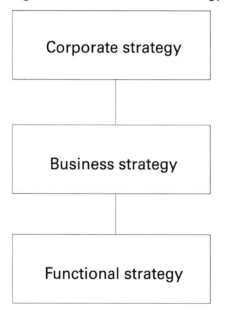

A textbook written 20 years ago would have assumed that all strategy was formulated at corporate level and then implemented in a 'top-down' manner by instructions to the business divisions.

Corporate strategy determines the overall purpose and scope of the organisation.

Business strategy should be formulated within the broad framework of objectives laid down by the corporate centre to ensure that each SBU plays its part. Business strategy is often termed 'competitive strategy' as it concerns the pursuit of competitive advantage.

Functional strategies are the long-term management policies of the major functional areas of a business. They are intended to ensure that the functional area plays its part in helping the SBUs achieve the goals of their business strategies. The supply chain strategy of an organisation is an example of such a strategy.

Learning activity 10.1

For your organisation (or one with which you are familiar), try to identify the supply chain (or procurement) strategy of the organisation.

Feedback on page 123

According to Handfield and Nichols (2002), the *supply chain* 'encompasses all those organisations and activities associated with the flow and transformation of goods from the raw materials stage through to the end user, as well as the associated information flow.' The same authors also define *supply chain management* (SCM) as 'the integration and management of supply chain organisations and activities through cooperative organisational relationships.'

The overall goal of any supply chain strategy, according to Dam Jespersen and Skjott-Larsen (2005), is to 'fulfil the end customers' needs and expectations in a cost-effective manner'. The same authors suggest that 'this overall goal can be broken down into a more operational range of subgoals, such as order cycle time, production lead time, rate of turnover, punctuality of delivery and product availability.' Supply chain strategy is therefore very diverse and impacts on many aspects of the organisation.

The specific supply chain strategy pursued by an organisation also depends on the type of supplier being dealt with, so an organisation might have different strategies for different supplies. Kraljic (1983) proposed a matrix approach to the strategic management of supplies. With the two dimensions of his matrix being the importance of the purchase and the risk and complexity of the supply market, Kraljic gave us four supply categories:

1 *Non-critical supplies*: those with low importance and low risk/complexity. For these, the number of suppliers should be reduced and the cost of procurement minimised.
2 *Leverage supplies*: those with high importance but low risk/complexity. For these supplies, competitive bidding should be encouraged.
3 *Bottleneck supplies*: those with low importance but high complexity/risk. Alternative suppliers should be identified and supply secured.
4 *Strategic supplies*: those with high importance and high risk/complexity. A performance-based partnership is appropriate.

In many cases, it is clear that the supply chain strategy can directly support the corporate or business strategies of the organisation or its SBUs. Examples of this can be seen in table 10.1.

10

Table 10.1 Corporate and supply chain strategies

Corporate or business objective	Supply chain objective
• Increasing product or service quality.	• Improving the quality of supplies.
• Improving profitability.	• Reducing the cost of supplies or simplifying logistics.
• Increasing market share.	• Securing the supply of critical components at the level required.
• Improving cashflow.	• Minimising inventory levels or extending payment terms.
• Developing new products.	• Securing the supply of critical inputs to allow new products to be produced.
• Entering new markets.	• Ensuring that supplies can be made available where they are required.

Self-assessment question 10.1

On the basis of your findings in learning activity 10.1 above, discuss how well the organisation's supply chain strategy supports its corporate objectives.

Feedback on page 123

10.2 How to integrate supply chain strategy with other strategies

In any organisation, the purchasing function should play an important role in helping to shape the competitive position of the organisation in the marketplace. It is also well understood that, to a great extent, the competitive capability of any manufacturing organisation (and many others) is influenced heavily by the performance of its suppliers.

Learning activity 10.2

Look at your organisation (or one with which you are familiar) and try to identify the processes and structures used to ensure that the supply chain (or procurement) strategy of the organisation supports the corporate strategy.

Feedback on page 124

A number of formal and informal measures are available to ensure that supply chain strategy is integrated into the corporate strategy process.

The formal processes are:

• Procurement has its own formal long-range plan, or a section of the corporate plan is devoted to supply chain management.
• The purchasing manager has a high status in the organisation's hierarchy (board-level representation, perhaps).

The informal processes are:

- The purchasing function actively participates in the planning process within the organisation.
- The supply chain management goals and plans are aligned with the organisation's strategic business goals.
- The corporate culture is such that supply chain management is seen as a key function.
- The supply chain managers frequently meet with the senior managers of other functions.

Self-assessment question 10.2

Identify the formal and informal structures and processes through which supply chain strategies may be integrated with corporate strategy.

Feedback on page 124

10.3 Strategic make/do or buy decisions

This section looks at key 'boundary of the firm' decisions. These are the decisions a firm makes over whether to make components (or perform activities) itself, or whether to subcontract or outsource such production (or process) to a supplier.

The advantages of outsourcing are:

- The opportunity to reduce cost by subcontracting to a specialist with economies of scope or scale.
- Receiving a better service/product as a result of the supplier's 'expert' status.
- Reduced management effort in planning, organising and supervising the activity.

The disadvantages of outsourcing are:

- Increased transaction costs, as a customer/supplier relationship is created.
- Risk that the supply might not meet the expectations in terms of cost, quality or delivery.
- Increased adversarial activity between the customer and supplier.

Learning activity 10.3

Identify a few activities or components that your organisation has outsourced, and consider why they may have chosen to do this.

Feedback on page 124

You should remember, from study session 3, that a *competence* is an activity or process through which an organisation deploys or utilises its resources. It is something the organisation does, rather than something it has.

In study session 3, we said that strategic competences could be classified as follows:

- *Threshold* competence is the level of competence necessary for an organisation to compete and survive in a given industry and market. For example, an online bookseller must have a logistics system that allows books to be delivered as promised, to the customers who have bought them.
- A *core* competence is something the organisation does that underpins a source of competitive advantage. For example, if an online bookseller is able to deliver books a day or two earlier than its rivals, this represents a core competence.

Reve (1990) argues that the core competetences of an organisation are of four different types, each based on a different kind of what is known as 'asset specificity'. This is the degree to which assets of the organisation are committed to the performance of a particular core competence. A high degree of asset specificity therefore denotes a core competence. The four types of core competence are:

1 *Site specificity*, where the advantage is based on immovable assets (such as raw materials, for example).
2 *Physical asset specificity*, where the advantage is based on some technological advantage (such as a production technology, for example).
3 *Human asset specificity*, where the advantage is based on know-how (such as intellectual property, for example).
4 *Dedicated asset specificity*, where the advantage is based on some specialised investment (such as a brand, for example).

Bearing in mind these arguments about asset specificity, Cox (1996) has developed a different way of looking at competences in terms of strategic supply chain management. He suggests that competences come in three types, as follows:

1 *Core competences*, where there is high asset specificity. These are areas where the organisation should never consider outsourcing, as it is the core competences that give a competitive advantage. In this case, the decision should always be to make or do.
2 *Complementary competences*, which are areas where the organisation has medium asset specificity. In this case, the firm should outsource, but only to trusted key suppliers who have the skills to supply as required. The firm would also enter into a strategic relationship with the supplier.
3 *Residual competences*, where there is a low level of asset specificity. In these areas, the organisation should outsource by means of an 'arm's length' relationship – a simple 'buy' decision.

Thus, when making strategic 'make/do or buy' decisions, the organisation should look at the degree of asset specificity to determine what type of competence is being considered. These decisions can be summarised as shown in table 10.2.

Table 10.2 Asset specificity and outsourcing decisions

Degree of asset specificity	Strategy
Low asset specificity (residual competence)	• Adversarial (arm's length) procurement
Medium asset specificity (complementary competence)	• Preferred supplier relationship • Single sourcing • Network sourcing
High asset specificity (core competence)	• Merger or acquisition • In-house process.

The six available strategies are explained as follows:

1 *Adversarial procurement* is the typical competitive resource acquisition process, where the buyer puts pressure on the supplier to meet quality expectations at the lowest possible cost.
2 *Preferred supplier relationship* is where a small number of suppliers are given special status, and competition to supply is limited to these.
3 *Single sourcing* is where there is a 'sole supplier' relationship, with one key supplier and a blurring of the 'boundary of the firm'.
4 *Network sourcing* is where the organisation creates a 'virtual company' at different stages of the supply chain by creating strategic partnerships at each stage.
5 *Merger or acquisition* is where the organisation vertically integrates with a supplier or suppliers.
6 *In-house process* is where the organisation decides to retain responsibility for performing the process, rather than involving a supplier.

While these arguments seem reasonable, other authors have argued that the concepts of core competence and asset specificity should not be linked in the simplistic, linear way that Reve and Cox do.

As was made clear in study session 3, the core competence/competitive advantage argument is about those activities which make an organisation's products or services unique and valued in the market and which cannot easily be copied. The issue of asset specificity, on the other hand, is about the extent to which the assets used to support a particular transaction are specific to that transaction and would lose value if they were transferred to an alternative transaction. Highly specific assets (site, physical, human) create a sunk cost which, it is argued, is best managed in-house rather than between a separate buyer and supplier. The logic is that the higher the sunk cost the more significant the degree of lock-in and therefore the more damage might be caused by opportunistic behaviour if the transaction (and the asset) is outsourced. As the level of asset specificity falls it becomes progressively less risky to use external suppliers because the threat of switching, if a supplier becomes unreliable, becomes more credible.

The problem with the Cox and Reve models is that they are bolting together two different sets of issues, which relate to different aspects of the outsourcing decision (competitive advantage and risk management). An activity regarded as a core competence might involve highly specific assets, but there is no reason why it necessarily should. It is equally plausible that

10

a core competence might be the result of the unique way an organisation combines and uses assets and resources that are entirely non-specific.

There are a number of alternative views on outsourcing, which do not relate to asset specificity. Quinn and Hilmer (1995) state four advantages of what they term 'strategic outsourcing':

- Managers can concentrate their efforts on what the enterprise does best and therefore get the best returns on internal resources.
- Well-developed core competences provide barriers to entry that can be used to protect competitive advantage.
- Organisations can fully leverage the investments, innovations and capabilities of their suppliers, in a way that would be prohibitively expensive or even impossible to duplicate in-house.
- Such collaborative strategy decreases risk, shortens life cycles and creates better responsiveness to changing customer needs.

In order to gain these benefits, Quinn and Hilmer suggest, organisations need to resolve three key issues:

1   What exactly are their core competences?
2   Having identified the core competences, does that mean the organisation should outsource everything else?
3   How can managers identify and manage the risks of those activities that it is desirable to outsource?

Core competences, according to Quinn and Hilmer, are:

- Skills or knowledge sets, not products or functions.
- Flexible long-term platforms for competitive advantage – capable of adaptation or evolution.
- Limited in number.
- Unique sources of leverage in their supply chain.
- Areas where the company can dominate.
- Elements important to their customers, in the long run.
- Embedded in the organisation's systems.

Quinn and Hilmer put forward three tests for whether any non-core activity should be outsourced:

1   What is the potential for gaining competitive advantage from this activity, taking account of transaction costs? The lower the potential, the more sensible it is to outsource.
2   What is the potential vulnerability to market failure that could arise if the activity was outsourced? Once again, the lower the risk, the more sensible to outsource.
3   What can be done to reduce these risks by structuring arrangements with suppliers in such a way as to protect ourselves? In this case, the more we can protect ourselves, the more sensible it is to outsource.

Quinn and Hilmer suggest that the main risks of outsourcing are:

- Loss of critical skills, that later become a potential source of competitive advantage.

- Loss of cross-functional skills, that later become essential to support other core competences.
- Loss of control over the processes or activities carried out by a supplier, rather than in-house.

Self-assessment question 10.3

For each of the examples identified in learning activity 10.3 above, identify what type of competence was involved, and what strategy was chosen.

Feedback on page 124

Revision question

Now try the revision question for this session on page 259.

Summary

This session has looked at the relationship between supply chain strategy and the corporate and business strategies of the organisation, including the contribution of strategic 'make/do or buy' decisions to corporate strategy.

Suggested further reading

Dam Jespersen and Skjott-Larsen (2005), chapters 1 to 3.

Watts, Kim and Hahn (1995), pages 2–8. (Available by logging in to the CIPS website, then following the link to the ISM website and searching their articles database.)

Quinn and Hilmer (1995). (Available from libraries, subscription services, or on a number of websites.)

Feedback on learning activities and self-assessment questions

Feedback on learning activity 10.1

Remember, from the definitions of strategy, you are looking for 'clear objectives and a prescribed course of action' or 'a pattern in a stream of decisions'.

Feedback on self-assessment question 10.1

If the organisation's supply chain strategy is 'deliberate' (that is, crafted as part of some formal process), it should be fairly easy to see whether it is goal congruent with the corporate strategy. You might even be able to see the supply chain strategy documented as part of the corporate strategy document.

10

If the organisation has a formal corporate strategy but no deliberate supply chain strategy, you will need to look for a 'pattern in a stream of decisions' as evidence of some sort of emergent strategy. You then need to make a decision whether that emergent strategy appears goal congruent with the corporate strategy.

If the organisation has no formal strategic planning process, it is unlikely to have a supply chain strategy. In that case, you will have a much more difficult task, as you will need to identify the emergent corporate and supply chain strategies (or choose a different organisation to study!).

Feedback on learning activity 10.2

Does the procurement function senior manager get involved with strategy formulation? Does the function have a seat on the board? Are there regular meetings between the head of procurement and the 'strategy makers'?

Feedback on self-assessment question 10.2

The formal processes are:

- Procurement has its own formal long-range plan, or a section of the corporate plan is devoted to supply chain management.
- The purchasing manager has a high status in the organisation's hierarchy (board-level representation, perhaps).

The informal processes are:

- The purchasing function actively participates in the planning process within the organisation.
- The supply chain management goals and plans are aligned with the organisation's strategic business goals.
- The corporate culture is such that supply chain management is seen as a key function.
- The supply chain managers frequently meet with the senior managers of other functions.

Feedback on learning activity 10.3

All organisations make outsourcing decisions, even if it is in a simple area such as office equipment or stationery. You don't have to look for whole functions being outsourced, just simple 'components'. There are a number of reasons why functions might have been outsourced, the most common of which seems to be 'we didn't understand it' or 'we couldn't be bothered with it'. Contrast these arguments with the 'advantages' listed at the start of section 10.3.

Feedback on self-assessment question 10.3

Hopefully this analysis will fit with the summary in table 10.2. If it doesn't, you should think through the consequences of the decision made.

Innovative supply chain strategies

'It ain't what you do, it's the way that you do it.'
Bananarama

Introduction

This session looks at a range of supply chain strategies that may be used by organisations to meet corporate and business objectives. The first three sections of this session look at ways of improving the supply chain strategy of the organisation in its current position, and the fourth at repositioning along the supply chain. The final section looks at improving the way the whole supply chain works, to gain a mutual competitive advantage for all the players.

Session learning objectives

After completing this session you should be able to:

11.1 Develop better supplier relationships to meet corporate and business targets.

11.2 Propose cost improvement strategies to meet corporate and business targets.

11.3 Design quality improvement strategies to meet corporate and business targets.

11.4 Analyse supply/value chain positioning as a means of meeting corporate and business targets.

11.5 Develop innovative strategies to improve agility (flexibility/responsiveness) in the supply chain.

Unit content coverage

This study session covers the following topics from the official CIPS unit content document:

Statement of practice

- Explain the contribution of strategic supply chain management to corporate strategy.

Learning objective

3.4 Propose innovative supply chain strategies to meet corporate and business targets.
- Benefits and difficulties in developing better supplier relationships
- Methods of cost reduction and cost improvement
- Strategies for quality improvement
- Strategies for repositioning the organisation on the supply or value chain

11

Resources

Access to the following books is highly recommended for use throughout this session:

- Lysons and Farrington (2006), chapters 3, 9 and 12
- Dam Jespersen and Skjott-Larsen (2005), chapter 4
- Christopher (2005), chapters 3, 9 and 10.

Timing

You should set aside about 6 hours to read and complete this session, including learning activities, self-assessment questions, the suggested further reading (if any) and the revision question.

11.1 Supplier relationships

This whole study session looks at the different ways that supply chain strategy could be used to support corporate or business strategy. Although each section deals with different issues, they are, of course, all linked. High-level business strategy objectives such as cost leadership, differentiation or focus, require the support of a range of functional strategies (see study session 10) of which supply chain strategy is just one.

According to Dam Jespersen and Skjott-Larsen (2005), 'the overall goal for a supply chain is to *fulfil the end customers' needs and expectations* in a cost-efficient manner'. At first sight, this statement makes supply chain management illogical; indeed Christopher (2005) agrees that '...*supply chain* management is actually mismanaging. *Demand chain management* would be a better term, and would stress the fact that the chain is driven by market forces and not by the supply side'.

Although it is true that many organisations concentrate too much on facing upstream in their supply chain strategies, there is a need to develop relationships with suppliers. After all, relationships are two-way things. If they are your supplier, you are their customer.

Learning activity 11.1

Identify the benefits and difficulties of developing better supplier relationships from your own experience.

Feedback on page 136

In recent years, we have seen words and phrases, such as 'partnership', 'co-makership' and 'collaboration', used freely in both literature and practice within supply chain management. Such words and phrases reflect a belief that cooperation is a major path in developing inter-organisational relationships. Nonetheless, there is confusion about how and when *cooperative strategies* should be used, and the effectiveness of the tactics and operations that support these strategies.

Many writers have suggested that it is better to co-evolve rather than compete with a rival in business. Authors borrow metaphors from biology to suggest that business is an 'ecosystem', where mutual interdependence maintains the environment. They offer examples, such as the way Wal-Mart revolutionised retailing by exerting heavy pressure on suppliers, like Proctor and Gamble, to keep their prices down through cross-company information systems that attained maximum manufacturing and distribution efficiency.

For example, Wal-Mart and Proctor and Gamble (P&G) reached an unprecedented partnership that involved extensive electronic data interchange (EDI) between the companies, enabling both customer and supplier to better predict demand and adjust operations. P&G dramatically improved inventory levels, factory scheduling, purchasing economics, order and data handling costs, shipping mistakes, billing errors and stock-outs. More significant were the industry-wide changes from P&G's re-engineering of its entire distribution operation. By turning its customers into partners, P&G gave all participants a stake in contributing to the information system. To achieve these dramatic results, P&G had to exercise leadership, take risks and work with others. P&G sold its system to IBM after the industry standard was accepted and the rules of the game changed. Today, businesses are increasingly requiring their suppliers and customers to conduct these paperless transactions over the internet.

Implementing cooperative strategies involves a wide range of activities from contract design through to supplier selection and management. It should be noted that cooperative strategies are not in themselves 'good' or 'bad', they depend on a range of factors including industry climate (what has traditionally been practised in an industry), competitive pressure and resource availability. Where organisations choose a cooperative strategy, they often need to work at it for a considerable period of time, spend a lot of money and be prepared for disappointments.

Although collaborative relationships and strategies are seen as being optimal in some circumstances, there are others where *adversarial, arm's-length relationships* work best, and other industries where such strategies are normal. The adversarial strategy, a traditional approach, is to have several vendors for each product. This approach was developed in order to increase competition for the buyer's business, which is believed to lower prices while increasing the level of service and attention paid to the account. In one recent study, for example, having *multiple sources* reduced total costs for some purchases. At the same time, buying from a large number of suppliers can lower the quality of the relationship with suppliers, which can lead to availability problems during times of shortage, as well as other problems.

One instance of the use of such a strategy might be the purchasing of standard or commodity products, in which the *key criterion is price*, the interactions between the vendor and the buyer are simple and the need to

11

11

share knowledge is very limited. Under that set of constraints, buyers can generate significant short-term concessions by playing sellers off against one another. This drives up transaction costs, but these can often be dramatically offset against price reductions, and transaction costs may not be as high as those involved in developing a collaborative strategy. Nonetheless, overtly adversarial strategies are slowly becoming less popular. This does not, however, mean that cost-reduction strategies do not sometimes produce adversarial results.

The *benefits* of cooperation with suppliers are:

- A *reduction in transaction costs*, by automation and streamlining of the process.
- *Improvements in the quality* of product and service, such as shorter lead times, as a result of greater understanding.
- Better *utilisation of the supplier's competences*, leading to better responsiveness and improved innovation.
- *Improved planning*, as a result of cooperation in the planning process.

There are, however, potential *pitfalls* in the cooperation process:

- The closer relationship might lead to *complacency*, and a gradual erosion of cost reductions.
- Developing a close relationship with one supplier may lead to *high switching costs* if it becomes necessary to change to another supplier.
- Close relationships between buyers and sellers may increase the risk of *fraud*.

Self-assessment question 11.1

Discuss whether it is possible to improve the 'customer experience' by improving relationships with suppliers.

Feedback on page 136

11.2 Cost improvements

Recently we have seen cost-reduction strategies implemented by a number of enterprises, using price-cut mandates and new technology, such as online reverse auctions. Suppliers faced by forced price reductions are often hostile to these methods and claim that if they reduce material and part quality, this may lead to plant closures. Enterprises employing these methods respond by portraying the processes as improving supplier 'fitness' or the lean elements of a production system (see section 11.5).

Mandatory price reductions are, of course, fairly common in a number of industrial sectors. Toyota requires its suppliers to cut prices annually. Many manufacturers now require suppliers to cut prices as a contractual obligation. Other companies in the automotive sector, such as Daimler-

Chrysler AG and Fiat, are looking for cost reductions of 15% over three years. Still others may consider cost targets on an individual basis.

Learning activity 11.2

Identify the risks of pursuing cost-reduction supply chain strategies.

Feedback on page 136

According to Lysons and Farrington (2006), there are a number of techniques that can be used to obtain the best value for money from the purchasing process. These include the following:

- *Value analysis*, including the elimination of unnecessary product features.
- *Consolidation of demand* (that is, aggregating several orders to negotiate discounts).
- *Negotiating* contracts and/or prices *centrally*.
- Ensuring *competition* in the procurement process, often by challenging the use of preferred suppliers.
- *Buying complete* sub-assemblies, rather than components.
- *Refurbishing* existing items, rather than replacing them.
- *Encouraging standardisation*, thus reducing the costs of spares and maintenance.
- Adopting a *whole-life approach*, rather than an initial-price approach.
- *Eliminating unnecessary inventory.*
- *Eliminating non-productive costs*, such as travel expenses.

There are also significant cost-reduction benefits to be gained from the use of technology in the procurement process. The *online reverse auction*, in which suppliers are pitted against each other in a downward bidding spiral, is one of the most popular technologies, enabling manufacturers to reduce their overall spend. Using the internet for procurement can mean that decades of suppliers building relationships and profit margins can be lost in an hour of frantic price cutting. In some cases, there are stories of suppliers having been invited to bid in online reverse auctions to place pressure on existing suppliers, rather than with any real hope of obtaining a contract award, and such stories can shade cost-reduction strategies into the adversarial mode.

Online reverse auctions can create apparently dramatic savings, and in some cases opening prices can be reduced by up to 40% over the course of a few hours. The downside of such auctions is to drive good suppliers out of the market as they first diversify and then leave the market. Another upside is that some suppliers will diversify into more innovative product lines within the existing market, where the ownership of intellectual property gives more bargaining power. Unique or special technology that makes a product better, or different, will allow for a different type of relationship. Without those characteristics, however, price will tend to take over. In a global economy, production will tend to gravitate to the lowest-cost provider.

11

Self-assessment question 11.2

Explain how use of the internet can reduce procurement costs, and identify the risks in such an approach.

Feedback on page 136

11.3 Quality improvements

Note: If you have not studied quality management before, or need a review of the key issues, chapter 9 of Lysons and Farrington (2006) contains sufficient detail.

Juran (1998) defines quality as '*fitness for purpose*' and Crosby (1980) as '*conformity to requirements*'. Neither of these definitions is terribly exciting, nor is the pursuit of fitness for purpose exactly innovative (see the title of this study session). So why is quality so important?

Fundamentally, achieving conformity to the customers' requirements is a *critical success factor* for all businesses. Producing products or services that disappoint will lead to an organisation that has no customers in the truest sense of the word. Instead, it will survive in the short term by generating a series of one-off sales. In the long term the organisation will fail, as it will run out of new customers.

Learning activity 11.3

Identify the quality improvement strategy used with a supplier/suppliers of any product or service to your organisation, or one with which you are familiar.

Feedback on page 136

One of the main problems with quality improvement is that it is difficult to measure its benefits. It is, however, easy to measure the cost of quality. There are thought to be four costs, in two categories:

Costs of conformance

1   *Prevention costs.* These are the costs of actions taken to prevent or reduce defects or failures, such as the costs of training staff or maintaining equipment.
2   *Appraisal costs.* These are the costs of assessing the level of quality achieved, such as the costs of inspection and testing.

Costs of non-conformance

1   *Internal failure costs.* These are costs, related to quality failure, that arise in the organisation (before the product or service reaches the customer), such as scrap and rework costs.

2   *External failure costs.* These are costs, related to quality failure, that arise after the product or service reaches the customer, such as the costs of replacing products that fail 'in service'.

Logically, there is a trade-off between the costs of conformance and non-conformance. In order to reduce failure costs, it may be necessary to increase prevention and appraisal costs.

There are a number of different *quality strategies* that organisations might pursue, incrementally increasing the costs and benefits to the organisation:

- *Product inspection*, to ensure that sub-standard products do not find their way to the customer.
- *Quality control*, so that the processes of the organisation can be incrementally improved, and there can be improved product quality and reduced costs of quality failure.
- *Quality assurance*, so that customers and potential customers of the organisation can buy the product with confidence.
- *Total quality* initiatives, where the principles of quality control and assurance are applied throughout the organisation

These strategies can also be applied to the supply chain, as follows:

- Goods may be inspected, either before they leave the supplier or as they reach the customer.
- Organisations can collaborate on the development of quality improvement programmes, sharing information relating to costs of quality and opportunities for improvement.
- Supply chains can be inspected and certified by third parties, and such certification publicised.
- Total quality partnerships can be established between adjacent organisations in the supply chain. These organisations will then develop a continued dialogue on quality-related issues, and collaborate on quality improvement initiatives. These initiatives will not just look at improving the products that are exchanged, but at improving the quality of every aspect of the relationship between the organisations.

For organisations seeking a competitive advantage, quality improvement is an obvious place to look. In any buying situation, potential customers will compare the price-quality characteristics of the choices, so an improvement in product quality is at least as valuable as a price reduction. However, there is a fundamental problem with any tangible source of competitive advantage – it is too easy to copy. This has led to two trends in the quality improvement initiatives pursued by organisations:

- They have become *more complex and sophisticated* (see, for example, six-sigma).
- Their emphasis has shifted away from clear, tangible improvements in product or service quality (such as quality inspection) to *intangible, cultural change* programmes (such as total quality management (TQM)).

There has been such focus on developing increasingly complex quality management philosophies, that it is now questionable whether such

11

exercises add value at all. Many organisations wish to be 'seen to be doing something about quality', even though there are no discernible benefits to customers. Perhaps it is time that such attributes as TQM and six-sigma be seen as threshold competences, allowing organisations to look elsewhere for sources of competitive advantage.

Self-assessment question 11.3

Identify and assess various approaches to quality improvement.

Feedback on page 137

11.4 Supply chain positioning

A supply chain consists of a series of organisations, each of which adds value by performing a number of tasks in series or parallel. The chain starts with a raw material and ends with a final consumer.

An organisation can reposition itself in the supply chain by two methods:

- By organic development, either one step upstream or downstream, or further, away from its original position.
- By acquisition, normally one step upstream (known as 'backward vertical integration') or downstream (known as 'forward vertical integration').

All this depends, of course, on two factors:

- The move has to be desirable, in that it has to result in the organisation ending up in a better strategic position (that is, one that yields greater shareholder wealth).
- The organisation must be able to exploit their new position, in other words they need to have (or be able to acquire and leverage) the required competences.

Learning activity 11.4

Look at the supply chain for any input into your organisation. Draw it out from the original 'raw material' to the final consumer good. Who seems to be making the most money in the supply chain? Is it because of the size and power of that organisation or is it because of the position they occupy in the supply chain?

Feedback on page 137

The idea of an organisation positioning itself strategically within a supply chain is an underdeveloped area of thinking in business strategy. While Porter was clearly aware of the importance of buyer-supplier power when he developed the value chain and value system models, he put forward little in the way of advice as to how an organisation might reposition itself.

If we are happy with the idea of strategy based on core competences (section 11.3) we must accept that organisations will think seriously about where they position themselves in any supply chain they choose to enter. At one extreme, they could decide to vertically integrate the entire supply chain from raw material to end consumer. At the other, they may decide to focus on only one or two core competences at one stage of the supply chain. The decision as to how many supply chain stages to carry out is simply an extension of the 'boundary-of-the-firm' decisions (as discussed in study session 10), but extended over the supply chain.

Any decision as to where to position the organisation in the supply chain must logically be based on the answer to two questions:

- At which stage in the supply chain does the organisation possess (or can the organisation acquire or develop) the core competences required to dominate the supply chain?
- At which stage, or stages, in the supply chain are there the best opportunities to earn high margins?

Clearly, in an ideal world, organisations should position themselves strategically to own those supply chain resources and competences that are most difficult to imitate, and around which they can build maintainable barriers to entry. This should necessarily lead to the organisation earning and maintaining higher margins, a clear sustainable competitive advantage.

Historically, business strategy has been concerned with competing horizontally across supply chains, rather than vertically within them. If it is accepted that business is about appropriating value for oneself, rather than passing it to the end consumer (unless there is no alternative) then positioning within the chain must be a rational strategic decision. To exert power over the supply chain in this way, however, conflicts directly with the idea of 'mutual trust' that is at the core of lean supply chain thinking. (See section 11.5 and study sessions 17 and 20 for a detailed discussion of lean supply chains, and study session 18 for a discussion of power in supply chains.)

Self-assessment question 11.4

Analyse any of your organisation's supply chains and recommend a strategy to improve the position of your organisation in that supply chain.

Feedback on page 137

11.5 Flexibility and innovation

Flexibility is a measure of how quickly the organisation or supply chain responds to changes in the environment, such as customer requirements.

Innovation is a measure of how many new ideas are developed within the organisation or supply chain.

Agility is the ability of the organisation or supply chain to respond to changes in demand. In other words, it needs to be able to adjust both quantity and specification in order to meet changing needs. Agility requires both flexibility and innovation.

Learning activity 11.5

Identify various examples of agility in the supply chain involving your organisation, or one with which you are familiar.

Feedback on page 137

You will be familiar with the concept of a lean supply chain from your earlier studies. *Leanness* in a supply chain is achieved by reducing the inventory levels throughout the chain. While it is tempting to see agility as being the same as leanness, they are by no means the same. Although leanness may make agility easier to achieve, it may also reduce flexibility (and therefore agility). The features of the two approaches are compared in table 11.1:

Table 11.1 Lean v agile

Feature	Leanness	Agility
Purpose	Meeting predictable demand as efficiently as possible	Meeting unpredictable demand as quickly as possible
Focus	Improving utilisation	Deploying capacity effectively
Inventory	Minimum inventory	Holding buffer stocks to allow responsiveness
Lead time	Shorter	Shortest
Selection criteria	Cost and quality	Speed, flexibility and quality
Linkages	Long-term partnerships	Virtual and temporary
Performance measures	Quality and productivity	Delivery promises met
Organisation	Standardised	Responsive
Planning and control	Synchronisation and waste reduction	Instantaneous response

According to Christopher (2005), '…the key to agile response is the presence of agile partners upstream and downstream of the focal firm'. This leads to the idea that agility resides in the supply chain, rather than in the organisation. An organisation cannot be agile in isolation – it depends on support from the other organisations in its supply chain. A supply chain is only as agile as its least agile member organisation.

While it may seem desirable for all supply chains to be agile, this is unnecessary. Christopher suggests four different 'generic supply chain strategies', each dependent on different supply and demand characteristics (see table 11.2):

Table 11.2 Generic supply chain strategies

Strategy	Supply characteristic	Demand characteristic
Lean	Long lead times	Predictable demand
Hybrid	Long lead times	Unpredictable demand
Kanban	Short lead times	Predictable demand
Agile	Short lead times	Unpredictable demand

Gunasekaran (1998) identified seven 'enablers' of agile manufacturing, most of which can be applied in non-manufacturing contexts as follows:

1 *Virtual enterprises*, working collaboratively.
2 *Physically distributed* work teams.
3 *Rapid partnership formation*, enabled by IT.
4 *Concurrent (in parallel) planning and process redesign*, leading to rapid response.
5 *Integrated information systems* through the supply chain.
6 *Rapid development* and 'trialling' of new processes.
7 *E-commerce*, improving responsiveness to customer demands by directly collecting their requirements.

Alternatively, Christopher (2005) suggests that the characteristics of an agile supply chain are:

• *Virtual*: using technology to create an information-based, rather than inventory-based, supply chain.
• *Market-sensitive*: capable of reading and responding to changing customer needs.
• *Process-aligned*: using common systems, as a result of collaboration and information sharing.
• *Network-based*: managed as a supply chain, rather than as a collection of competing organisations.

Christopher also proposes seven steps towards an agile supply chain:

1 Synchronise activities through shared information.
2 Work smarter, not harder.
3 Partner with suppliers to reduce inbound lead times.
4 Seek to reduce complexity.
5 Postpone the final configuration/assembly/distribution of products.
6 Manage processes, not just functions.
7 Utilise performance metrics based on agility.

Self-assessment question 11.5

Make recommendations to your manager for adopting an 'agile' strategy in respect of any one of your organisation's supply chains.

Feedback on page 137

Revision question

Now try the revision question for this session on page 259.

Summary

This session has looked at a series of innovative supply chain management strategies, including:

- developing better supplier relationships
- implementing cost improvement strategies
- designing quality improvement strategies
- analysing supply/value chain positioning
- improving agility in the supply chain.

Suggested further reading

Case studies in Johnson, Scholes and Whittington (2007), Dam Jespersen and Skjott-Larsen (2005), and Lysons and Farrington (2006), to identify innovative supply chain strategies.

Feedback on learning activities and self-assessment questions

Feedback on learning activity 11.1

You may need to talk to a purchasing specialist to be able to answer this question. Compare your list with the benefits and pitfalls identified in the continuation of section 11.1.

Feedback on self-assessment question 11.1

If you can create added value, and pass some or all of that value on to the customer, then the answer is 'yes'.

Feedback on learning activity 11.2

Have a look at a few case studies, either from the suggested texts (such as 'Wal-Mart' in Christopher (2005), or 'ESU' in Lysons & Farrington (2006)) or from the internet.

Feedback on self-assessment question 11.2

The first part of your answer can be a précis of the explanation of online auctions in section 11.2, and the second a reworking of your findings in learning activity 11.1.

Feedback on learning activity 11.3

Strategies can range from simply inspecting (and accepting or rejecting) to a total quality partnership approach (see the continuation of section 11.3).

The degree of investment in quality improvement may reflect the perceived 'strategic value' of the particular supply.

Feedback on self-assessment question 11.3

Pick three or four 'approaches' – such as quality inspection, quality assurance or total quality. Briefly explain each of them, and discuss the advantages and disadvantages of each – refer to section 11.3 for explanation and discussion.

Feedback on learning activity 11.4

Think about the Five Forces model that you studied in study session 3. Porter suggested that competitive advantage might result from an imbalance between the 'bargaining power of suppliers' and the 'bargaining power of buyers' (customers). Does this explain the split of profit, or is it more complicated than that?

Feedback on self-assessment question 11.4

In order to do this, you will need to consider the Five Forces model and the issues discussed in section 11.4.

Feedback on learning activity 11.5

Concentrate on the responsiveness of the organisation immediately upstream, and of your own organisation.

Feedback on self-assessment question 11.5

Work through Christopher's seven steps (for example) for any of your organisation's supply chains, proposing changes to bring the processes in line with Christopher's suggestions.

11

11

Aligning organisational structures and processes with supply chain strategies

Introduction

In this study session, we remind ourselves that structure should follow strategy. We also look at some 'modern' supply chain management structures.

'The mechanics of industry is easy. The real engine is the people: Their motivation and direction.'
Ken Gilbert

Session learning objectives

After completing this session you should be able to:

12.1 Analyse and align organisational structures with supply chain strategies.
12.2 Assess the appropriateness of centralised, decentralised and mixed structures for effective alignment.
12.3 Analyse the use of cross-functional teams to support supply chain strategies.
12.4 Identify the inter-organisational networks necessary to achieve supply chain strategies.

Unit content coverage

This study session covers the following topics from the official CIPS unit content document:

Statement of practice

- Distinguish and assess various models of supply chain structures and relationships.

Learning objective

3.3 Analyse and align organisational structures and processes, with supply chain strategies.
  - Alignment of organisational structures and processes with strategic supply chain strategies
  - Centralised, decentralised and mixed structures
  - Future trends in purchasing organisation and processes (Carter and Narasimhan, Van Weele and Rozemeijer)
  - Use of cross-functional teams to support supply chain strategies
  - Use of inter-organisational networks to achieve strategic supply chain strategies

Resources

Access to Lysons and Farrington (2006), especially chapter 5, is highly recommended for use throughout this session.

12

Timing

You should set aside about 5 hours to read and complete this session, including learning activities, self-assessment questions, the suggested further reading (if any) and the revision question.

12.1 Supply chain strategy and organisational structure

Having looked (in study session 4) at the way in which organisational structures are developed, and the types of dilemma that they are designed to resolve, we can now look at the structure of the purchasing function within the organisation. The way in which a department is organised reflects, in some ways, the way in which an organisation is structured, although it is possible to suggest that the organisational environment can be slightly less complex than the industry or global environment. In addition, purchasing and supply function structures can utilise any of the forms identified in study session 4, such as project teams, matrix forms and even adhocracies.

Learning activity 12.1

Identify and categorise (functional, divisional, matrix and so on) the structure of the purchasing function in your organisation, or one with which you are familiar.

Feedback on page 148

The days of large purchasing departments concerned with order processing, invoicing and order handling are passing, under the pressures of new technology and outsourcing initiatives. Nonetheless, issues such as monitoring and managing performance can still be an issue in larger purchasing departments.

Deciding the *nature of the purchasing and supply task* is a critical first step in the developing structure. Some critical issues here may include:

- size of spend
- nature of spend
- use of technology within the organisation, such as ERP
- use of technology within the supply network, such as e-procurement
- available budgets
- risk profile
- existence and nature of contracting strategy.

Another key issue in structuring is the *choice of alignment* for the function, the function might be organised as follows:

- supplier groups
- product categories

- manufacturing units
- demand categories
- internal customer groups.

The *environment* in which purchasing operates is also a critical factor in choosing an organisational structure. Purchasing here has two sets of critical relationships. The first of these is with *other internal constituencies* within the organisation:

- Is purchasing a direct provider of services?
- What are the demand patterns for these services?
- Does purchasing carry out a consulting and advisory role?
- Does purchasing carry out a regulatory role?
- What are the purchasing core skills?
- What are the core values?
- What are the critical performance measures used within the organisation to assess purchasing performance?
- What function does purchasing report to?
- Which functions is purchasing interdependent with?
- At what level does purchasing report?
- What is the overall organisational structure?
- What is the organisational culture?

The second set of critical relationships is with the *supply base*:

- What are the critical performance measures used within the supply base?
- What is the size of the supply base?
- What is the geographical spread of the supply base?

In many ways, purchasing occupies a difficult position within many organisations as it mediates between the supplier and other internal functions. This means that the function often has to face two ways and manage both internal customer expectations and needs, and activity within the supply base.

The overall *objectives of the function* will also have an impact on structure. Strategy should always dictate structure, whether at the departmental or organisational level. Here, the sorts of issues which may need to be taken into account include:

- Is the function's primary goal *cost reduction*? In this case, a centralised structure may allow the exploitation of economies of scale.
- Is the primary goal *customer service*? A decentralised structure, with small purchasing departments that are 'close to the customer' may be appropriate.
- Is the primary goal *supply performance improvement*? In this case a structure based on supplier groupings or commodities may be most appropriate.
- How will this change over the strategic planning period?

In designing a structure for a purchasing and supply function, many of the lessons learned from designing an overall organisational structure can be

12

applied. Different elements, such as size, skills, culture and nature of task, need to be taken into account when designing a structure. The solution, in any particular case, will involve trade-offs between the factors identified, as well as value judgements regarding the ranking of the various factors.

By designing an effective structure – and each structure will be unique, because each purchasing and supply function is unique – the manager or staff member has an opportunity to ensure that the function can both make a value-adding contribution to the strategy of the organisation and demonstrate the nature of that strategy.

Self-assessment question 12.1

How might the following factors affect the structure of the purchasing function:

1   If the function's primary goal is *cost reduction?*
2   If the function's primary goal is *customer service?*
3   If the function's primary goal is *supply performance improvement?*

Feedback on page 148

12.2 Centralising or decentralising the purchasing function

One major issue in structuring the purchasing function, as mentioned briefly before, is the balance between centralisation and decentralisation within the department. This refers to the extent to which purchasing authority is delegated. In a centralised purchasing department, the main decisions are made by senior management and little authority is passed down the organisation.

Learning activity 12.2

List the arguments for and against centralisation and decentralisation.

Feedback on page 149

The *advantages of centralisation* include the facts that:

*   Decisions are made by experienced people, with an overview of the company.
*   Policies are consistent throughout the company.
*   Quick decisions can be made without consultation.
*   Procedures, such as ordering and purchasing, can be standardised throughout the company, leading to economies of scale.

The *disadvantages* include the facts that:

- Centralisation reduces the input of the day-to-day experts – for example, the shop floor staff cannot make purchasing decisions.
- It risks demoralising managers who may feel mistrusted or powerless.

There has been a trend in the face of the introduction of information technology to decentralise and provide greater flexibility in purchasing, aggregating spend using procurement software, and leaving purchasing and supply to manage the more complex aspects of the task.

The *advantages of decentralisation* include the fact that it can:

- Reduce the stress and burdens on purchasing departments.
- Empower local managers and staff, encouraging them to be more innovative in the use of budgets.
- Reduce the volume of transactions, therefore leaving staff free to concentrate on value-adding tasks.
- Allow non-purchasing staff to make more informed choices, because they may have a better knowledge of local conditions affecting their areas of work.
- Give non-purchasing staff the experience of purchasing decision making.
- Allow greater flexibility and a quicker response to changes. Since decisions are quicker, they are easier to change in the light of unforeseen circumstances.

In practice, it is unlikely there will ever be complete centralisation or decentralisation of the purchasing function. Any solution is, however, likely to be characterised by a 'tight/loose' pattern, whereby there is 'tight' or centralised control over the major objectives that is then joined by 'loose' or decentralised discretion over the ways in which those objectives are achieved, to varying degrees.

In general terms, the main reasons for centralising any function are either to support a cost-reduction strategy, or to ensure there is firm control. Another argument is that centralisation allows better communication and knowledge sharing between professionals, but this argument is pretty much obsolete in a world of intranets, videoconferencing and email.

A way of sidestepping the debate is to employ a hybrid model, such as the *centrally led action network* (CLAN), whereby some features of a centralised department, such as spend aggregation, are kept, but in which local decentralised purchasing is responsible for contract management under a local strategy.

12

Self-assessment question 12.2

For each of the following strategic objectives, suggest whether it should lead to the purchasing function being centralised or decentralised:

- Close supplier and customer relationships to improve the agility of each supply chain.

(continued on next page)

12.3 Cross-functional teams

Cross-functional collaboration, when individuals attempt to integrate their diverse knowledge and experiences into solutions that provide synergy (more than the sum of the parts) or add value is often difficult. Cross-functional teams involve a complex set of factors from a range of disciplines such as psychology, management, social psychology, computer science, design, architecture and many more.

As we have seen, one of the common approaches to organisational design is the bureaucratic organisation in which managers coordinate the work of multiple functional specialists, on various tasks, which are then integrated into a common whole. Traditionally, the most common attitude used to be 'you do your job, and I'll do mine'. An assumption was made that, somehow, if all the parts are done right, they will fit together into an effective whole.

Of course, there are good reasons for this. A great deal of our civilisation's economic success has come from dividing complex tasks into simpler ones, which could be done by less talented people. Adam Smith tells the story of pin making, where dividing the work formerly done by master craftsmen into simple steps done by people with far less training allowed a quantum leap in productivity and profitability.

However, this situation is changing in response to a variety of driving forces. These include the need to control costs in the face of higher levels of competition and increasingly demanding customers. They also include the introduction of new technology such as enterprise resource planning (ERP) systems which, as we have seen, have a major impact on accountability and the elimination of the 'you do your job, and I'll do mine' mindset.

Nonaka and Takeuchi (1995), two Japanese academics, identified the idea of the 'knowledge creating company' and considered multifunctional teams in detail. Interestingly, at a time when middle managers were being eliminated by information technology, Nonaka argued that only they were equipped to lead and manage the collaboration between functional departments, which is the knowledge-creating engine of organisations. Unfortunately, many of these managers are promoted specialists who have little education or experience of the type of leadership and management necessary to make team collaboration across disciplines effective.

Two issues make this teamwork problematic. The first is that when individual professionals and groups work on projects, a new kind of complexity develops as individuals and groups bring specific mental models with them. Each mental model will have a specific set of truths or 'taken for granteds', and the truths of different perspectives conflict with each other. The second is that people not only bring diverse knowledge sets, they *differ in cognitive style, cultural backgrounds, personality and values* in ways that can quickly destroy all hopes of collaboration. Attempts to establish cross-functional working must succeed in dealing with, and even take advantage of, these complexities.

One critical difference in collaborative projects is that every member brings knowledge and processes that cannot be checked in detail by other team members. The marketer can't really check the engineering calculations and the engineer is rarely equipped to check the allocation decisions of the accountant. This reality strongly affects team performance and requires a different type and level of *trust* from each team member. This is a critical team dynamic, and often requires time and process support to develop.

Purchase relationships, from both the customer and buyer perspective, are necessarily multi-actor relationships. Making a single sale might involve staff from several departments of both the selling organisation and the buying organisation. Cross-functional management has always been needed, but the need was never formalised by giving it a name. The idea of cross-functional teams also fits nicely with the concept of agile supply discussed in study session 11. If we are to give excellent service to our customers, and shorten lead times on new or revised products, we need to encourage collaboration within the organisation.

12

Self-assessment question 12.3

Identify the benefits and difficulties of cross-functional working in the context of supply chain management.

Feedback on page 149

12.4 Inter-organisational networks

Note: study session 13 will explore the issue of supply networks in more detail.

As well as intra-organisational cooperation, alliances and collaboration between organisations is becoming more common. In the network perspective, the fundamental principle is one of perceived interdependence. Individual organisations depend on resources controlled by other organisations. The organisation gains access to these resources through ongoing interaction with other organisations. This interaction is economic and social in character as individuals within the organisations learn to work together.

Learning activity 12.4

Give examples of inter-organisational networks from your experience, or from case studies in the core texts. Draw simple diagrams (if that is possible) to illustrate the various relationships.

Feedback on page 149

Industrial networks develop over time. The players, who may be individuals or organisations, invest in relationships with other players, thereby gaining knowledge of their network partners. This ongoing investment tends to make relationships stronger and more stable over time. Network theory is based on three components and their interaction to analyse and explain the way in which industrial networks operate. These are:

- activities
- actors
- resources.

You should be very familiar with the concepts of 'activities' and 'resources'. 'Actors' are defined by the resources they control, and the activities they perform. The relations between organisations in a network are developed through three separate, but closely linked, interaction process types:

- *Exchange processes* are not simply cash for goods or services. They also include the exchange of information and what are termed social processes.
- *Social processes* include personal relations but also technical, legal and administration processes. Through the social exchange processes the parties gradually build up a trust in each other. Large enterprises involved in process alignment with their suppliers might be seen as carrying out exchange processes.
- *Adaptation* is about the degree to which an individual organisation makes process modifications, such as products, administrative systems, production processes, in order to achieve a more efficient exploitation of resources within the network. Adaptation processes are important to network theorists for a number of reasons. They help strengthen the bonds between the parties. If a supplier has adjusted internal processes to meet the needs of a specific customer, interdependence is increased. Secondly, by adjusting to each other's needs, the parties signal that they consider their mutual relations as stable and lasting, and not governed by short-term profit opportunities. This signalling also can be seen in game theory where players react to the moves and signals of other players.

Through interaction, the parties in a network will develop various kinds of mutual bonds and linkages. These may include:

- *Technical bonds*, attached to the technologies applied by the organisations.

- *Social bonds*, in the form of personal trust.
- *Administrative bonds*, resulting from adjusting administrative routines and systems
- *Legal bonds*, in the form of contracts between the organisations.

Such bonds tend to create lasting relations between organisations operating in a network. Networks are stable and dynamic at the same time. New relationships are established, and old relations come to an end for a variety of reasons. Relations differ in terms of the strength of the ties that exist. Some are strong; others are weak. Relations will also change over time. This means that networks do not seek an optimal state of equilibrium, but are in a constant state of movement and change.

In all networks a *power structure* exists, with different players having different levels and types of power, which they can use to influence the actions of the other players. This power structure interacts in complex ways with the players' contradictory and common interests influencing the development of the network. The power structure also determines the role and position of the individual organisation in relation to the other organisations in the network. The organisation's role and position in the network also influences its strategic identity. The issue of relative power in supply chains is discussed in more detail in study session 18.

The strategic identity of an organisation is shaped and developed through interaction with other organisations. The interaction between the strategic identity of an organisation, the development of the organisation's industrial activities and its relations with other organisations in the network shapes the structure of the network. The shape of any specific network is one of a large number of possible structures. By establishing new relations, finding new cooperators and making new investments, the organisation is able to use the network and position itself competitively. A central element in any network strategy is the ability to influence not only the direct players, but also the indirect players through the direct players. Thus, an organisation in a supply chain is, in network theory, able to influence both its suppliers and customers, and also its suppliers' suppliers and its customers' customers.

According to the network theory, an organisation's relationship with other organisations is often the gateway to its most valuable resources. The players are connected within the network through different types of activity chain. Therefore, the performance of an organisation not only depends on its own relational efficiency, but also on the relational efficiency of its partners and their partners. This relational efficiency may involve both formal (organisational contracts) and informal (personal friendships) processes. Both formal and informal relationships can create entry barriers against external players, but also exit barriers for the parties involved. It is precisely this kind of inter-organisational relationship that is necessary if the supply chain is to become agile. Fast response to changing consumer needs can only be achieved if the supply chain actors collaborate between, as well as within, organisations.

Network theory rests on the assumption that an individual organisation's continuous interaction with other organisations is a critical factor in the development of new resources and skills. This means that enterprises must make a basic shift in perspective. It moves from an emphasis on the allocation and structure of internal resources to an emphasis on the way in which activities and resources can be related to other players' activities and resources within the network. In study session 17 we will look at Michael Porter's 'value chain' model. This kind of inter-organisational relationship is what Porter meant by 'linkages between value chains'. It is also the kind of mindset needed if a supply chain is to gain a sustainable competitive advantage, as discussed in study session 11.

Self-assessment question 12.4

Explain the differences between 'exchange', 'social' and 'adaptation' processes.

Feedback on page 149

Revision question

Now try the revision question for this session on page 259.

Summary

In this session we have discussed issues relating to the structuring and management of the supply chain function of an organisation – in particular:

- aligning organisational structures with supply chain strategies
- assessing the appropriateness of centralised, decentralised and mixed structures for effective alignment
- analysing the use of cross-functional teams
- identifying appropriate inter-organisational networks.

Suggested further reading

Read some of the cases in Johnson, Scholes and Whittington (2007), and identify examples of cross-functional and inter-organisational collaboration.

Feedback on learning activities and self-assessment questions

Feedback on learning activity 12.1

Look back at study session 4. You are looking, firstly, for the structural form of the organisation. Secondly, look at the way the purchasing function is structured – is it split between divisions? Is it decentralised or centralised?

Feedback on self-assessment question 12.1

1 A centralised structure may allow the exploitation of economies of scale.
2 A decentralised structure, with small purchasing departments that are 'close to the customer' may be appropriate.

3   A structure based on supplier groupings or commodities may be most appropriate.

Feedback on learning activity 12.2

The arguments are very similar for purchasing as for any function. See the continuation of section 12.2.

Feedback on self-assessment question 12.2

It is obviously far too simplistic to take each of these situations in isolation, but in general terms the answer is probably:

- decentralised
- centralised
- centralised (but not really!).

Feedback on learning activity 12.3

Depending on the type of organisation(s) you have worked for, you may or may not have had experience of this. If not, think about some 'missed opportunities' where cross-functional working would have been of benefit.

Feedback on self-assessment question 12.3

Benefits include: synergies, better and faster problem solving, improved motivation levels, reduced conflict.

Disadvantages include: reduced effectiveness as people 'discuss' rather than 'do', complex to manage, accountability for failure may be blurred.

Feedback on learning activity 12.4

There are many examples in Johnson, Scholes and Whittington (2007) such as Wal-Mart.

Feedback on self-assessment question 12.4

- Exchange processes are not simply cash for goods or services. They also include the exchange of information.
- Social processes include personal relations but also technical, legal and administration processes.
- Adaptation is about the degree to which an individual organisation makes process modifications, such as products, administrative systems, production processes, in order to achieve a more efficient exploitation of resources within the network.

12

The 'supply chain' concept

Introduction

This session looks at the metaphor of 'the supply chain' and alternatives to it.

'The weakest link in a chain is the strongest because it can break it.'
Stanislaw Lec

Session learning objectives

After completing this session you should be able to:

13.1 Assess the validity of assumptions about the nature of supply underlying the supply chain concept.

13.2 Assess the validity of the chain metaphor underlying the supply chain concept, and distinguish between supply network and supply chain models.

13.3 Assess the empirical evidence in relation to supply chain management.

Unit content coverage

This study session covers the following topics from the official CIPS unit content document:

Statement of practice

- Distinguish and assess various models of supply chain structures and relationships.

Learning objective

4.1 Assess the validity of the supply chain concept both in terms of the nature of supply and the chain metaphor.
- Concepts of supply and supply chain
- Assumptions about the nature of supply (Lamming and Cox 1997)
- Supply chain metaphors: chain, pipeline, network, channel
- Critiques of the supply chain concept (New and Ramsay 1997)
- Types of supply networks and supply chain models: internal supply chains, dyadic supply relationships, inter-business chains, inter-business networks (Harland 1996)
- Arguments and evidence for and against the application of supply chain management

Resources

Access to the following books is highly recommended for use throughout this session:

- Lysons and Farrington (2006), chapters 3, 4 and 13
- Dam Jespersen and Skjott-Larsen (2005), chapters 1, 2, 3 and 7
- Christopher (2005), chapters 1, 6 and 10.

13

Timing

You should set aside about 4 hours to read and complete this session, including learning activities, self-assessment questions, the suggested further reading (if any) and the revision question.

13.1 The supply chain concept

You should remember from study session 10 that, according to Handfield and Nichols (2002), the *supply chain* 'encompasses all those organisations and activities associated with the flow and transformation of goods from the raw materials stage, through to the end user, as well as the associated information flow.' The same authors also define *supply chain management* (SCM) as 'the integration and management of supply chain organisations and activities through cooperative organisational relationships.'

According to Dam Jespersen and Skjott-Larsen (2005), 'the competitiveness of international companies is highly dependent on their ability to deliver customised products quickly and timely all over the world. Therefore, focus has moved from competition between firms at the same level in the production process to competition between supply chains, from raw materials to end customers.'

Learning activity 13.1

Draw a diagram of a supply chain in which your organisation (or one with which you are familiar) is positioned.

Feedback on page 156

13

Linkages within a supply chain are either *upstream* or *downstream*. These terms relate to the 'direction of flow' in the supply chain, so downstream refers to towards the customer, and upstream towards the supplier.

From a purchasing perspective, the supply chain processes are as follows:

- search
- acquire
- use
- maintain
- dispose.

From the supplying perspective, the processes are:

- research
- design
- manufacture or provide
- sell
- service.

Supply chains are often described diagrammatically, as shown in figure 13.1.

Figure 13.1: A typical supply chain

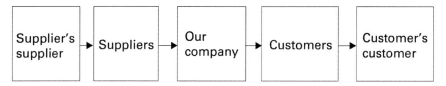

Of course, real supply chains are a lot more complicated than shown here. Suppliers and customers in a supply chain are often referred to as being in *tiers*. In figure 13.1, the supplier would be a tier 1 supplier, and the supplier's supplier a tier 2 supplier. A more complex supply chain can be seen in Dam Jespersen and Skjott-Larsen (2005: 15).

According to Cox and Lamming (1997), this view of a supply chain being a series of dyadic (one-to-one) relationships is based on a model of business dating from the nineteenth century. At that time, 'the manner in which firms dealt with one another reflected their competences' – in other words, each organisation (or, more often, individual) used their own skills as part of a 'joint wish to provide' products to the end consumer, and a 'commercially based respect for the technical capabilities available from both companies'. Mass production principles destroyed this model, and replaced it with a high volume model serving consumers that were 'easily led and presented manufacturers with a ready, tempting opportunity for exploitation'.

This meant, according to Cox and Lamming, that 'for the first three quarters of the twentieth century, the mass producers could thus force their "vanilla" products upon their sales markets.' There was, therefore, no incentive for organisations to have any kind of sophisticated relationship with their 'compliant supply market', particularly where the purchaser had a wide spread of potential suppliers who could be controlled in one of two ways:

- By being bought, leading to the development of vertically integrated 'mass production leviathans'.
- By extracting their expertise under threat of the loss of business.

13

Self-assessment question 13.1

Explain what is meant by a supply chain, illustrating your answer with examples related to a specific situation.

Feedback on page 157

13.2 The supply chain metaphor

There is some academic argument as to whether it is reasonable to view the supply chain as a chain. Indeed, many definitions cannot help referring to the supply chain as something other than a chain – for example, 'a supply chain is a network of organisations'.

Learning activity 13.2

Look at the diagram you drew in learning activity 13.1 above. Is the supply chain really just a simple chain or would it be better described as some kind of network?

Feedback on page 157

According to Harland (1996) there are four different applications of the term 'supply chain':

1 The internal supply chain, which integrates business functions involved in the flow of materials and information from 'inbound' to 'outbound'.
2 A dyadic (or two-party relationship) between a supplier and a customer.
3 A series of businesses, including an organisation, its supplier, its supplier's supplier, its customer and its customer's customer, and so on.
4 A network of interconnected businesses involved in the ultimate provision of product and service packages required by end customers.

According to Hakansson (1987) a network is based on linkages between actors, resources and activities, as follows:

• Actors may range from individuals to groups of companies, but they all aim to increase their control of the network. They perform activities and own and control resources (either alone or jointly).
• Resources may be human or physical and are often mutually dependent. They are owned by actors and are either used in the performance of activities or are the subject of those activities.
• Activities include those concerned with transformation and those with transaction. Activities use and act on resources and are performed by actors.

Lamming et al (2000) suggest that there are three factors driving the way that supply networks should be managed:

1 Whether the product is 'innovative' or 'functional'. An innovative product is one with unpredictable demand and a short product life cycle.
2 Whether the product is 'unique' – that is, valuable, rare and difficult to imitate.
3 The degree of complexity of the product.

The authors find close links between 'innovation' and 'uniqueness', in products, so they do not distinguish between these two characteristics any further. This gives a 2×2 matrix of supply network management approaches, as summarised in table 13.1:

13

Table 13.1 Four generic supply network management approaches

	Innovative/unique products	Functional products
Higher complexity products	• Speed • Flexibility • Innovation • Detailed knowledge sharing	• Cost reduction • Quality sustainability • Service • Strategic knowledge sharing.
Lower complexity products	• Speed • Flexibility • Innovation • Quality supremacy • Sensitive knowledge sharing	• Cost • Service • Cost and strategic knowledge sharing

There are a number of reasons why we should regard supply chains as networks:

• We are more likely to take a view across the supply chain when formulating strategy, rather than just concentrating on tier 1 suppliers and customers.
• We should become more responsive and innovative, as the supply chain is better informed and can react in a consistent manner.
• Throughput times will be shortened, leading to a reduction in inventory levels throughout the chain and subsequent improvements in cashflow and margins.
• Inter-firm relations are more likely to be mutually beneficial, leading to more stable supply chains and improved service levels.

Christopher (2005) suggests that the development of supply networks requires organisations to respond to three major challenges:

• *Collective strategy development.* The organisations in a supply chain must work together, as part of a marketing network, and must develop strategies that are in the best interest of the network, rather than each individual organisation.
• *Win-win thinking.* The organisations need to 'break free of the often adversarial nature of buyer–supplier relationships' that have existed in the past. While win-win need not mean 50–50, the benefits of improved performance should be shared among the members of the network.
• *Open communication.* All parties must share information in order for the network to become innovative, flexible and efficient. This includes information about costs, as well as about quality and delivery expectations. Information can no longer be thought of as flowing only 'upstream' in the supply chain.

Self-assessment question 13.2

Explain why organisations would be more successful if they regarded their supply chains as networks.

Feedback on page 157

13.3 Supply chain management in practice

Despite having been in existence for many decades, and the subject of many academic studies and business qualifications, supply chain management (SCM) is still not practised by anywhere near all organisations. If you are to recommend it to your organisation, you need to be familiar with how SCM works in a range of real organisations.

Learning activity 13.3

Search the internet and/or library articles for practical examples of supply chain management practice. Make brief notes summarising the main approaches used by a range of private and public sector organisations.

Feedback on page 157

Now try the following question.

Self-assessment question 13.3

For five different organisations, classify their SCM strategy in accordance with Christopher's 'generic supply chain strategies', summarised in table 11.2.

Feedback on page 157

Revision question

Now try the revision question for this session on page 259.

Summary

This session has looked at the 'supply chain' metaphor, and alternative approaches to supply chain management.

Suggested further reading

Following on from learning activity 13.3 above, find as many SCM case studies as you can.

Feedback on learning activities and self-assessment questions

Feedback on learning activity 13.1

For a model diagram of a typical supply chain, see figure 13.1.

Feedback on self-assessment question 13.1

A supply chain 'encompasses all those organisations and activities associated with the flow and transformation of goods from the raw materials stage, through to the end user, as well as the associated information flow.'

For example, figure 13.2 illustrates a car industry supply chain.

Figure 13.2: Car industry supply chain

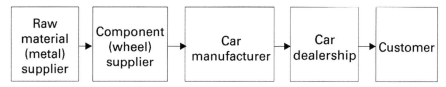

Feedback on learning activity 13.2

The continuation of section 13.2 provides the answer to this question.

Feedback on self-assessment question 13.2

There are a number of reasons for regarding supply chains as networks:

- We are more likely to take a view across the supply chain when formulating strategy, rather than just concentrating on tier 1 suppliers and customers.
- We should become more responsive and innovative, as the supply chain is better informed and can react in a consistent manner.
- Throughput times will be shortened, leading to a reduction in inventory levels throughout the chain and subsequent improvements in cashflow and margins.
- Inter-firm relations are more likely to be mutually beneficial, leading to more stable supply chains and improved service levels.

Feedback on learning activity 13.3

There are lots of case studies and articles available free of charge on the internet. Many of them relate to Toyota as they were responsible for the birth of the lean supply chain. There are others, however, and it will be a very useful exercise for you to find them for yourself.

If you are finding it difficult to track down case studies relating to supply chain management, there are some in the recommended textbooks. You could look at the following:

- Gattorna (1998): chapters 33–38.
- Christopher (2005): Cisco (p171), Smart (p185), Nike (p210).
- Dam Jespersen and Skjott-Larsen (2005): B&O (chapter 2), Arla Foods (chapter 4), Carlsberg (chapter 5), Sanistaal (chapter 8).

Feedback on self-assessment question 13.3

See table 13.2.

13

Table 13.2 Generic supply chain strategies

Strategy	Supply characteristic	Demand characteristic
Lean	Long lead times	Predictable demand
Hybrid	Long lead times	Unpredictable demand
Kanban	Short lead times	Predictable demand
Agile	Short lead times	Unpredictable demand

Study session 14

Internal and external supply chains in different sectors

'When a customer
enters my store,
forget me. He is
king.'
John Wanamaker

Introduction

In this session we will look at various internal and external supply chains
and consider how they may differ according to the different types of
organisation.

Session learning objectives

After completing this session you should be able to:

14.1 Map and assess models of the supply chain.
14.2 Analyse the internal supply chain.
14.3 Identify customers in the supply chain.
14.4 Analyse the flows across organisational boundaries upstream and
downstream.
14.5 Distinguish the nature of supply chains in the manufacturing, retail and
financial sectors.
14.6 Distinguish the nature of supply chains in different public sector
organisations, such as health and social care, defence, transportation.

Unit content coverage

This study session covers the following topics from the official CIPS unit
content document:

Statement of practice

- Distinguish and assess various models of supply chain structures and
relationships.

Learning objectives

4.2 Analyse internal and external supply chains and the flows across
organisational boundaries upstream and downstream.
  - Internal and external supply chains
  - Interface and integrated models (Syson 1992)
  - Roles of internal and external customers within supply chains
  - Flows across organisational boundaries upstream and downstream
  - Problems with forecasting demand accurately within supply chains
4.3 Compare and contrast the nature of supply chains in different sectors.
  - Nature of supply chains in the manufacturing, retail and financial
sectors
  - Nature of supply chains in different public sector organisations:
health and social care, defence, transportation

14

159

Resources

Access to the following books is highly recommended for use throughout this session:

- Lysons and Farrington (2006), chapter 13
- Dam Jespersen and Skjott-Larsen (2005), chapters 2 and 8
- Christopher (2005), chapters 4 and 6.

Timing

You should set aside about 5½ hours to read and complete this session, including learning activities, self-assessment questions, the suggested further reading (if any) and the revision question.

14.1 Internal and external supply chains

If we consider that supply chain management is 'the management of relations and integrated business processes across the supply chain that produces products, services and information that add value for the end customer', we can see that this obviously encompasses activities which are both upstream from the focal organisation and downstream. We can illustrate this with a simplified diagram (see figure 14.1).

Figure 14.1: A simplified industry supply chain

Flow of customer's expectations

Supplier's supplier → Supplier → Organisation → Customer → Customer's customer

Flow of goods or services

This is very simplified because, depending on the nature of the industry, the 'organisation' may have many suppliers who, in turn, have many suppliers. Similarly the organisation may have many customers who also have many customers buying from them. (We discussed this in study session 13 when we talked about supply networks.) If you think of the 'organisation' as a packaged food manufacturer supplying a major supermarket with cakes and fruit pies, it may have only a few suppliers: for the supply of the ingredients, the plant and equipment and the packaging; and it would only have one, or possibly two, customers – the supermarkets themselves. However, if they are successful, the supermarkets will have many thousands of customers.

The relationships between the various stages in this supply network are all important but some are more important than others. You might want to refresh your memory about Porter's Five Forces model (see section 3.1), since this will help you to consider the different relationships at each of the stages.

In the case of a food manufacturer, some of those relationships might be quite stable. For instance, there may be a long-term contract for flour and sugar and the relationship with the supplier could be quite close. Hopefully, the relationship with the supermarket will, similarly, be long term. However, the relationships with suppliers of fresh fruit for the pies are likely to be more dynamic, since the fruit is seasonal and subject to complex issues like the weather.

We can also consider the balance of power in these relationships as well. Doubtless, the supermarkets will be more powerful than our organisation and it may be that the suppliers of flour and sugar are of similar size and equal power, but the farmers producing the fruit are likely to be in a weaker position. These factors will affect the management of the supply chain between the respective firms and will affect the degree of cooperation and integration that is necessary for all players to add the most value to their customers' experience. We have discussed the effect of these different relationships in study sessions 3 and 4.

Learning activity 14.1

For a particular product or service with which you are familiar, map the supply chain. Considering the stages you have identified, should this involve direct (production) expenditure or indirect (support) expenditure?

Feedback on page 171

If we are to model the supply chain relationships we can use an 'evolutionary framework'. For instance, some companies have focused their efforts at developing a supply chain purely inwardly. They have placed reliance on internally generated process improvements aimed at reducing costs in specific functional areas. Although offering gains, these efforts fall far short of industry leaders. Others have made some progress at integrating a few of their external partners into the process and have gained from that. However, they still lag behind the lead companies who have fully utilised collaboration and information technology to gain the maximum competitive advantage.

We can recognise four levels of supply chain sophistication:

1   At level one the company is internally focused on functional and process improvement. The efforts made are purely internal, oriented towards enterprise integration and focused on functional areas. Most companies will be using the supply chain operation reference model (SCOR) developed by the Supply chain Council: 'plan, source, make and deliver'. In most cases, organisations will initially focus their efforts on procurement and logistics, usually resulting in a significant reduction in the number of suppliers of goods and logistics, product rationalisation and economies of scale in purchasing. The problems at this stage tend

14

to be a lack of cooperation between functional areas and a lack of any organisation-wide communication system.

2   By *level two* the company is still internally focused but, having recognised the savings being made at level one, *starts to evaluate various supply chain assets* with a view to outsourcing to expert third-party providers. The focus at this stage is on providing best end-to-end product or service delivery within the company. The supplier base is likely to be segmented with the lower value components being dealt with by electronic purchasing, and the purchasing staff, who now enjoy a higher status, dealing with the vendors with strategic importance. The flow of information is more sophisticated and a number of transaction activities will be automated. The company will recognise the problems caused to accurate planning and manufacturing by poor forecasts and demand management will be introduced, often by a sales and operations (S&OP) system. Enterprise resource planning (ERP) systems will be in operation.

Some organisations never get beyond this level since, to move on to level three, it is necessary for a visionary leader to manage a serious business transition. The company will need to get rid of the 'not invented here' mentality and be prepared to share information with a few trusted partners. This is the stage at which the firm moves from interface relationships to integration relationships.

3   At *level three*, strategic suppliers are invited to take part in the S&OP process, working on *collaborative designs of solutions* that match supply and demand more closely. At the same time, marketing and sales will be forming the same relationships with important customers in joint development processes. Design and joint development are very important at this stage. Logistics, transportation and warehousing benefit from sophisticated communications tools, often extranet based, which shortens the time from concept to completion. At this level there is a transition to business allies working together to find mutually beneficial approaches to reduce cycle times, utilise assets more effectively and achieve faster times to market so that all may maximise value added. With information now being shared via an extranet, organisations can now identify opportunities and advise allies where cost can be saved. The focus moves towards establishing an industry-dominant position for the network rather than just the individual company. The 'end-to-end' focus now extends beyond the boundaries of the organisation. It is likely that all players in the system will be using activity-based costing and some form of balanced scorecard as they work, jointly, towards the same strategic objectives. Supplier relationship management (SRM) and customer relationship management (CRM) will be practised by all members of the network.

4   At *level four*, end-to-end visibility across the whole network is achieved by the rigorous application of *e-commerce and e-business* techniques. Design and manufacture will be done collaboratively as will planning, forecasting and replenishment. As you can imagine, very few companies have reached this level of integration with their suppliers and customers.

You might want to ask yourself if it is necessary for organisations to evolve to these higher levels. Much will depend upon the strategic importance of the asset being acquired. If assets are of low specificity there will limited value in going beyond level two since there is little to be gained from a closer relationship with the supplier. The firm will do better to leverage any market power that they have to achieve the best result and capture as much of the available value for themselves.

If an asset is of medium specificity and there are advantages to be gained from the complementary competences that the supplier and the focal organisation share then a closer relationship is worthwhile and migration to level three or even four will offer advantages.

Progression from level one to level four will involve considerable expenditure and this must be weighed against any perceived benefit of closer working relationships.

Self-assessment question 14.1

Discuss the usefulness of the evolutionary framework as a tool for describing what an organisation is doing, and what it ought to de doing, in its management of the supply chain.

Feedback on page 171

14.2 The internal supply chain

When we consider the internal supply chain we are looking at the activities *within* the company, and are dealing with the area upon which a level one or two organisation has focused its efforts whilst seeking improvements. These aren't only about the flow of product or service towards the customer but about the flow of information, often in the other direction, to help satisfy the customer.

Learning activity 14.2

Identify the internal functions with which you interact in your organisation, and how often you do so.

Feedback on page 172

We can think about the internal supply chain in terms of a set of flows characterised under the headings: information, material and finance. A few examples are given in table 14.1.

Table 14.1 Flows in the internal supply chain

From supply side to demand side, flows would be:	
Information	Capacity, promotion plans, delivery schedules
Material	Raw materials, work in progress, finished goods
Finance	Credits, consignments, payment terms, invoices

(continued on next page)

14

Table 14.1 *(continued)*

From demand side to supply side, flows would be:

Information	Sales, orders, inventory, quality, promotion plans
Material	Returns, repairs, servicing, recycling, disposal
Finance	Payments, consignment

These are just a few of the items in each category. Traditionally, there were many opportunities for inefficiencies within the internal supply chain but increasingly, as organisations seek competitive advantage, these are being removed. As we can see from table 14.1, the efficiency of the processes depends to a large extent on the flow of accurate and timely information within the organisation. This flow is facilitated by enterprise resource planning (ERP) systems, which are designed to add value by managing the complex processes that go on within a business. ERP systems are a development from materials requirement planning (MRP) and manufacturing resource planning (MRPII) systems. These were developed to link the supply side of the firm with the demand side by breaking down orders into requirements for components or raw materials and then automatically placing those orders with suppliers and thus maintaining the inventory levels. These systems worked well with 'standard' businesses. Data flows were integrated across the basic business functions and included optimisation and reporting packages.

ERP systems are an extension of these capabilities and will include: planning and execution of some marketing activities; allowing the customer to place orders directly; factory floor and stock management; and ordering and invoicing. The optimisation of the logistics function is also, usually, included. Since most modern packages are now internet-enabled, much of the functionality can be extended to both customers and suppliers in a limited step towards level three supply chain management.

14

Self-assessment question 14.2

Describe how an enterprise resource planning package could add value in an organisation that was seeking to gain competitive advantage by a cost leadership strategy.

Feedback on page 172

14.3 Relationship marketing

The buying process has traditionally been considered to consist of the following stages: initiator, influencer, decider, purchaser and, finally, user. It can be argued that each of these stages can be described as a 'customer' since, at any point in time, you as a customer could take all of those roles. For example, if in the middle of this study session you feel hungry and decide to go for a coffee and a cake, you will fulfil all of the roles. However, for some of the products and services you are involved in at work you may just take the role of purchaser, or possibly decider. Traditionally marketers liked to refer to the decider and the purchaser as the gatekeepers since these were the 'customers' you really had to impress if you were to make a sale.

The concept of relationship marketing is a fairly recent one and recognises that companies have both internal and external customers. The broad idea was that transaction marketing placed the emphasis on the individual sale whereas, by the 1990s, relationship marketing placed the emphasis on the individual customer and sought to develop a long-term relationship between customer and company.

Learning activity 14.3

Identify and distinguish the roles of internal and external customers within any of your organisation's supply chains.

Feedback on page 172

The fundamental message of relationship marketing is that ongoing, long-term relationships should be the norm with all of the customers that the company deals with. Naturally, marketers are encouraged to build these kinds of relationship with external customers but the theory indicates that value will be added if similar relationships are established with other groups as well. The groups are defined in the 'six markets' model:

1   Customer markets – that is, the purchasers of the final product or service that the company sells.
2   Referral markets – that is, those who can advise our final customers and promote our product or service.
3   Suppliers who can make our life easier in dealing with customers.
4   Employee recruitment markets, with which a cooperative and collaborative relationship will get us the most appropriate staff to deal with our final customers.
5   Influencer markets, such as government bodies at any level whose approval will enhance our reputation with final customers.
6   Internal markets, who are the staff we employ who can impress the final customers by doing their job well.

This final market recognises the damage that can be done if all employees do not understand their role in the total marketing process. Internal marketing focuses on the concept that every member of the organisation has a 'supplier' and 'customer' relationship with every other member of the organisation. In order to exploit this internal market effectively it is necessary to establish: communication channels; leadership qualities and soft skills; information content that is readily accessed and shared; user-friendly IT support systems; clear internal management controls and other priorities for which employees are the principal targets.

There is a focus on the development of a unified and responsive sense of purpose amongst the workforce and to develop a sense of both internal and external customer focus. High levels of external customer service

14

require individuals to ensure that their customers and suppliers enjoy the interaction they have with them. The concept requires there to be a highly cooperative and supportive atmosphere, with everyone working in tune with the organisation's mission, strategy and goals so that the company is represented in the best possible light to the outside world.

In order to achieve this internal cohesion, six steps are proposed:

- The creation of internal awareness.
- Identification of internal 'suppliers' and 'customers'.
- Determination of internal customers' expectations.
- Communication of those expectations to internal suppliers.
- Modification of internal suppliers' actions to meet those expectations.
- Establishment of measurements of internal service quality and feedback to ensure a satisfactory exchange between all participants.

As you can see, this suggests that everyone you deal with should be treated as a customer and that, in the main, their wishes are the most important. But is this true? Essentially, business is about achieving value for your own company and not about passing value to customers unless it is the only way that one can satisfy them. This means that an ideal situation for the focal organisation is to be so powerful that no other player, including the customers, in the supply chain can leverage power over the focal organisation. With that in mind the opening statement for this chapter that the customer is king might not always be true.

Self-assessment question 14.3

Use the 'six markets' in the relationship marketing model to identify customers within any of your organisation's supply chains.

Feedback on page 172

14.4 Forecasting demand

If we think of a simple linear supply chain, with a series of organisations, each ordering from its immediate upstream supplier, the final end user is creating the demand all the way up the supply chain. Each predecessor in the chain is enjoying something called 'derived demand'. This means that the demand for their product is derived from the demand for their customer's product. There are invariably problems with forecasting demand with any accuracy in all but the simplest of situations.

Learning activity 14.4

By talking to the people within the marketing department of your organisation, or one with which you are familiar, find out how the organisation forecasts demand.

Feedback on page 173

The further upstream we go, the greater will be the fluctuation in demand and the inaccuracies that will creep into the system, since the orders are a compilation of information from further down the supply chain. This may be due to perceived seasonality, environmental changes (think of forecasting ice cream sales) or human error. There may also be changes as those further down the supply chain decide to cut back on inventory levels since they have financial problems or believe that they can eliminate waste by tighter forecasting. If they are right, then orders will be lower; if they are wrong, orders will suddenly be higher! This leads to a phenomenon known as the bullwhip (or whiplash) effect whereby:

- orders to the upstream organisation in a supply chain exhibit a greater variance than actual orders at the final consumer stage (demand distortion)
- the variance in orders placed increases as one moves upstream (variance propagation).

The effect even occurs in what might, at first sight, be considered very stable markets. Proctor and Gamble have reported the effect in their sales of disposable nappies. Whilst babies tend to use these at a fairly steady rate, demand order variations in the supply chain were amplified as they moved upstream from retailer, through various stages of distribution, to Proctor and Gamble.

The bullwhip effect has a variety of causes:

1 *Behavioural causes.* When managers perceive a threat to product supply because of a perceived fluctuation in demand, they will increase safety stock. Without good communication, this will give the impression upstream that there is a general increase in demand, as all stages in the supply chain increase their inventory. The organisation may have inappropriate performance measurements in place with stock-outs being 'punished' more rigorously than stockholding. The imbalances caused by a lack of communication between sales, marketing, manufacturing and distribution can also cause similar effects. Remember that, with the value chain, the linkages across functional areas can be as important as what goes on within the functions.

2 *Non-behavioural causes.* Demand forecast updating, where the processing of demand signals by many of the common forecasting methods, such as exponential smoothing, can often lead to inaccurate information passing up the supply chain. Order batching, whereby an organisation will seek economies of scale by reducing the number of orders placed (because of the transaction costs), can lead to inaccurate information being passed upstream. Price fluctuations due to special promotions and trade deals can encourage excess purchasing to take advantage of the economies on offer. This is common in the middle of a supply chain and can have quite an expensive effect both for the organisation making the purchase, if they cannot encourage increased demand further downstream, and for the supplier who has to increase production. Shortage gaming, whereby a customer will over-order in periods of short supply and cancel orders in times of plenty. Motorola faced serious problems in meeting demand for handsets in 1992 and 1993 when they rationed supply at the end-of-year shopping

14

seasons. The subsequent year, retailers over-ordered in anticipation of the rationing only to find that demand had cooled and they were overloaded with inventory. Motorola's stock price lost 10% in the period afterwards.

Self-assessment question 14.4

In the supply chain from farmer, miller, baker, wholesaler, retailer and customer, give two examples to explain how the baker might be affected by the bullwhip effect.

Feedback on page 173

14.5 Supply chains in the private sector

Most of our discussion of supply chains so far has concerned the private sector and, as discussed in earlier study sessions, the objectives of those types of organisation are fairly clear-cut. As commercial organisations, their primary objective is to increase shareholder value. There may be secondary or supporting objectives. As you will remember (see section 5.1), according to Porter, they will do this either by cost advantage or by differentiation advantage. In general, identifying and satisfying customers is also fairly straightforward.

Learning activity 14.5

Identify key supply chain drivers in different private sector organisations from whom you purchase products or services.

Feedback on page 173

Although supply chain management is important to all organisations, the emphasis on how it will add value depends on the nature of the organisation. This is particularly true as organisations look to move their manufacturing base to low-cost countries. For manufacturing companies much will depend upon the complexity and uncertainty of the product being manufactured, for example:

* *High complexity/high uncertainty*: Super-value goods, such as aircraft, which are usually manufactured on a project basis. Inventory costs can be high; and agile supply, where there is flexibility and responsiveness by holding capacity or strategic inventory, is essential.
* *Low complexity/high uncertainty*: For example, fashion clothing. Rapid replenishment and short lead times are essential. Despite the product simplicity there are often problems with quality and, for example, although Benetton manufacture in low-cost countries they do the final

dyeing of the garments at the market end and not the manufacturing end.
- *Low complexity/low uncertainty*: Typically commodity products. Demand is reasonably well known and cost-competitiveness is the route to success. Since these products are cost-sensitive the purpose of supply chain management will be to squeeze out any cost in the system.
- *High complexity/low uncertainty*: Consumer durables such as the Nokia phone we referred to earlier or cars. Inventory can be an expensive affair and the best manufacturers will have an excellent working relationship with their component suppliers to achieve JIT supply. Many car manufacturers now use demand-pull as the basis for manufacturing programmes rather than forcing inventory onto dealers.

For retailers the issues are somewhat different as they face the final consumer, and the variations in demand, which we described earlier, must be dealt with. For instance, Wal-Mart who pride themselves on the cost-efficiency of their supply chain management have cut their logistics costs by sending electronic point of sales data to all of their suppliers on a twice-weekly basis, thus ensuring that they do not hold lots of stock. This reduces not only the cost of stock in the balance sheet but also the warehousing costs and the need to have end of range sales.

For service industries, you might think that the principles of supply chain management are not so important since there is no physical product to manage or transport. However, if we think of service firms as employing either 'hard assets' or 'soft assets', the usefulness might become clearer. By 'hard asset' organisations we mean those that use physical assets to provide a service to consumers or other organisations. For instance, an airline, a hotel or a logistics company are all hard asset service providers. All have the same problems as a manufacturing firm or a retailer since there is inventory to be managed, but the problem is possibly worse since it is perishable! For the 'soft asset' organisation such as a consultancy, where value is added by differentiation, or financial services where cost-efficiency is important, the internal value chain needs to be managed but so does the relationship with the customer. Like all organisations they are in the business of efficiently managing information and, increasingly, the most successful companies are managing information rather than inventory.

Where a tangible product is involved, the other substitution has been to exchange transportation for inventory. By the use of real-time electronic data, freight transport has effectively become 'inventory on wheels' with an enhanced transportation/ warehousing/ inventory control and tracking system.

Self-assessment question 14.5

Describe how supply chain management could improve overall performance of supply chains in the manufacturing, retail, or financial sectors.

Feedback on page 174

14.6 Supply chains in the public sector

There has recently been considerable pressure on the public sector to introduce best practice and to adopt some of the more successful approaches used by commercial organisations. This has included the concept of supply chain management. It has been suggested that strategic management in the public sector should 'strengthen the long-term health and effectiveness of government units and lead them through positive change to ensure a continuing productive fit with their environments'. This should mean that management take steps to ensure that value chains, resources (staff, finance and infrastructure) are in place to allow planning, implementation and evaluation of service delivery, on time and within budget.

Learning activity 14.6

Identify areas of the public sector where supply chain management may be appropriate.

Feedback on page 174

Objectives in the public sector can be difficult to set due to the wide stakeholder group. The requirement to achieve value for money is challenging because it is not always clear what this entails. The supply chain strategies will be heavily influenced by EU directives and need to adopt very prescriptive and formal mechanisms of sourcing. The culture is one of risk aversion, and accountability may reduce options for flexibility. There are considerable political interventions and challenges for funding which make longer-term planning and budgetary control difficult. Bureaucracy, micromanagement, silo management and lack of staff turnover can create a very static environment. This, along with, in some cases, a lack of recognition of purchasing, makes it difficult to recruit and keep appropriately skilled purchasing professionals.

Unfortunately for those who have the responsibility of managing on behalf of government, there are unpredictable political dimensions in the sector and decisions are often made for short-term expediency rather than long-term efficiency. Quite often the decision makers are only judged on their ability to stay within budget – despite the ad hoc demands placed upon them.

One of the major differences between the public sector and the private sector can be found if we revisit the concept of stakeholders (see study session 3). Whilst the identification of stakeholders, and their power, for a commercial organisation is relatively straightforward, for public sector organisations this is not the case.

In a recent exercise the stakeholders for the BBC World Service were mapped and there were found to be over a hundred groups. A similar exercise for the Royal Botanical Gardens at Kew found nearly two hundred. This means that the objectives of these organisations are often pluralistic and far from clear-cut.

14

In the vast majority of cases the end user is not a customer – for example, in the health service where treatment is 'free at the point of delivery'. In some cases it is difficult to identify an end user. It could be argued, for example, that the armed forces have nothing to do if there is no conflict. However, service personnel need to recruited, trained, clothed, equipped, transported and fed if they are to function effectively when needed. This means that all the factors relating to supply and demand discussed in this study session are just as relevant to those managing the armed forces as they are to someone managing a commercial organisation with similar characteristics.

Self-assessment question 14.6

Compare and contrast supply chains in the private and public sector and explore the difficulties of working in each sector.

Feedback on page 174

Revision question

Now try the revision question for this session on page 259.

Summary

This session has discussed internal and external supply chains in a variety of contexts, including both the private and public sectors. It has considered the concepts of:

- the degree of supply chain sophistication
- enterprise resource planning systems
- relationship marketing and the six markets model
- demand forecasting and the bullwhip effect
- the complexity and uncertainty of markets.

Suggested further reading

Look at some of the 'strategy' cases in Johnson, Scholes and Whittington (2007) and identify the nature of the supply chains in those organisations.

Feedback on learning activities and self-assessment questions

Feedback on learning activity 14.1

Depending on the organisation that you work for, this could turn out to be quite a complicated exercise. Looking back to study session 13 you might be wondering whether your company is in a supply chain or a supply network.

Feedback on self-assessment question 14.1

If you look at the stages of the evolutionary framework there are fairly clear-cut boundaries between the approaches taken at each of the levels. It is very

14

171

unlikely that the development of the organisation's approach will be that clear-cut, and transition from one level to another, where it does occur, is not guaranteed to follow those stages. It is also likely that the organisation will be using different approaches for different assets depending upon their specificity. Only the more strategically important will be acquired by the more sophisticated approaches described in the higher levels.

The name evolutionary implies that organisations should be progressing to the higher levels as a means of improvement – this is definitely not the case for all organisations or all supplies.

Feedback on learning activity 14.2

It is unlikely that there are many departments in your firm that you don't talk to, or communicate with in some other way. Naturally, you will talk to some more often than others. When you do talk to them, you may be in the role of customer or supplier. You might reflect on how efficient the process is, and how each side helps the other to do its job.

Feedback on self-assessment question 14.2

An ERP has the potential to reduce inventory and the cost of holding it, reduce transportation costs, reduce manufacturing bottlenecks and eliminate the waste of both materials and time. Inventory reduction will occur at the raw material, component, work in progress and finished goods stages of the production cycle. The automation of invoicing and billing will speed the process of getting payment from customers, whilst the facility of order taking should make the buying process easier for those customers. The error count should be reduced on all transactions thus eliminating a further waste of time and human resource.

Feedback on learning activity 14.3

To some extent your answer will depend on what you decided the 'product' was. If you decided it was 'information' then the answer would involve quite a long list. You might care to ask some of your colleagues to answer the same question – it might give you an idea of the way the organisation thinks about the employees and the relationship with them.

Have you recognised the gatekeepers, or does your organisation take a broader view? Much will depend upon the nature of the product or service being bought; many users will not be pleased if someone else specifies the tools they are to use. In other situations, where the company wishes to standardise on a particular make of software, the users will work with what they are given and which will have been specified by someone else.

Feedback on self-assessment question 14.3

You should be able to identify each of the following types of customer:

1   Customer markets: These are the purchasers of the final product or service that the company sells.

2   Referral markets: These are the institutions and individuals who refer customers to us because of our reputation. This is possibly the most powerful form of promotion.

3   Supplier markets: These are our business suppliers who provide the inputs to our value chain and collaborate to improve quality of inputs, JIT systems and to jointly satisfy the customer.

4   Recruitment markets: These are the suppliers of the well-trained and expert staff that the organisation will need to provide excellent service to the end customers. If our organisation uses a large number of temporary staff a good working relationship with the agency is vital.

5   Influencer markets: These are the institutions that can influence what customers will purchase. For instance, an aeroplane manufacturer will need to influence governments, as well as airlines, to assure them that their product is safe.

6   Internal markets: The interaction between the various departments within the value chain can have a pronounced effect on the smooth running of the organisation, and the relationship between individuals is just as important.

Feedback on learning activity 14.4

The answers you get will depend to a large extent on the nature of the organisation, the number of products on offer and how integrated the relationship is with the customers. It should be interesting to find out how they gather this information from the existing customers (repeat business), and how they estimate the amount of new business they will get each year.

Feedback on self-assessment question 14.4

In this supply chain the farmer grows the wheat, which is bought by the miller who cleans it, grinds it, packages it and sells it to the baking company. The baking company combines the flour with other ingredients to make bread, which is sold to a wholesaler. The wholesaler will bundle the bread with other packaged products and sell them to the retailer who will sell the bread to a final customer. Each player at any stage of a supply chain is dependent upon their immediate supplier or buyer for information, since they do not interact with anyone else. If there are rumours of a drought, which will affect the farmer, then people with freezers may well stockpile bread, thus creating demand that will ripple up the supply chain. Conversely, if there is a health study that shows that bran rather than wheat is a better staple for children, then demand will suddenly decline again rippling up the supply chain. Since these health fads rarely last for long, at what time will the demand increase? And will it return to its previous levels?

Feedback on learning activity 14.5

Generally, the main drivers of supply chain implementation can be described as the search for value added. This can be either by cost-efficiency or by differentiation.

If you use a computer made by Dell, for example, you have dealt with a company which claims that, 'Our supply chain is the biggest leverage point

14

we have' and, 'We substitute information for inventory and ship only when we have a real end customer.' By not holding stock of finished computers but holding small inventories of components with local assemblers, they produce computers based on actual consumer orders not forecasts of demand. This allows them to be very cost-efficient.

If you use the latest camera phone from Nokia, you will be benefiting from a company with a global research and development capability drawing on the expertise of scientists and engineers in a variety of countries. They were able to do this by initially using the same approach as Dell, and through global sourcing effectively commoditise the low-end handsets, forcing out their competitors and building a barrier to entry which allowed them sufficient power to build the global R&D network.

Feedback on self-assessment question 14.5

Supply chain management can assist any organisation to improve its cost-efficiency or differentiation advantage and thus make it more competitive. Within the manufacturing industry this will depend upon the nature of the product but, in general, the management of inventory and cost-effective sourcing will be the main gains within this sector. For the retail sector, the opportunity to provide better quality information about demand on a timelier basis will offer significant advantages. For the financial services industry, which deals with a commodity product, cost-efficiencies and the rapid management of information is the key to success.

Feedback on learning activity 14.6

The government is one of the largest purchasers of goods and services in the country. They are also, through their various departments (health, social care, transportation, and so on) one of the largest suppliers of services. It is difficult to imagine an area where supply chain management could not be productively employed!

Feedback on self-assessment question 14.6

Areas to discuss may include:

- political and legislative influences
- funding
- profit and not-for-profit
- organisational structures
- strategic approaches
- drivers for decision making
- bureaucracy
- flexibility of the supply chain
- accountability.

14

Drivers of change in global supply chains

'Telecommunications is creating a global audience. Transport is creating a global village. From Buenos Aires to Boston to Beijing, ordinary people are watching MTV, they're wearing Levi's jeans, and they're listening to Sony Walkmans as they commute to work.'

Renato Ruggiero, Director General, World Trade Organisation

Introduction

There is no doubt that the world is becoming increasingly globalised and companies have to deal with that if they wish to remain in business. In this study session, we shall look at the phenomenon of globalisation, what causes it and whether it is a good or a bad thing. We shall also consider the strategic decisions that successful companies have to make in order to remain competitive as the world becomes a smaller place.

Session learning objectives

After completing this session you should be able to:

15.1 Assess the impact of globalisation on your business or sector.
15.2 Evaluate the impact of globalisation.
15.3 Identify drivers of change in global supply markets.
15.4 Identify technological drivers of change in global supply markets.
15.5 Identify strategies which address the drivers of change in globalised supply chains.

Unit content coverage

This study session covers the following topics from the official CIPS unit content document:

Statement of practice

• Understand the nature of supply chains.

Learning objective

4.4 Diagnose drivers of change in global supply chains and propose strategies to address them.
  • Nature and impact of globalisation
  • Drivers of change in global supply markets: competition, cost reduction, technological advances, speed of new product
  • Development, changing customer demand, environmental factors, collaborations and joint ventures, outsourcing
  • Impact of drivers of change in global supply markets
  • Strategies to address drivers of change in global supply chains

15

Resources

Access to the following books is highly recommended for use throughout this session:

- Christopher (2005), chapters 1, 6 and 10
- Gattorna (1998), chapter 20.

Timing

You should set aside about 5 hours to read and complete this session, including learning activities, self-assessment questions, the suggested further reading (if any) and the revision question.

15.1 Globalisation

Global business is not a new phenomenon; business activities between individuals, governments, companies and non-governmental organisations have existed for centuries.

However, *globalisation* is much newer concept. It implies an integration of world economies and a rapid increase in the movement of goods, services and capital across national borders. Globalisation has been considered to consist of five monopolies based on: technology, finance, natural resources, mass media and weapons of mass destruction.

The IMF defines globalisation as: 'the growing economic interdependence of countries worldwide through increased volume and variety of cross-border trade in goods and service, freer international capital flows, and more rapid and widespread diffusion of technology'. There are, therefore, significant political, cultural, economic and technological elements to globalisation.

Globalisation is related to the increase in the importance of individual companies that operate in a range of countries, and that increasingly see the world as a single market.

15

Learning activity 15.1

Think about the goods and services that you have used, or sourced, over the past month. How many of them have been produced in other parts of the world, or were provided by companies that have their headquarters in a country other than your own?

Feedback on page 185

Further aspects of globalisation include:

- *Globalisation of economies.* There is an increasing interdependence between national economies throughout the world. In the next study session we shall look at some of the trading blocks and the attempts to regulate them.

- *Globalisation of markets.* In some markets, consumer tastes and preferences are becoming increasingly homogenised. We can see the effect of this in the popularity of global brands such as McDonald's, Burger King and Pizza Hut for fast food, Coca-Cola and Pepsi-Cola for soft drinks and for fashion clothing; Calvin Klein, Gap and Hugo Boss. Consumer needs throughout the world appear to have grown more similar. This has the advantage for consumers that their choice of products has widened and the price they pay has, in general, fallen. For companies, the advantage is that they are able to earn higher revenues because of the larger potential market; they enjoy economies of scale and are therefore able to reduce their unit costs. This enables companies like Nokia to develop a constant stream of new products and improved products and recoup the large R&D costs.

- *Globalisation of industries.* Increasingly, the production process is being globalised, with companies choosing to spread their value-adding activities around the world to take advantage of cost or differentiation advantages of particular areas. They are able to take advantage of different resources, cost levels, skill profiles and levels of quality. There are often benefits of lower cost, and higher quality, manufacturing which can be passed on to consumers, underpinning the increased choice and lower costs. Much designer clothing is produced in the Far East and made affordable to more consumers. Vietnam is the latest country to become a manufacturing site for Nike trainers. The manufacture of computers and the development of the software that runs on them is an excellent example. Different areas of the world will develop a particular field of expertise and become recognised throughout the world for it. This is known as the 'cluster effect' whereby similar companies cluster in a particular area. Examples include Silicon Valley, California's high tech area, Toulouse, for aerospace, and Bangalore for software outsourcing.

- *Globalisation of finance.* Increasingly, finance for businesses will be raised in one country and invested in another, as companies attempt to gain advantage by foreign direct investment (FDI) in developing markets. In 2005 Russia attracted $16.7 billion of FDI, with Coca-Cola acquiring a fruit juice manufacturer, Toyota and Volkswagen building automobile plants and Heineken acquiring local breweries. Similarly, Whirlpool established a joint venture with the Vestel Group, a Turkish domestic appliance manufacturer, and opened a plant in Turkey. Many other companies also entered the Russian market as its domestic economy grew at a significantly faster rate than most of the rest of the world.

- *Globalisation of culture.* From a sociological perspective, there is an increasing degree of cultural interaction and convergence between the various countries of the world.

There are a number of recognisable trends in the growth of globalisation:

- International trade in products has grown at a faster rate than output, and has averaged 12% per annum in recent years.
- Trade in services (banking, telecommunications, tourism and transport) has increased at a faster rate than that for tangible products.

15

- Global financial transactions have seen the fastest growth; the rate over the past decade has been sixfold, whilst the increase in trade of goods and services generally was just 50%.
- The majority of trade is between businesses in developed countries.
- Almost 70% of total world trade is conducted by just 500 companies, and the level of concentration is increasing.
- The vast majority of these companies have headquarters in North America, Europe and Japan.
- A large number of these organisations have annual revenues in excess of the GNP of many countries.

Self-assessment question 15.1

Using an industry with which you are familiar, describe the critical success factors for a global firm in that industry.

Feedback on page 185

15.2 Is globalisation a good thing?

As you can see from section 15.1, not everyone is going to feel that globalisation is a good thing and it has been the subject of much debate and even violent protest.

Globalisation changes the geographical dimensions of economic markets. Economies which were not viable in a world of protectionism, become viable. This has been of particular importance to smaller developing nations. New technology development related to the information society and the application of technology, most notably in computing and telecommunications, have reduced the time and space dimension of international transactions. Investment liberalisation, which has been taking place in many countries, has also contributed to the penetration of national markets. However, trade liberalisation has the perverse effect of widening the gap between the various economic markets which expand rapidly and the territorially limited areas of jurisdiction of nationally regulated markets. As such, globalisation can undermine governments in the management of the economy of their country.

Learning activity 15.2

Discuss with colleagues at work their view on the impact of globalisation.

Feedback on page 185

Those that argue for globalisation claim that not only do the companies in the developed world benefit from access to larger markets and alternative production facilities but consumers benefit from extended choice and sharper prices. Post-war western democracies have played a large part in emphasising the world market economy as a vehicle for economic growth and stability and good international relations. Even though their costs are lower companies like Nike pay well above the local average wage in Vietnam and other developing countries which benefit from the increased wages and levels of employment.

The importance of national boundaries has been diminished by the international ties that have been developed and by improved communications, particularly the internet. This has made populations more aware of what is, and should be, available. Many developing nations have benefited from the reduction of protectionist barriers by global organisations like the World Trade Organisation (WTO), which we shall discuss in more detail in study session 16.

However, there are counter arguments and you will be aware of the violent protests that have occurred at meetings of the WTO and the International Monetary Fund (IMF) where it is claimed that globalisation is harmful. It is argued that developed countries gain at the expense of developing countries, and that globalisation has brought no benefit to their populations. The global divide between the richest nations and the poorest is getting larger, that transnational companies exploit child labour and women by paying slave labour rates of pay. They have scant regard for working conditions and ignore health and safety considerations. In developed countries there have been significant job losses as transnational companies 'offshore' work to more cost-effective locations abroad. Initially affecting unskilled labour and blue-collar workers in manufacturing industry, the trend has now spread to software development and call centres for financial institutions. The ability of the transnationals to capture low costs and economies of scale has impacted upon a number of small businesses in developed markets, as they are unable to compete with the prices charged by firms such as Tesco and Carrefour.

Globalisation threatens national cultures through the internet and satellite television and countries, such as France, have introduced legislation to protect their language, insisting that only a small percentage of foreign music may be played on national radio stations. Large transnational companies are seen as a threat to democracy as their economic power is greater than some of the countries with whom they deal. The may focus unduly on profits at the expense of local social, cultural and political issues. It is also argued that they have limited regard for ecological issues in their pursuit of shareholder value as global consumption threatens reserves of non-renewable resources.

15

Self-assessment question 15.2

Discuss the advantages and disadvantages of globalisation to a country in developed world.

Feedback on page 186

15.3 Drivers for change

According to Yip (1992) there are four principal categories of drivers to be used to assess the extent of globalisation in an industry. These are: market, cost, government and competitive forces. The strength of each of these factors will vary from industry to industry and, to some extent, from market to market. There is usually a strong correlation between the forces in the macro-environment (remember PEST analysis) and the globalisation drivers. An analysis of these drivers is an important first stage for any company in determining the extent of globalisation that is appropriate for their business. Once that analysis has been done, then the company should be in a position to match the drivers to their core competences and distinctive capabilities.

Learning activity 15.3

List in order of importance the drivers of change that impact on your business or sector and explain their effect.

Feedback on page 186

Looking at the drivers for change in more detail we can describe them as:

- *Market globalisation drivers.* The similarities and differences in consumer needs for a product or service will depend on the degree of difference in the cultural environment, the stage of economic development and the physical environment. There is currently an increasing degree of cultural and economic convergence in most countries due to the impact of the internet and easier international travel. Some customers, often transnationals themselves, purchase goods and services on a global basis as they seek distinctive capabilities of their own. For instance, most major car manufacturers source their components globally but they are increasingly obtaining their supplies from a smaller and smaller group of larger and larger companies. Marketing efforts also increase the degree of globalisation as global brands are established and communicated around the world. As cultural differences diminish, global branding becomes ever more feasible. The clusters that we mentioned in section 15.1 tend to set global standards for products and services, create lead status for their countries and are able to seek, and hold, global markets for their products.
- *Cost globalisation drivers.* Where there are high capital costs in an industry, companies will aim to achieve economies of scale through large volumes of sales. Where a national market is of insufficient size the companies in the industry will be inclined to seek global markets. The same is true of economies of scope, where a company will try to gain advantage by selling two or more distinct products or services together rather than separately, capitalising on similar marketing, markets or distribution channels. This can be important for some companies where economies of scale are insufficient, both of whom manufacture and sell a vast range of detergents, toiletries and other household products and derive economies of scope by virtue of the marketing research into consumer needs and product research to satisfy them. Global sourcing will bring about cost reductions for a company and for the industry itself in what we might describe as a reinforcing, virtuous circle. Going back to our example of car manufacturers, as the car manufacturer seeks a cost-effective source of supply for a component, it will most probably identify a supplier who supplies more than one car manufacturer. As the supplier grows, it is able to offer, or is forced to offer, more cost reductions to the car manufacturer. In this way, global sourcing will

15

increase the incidence of globalisation. The logistics function will contribute to the rise of globalisation where the good is not perishable or urgent since the advantages of economies of scale can be fully taken up. This is particularly true of commodity products (where there is little differentiation) and bulk-reducing industries where the final product takes less space than the raw materials. The rate of new product development is also a driver for globalisation as consumers become more demanding and require the latest version, firms are forced to incur increased development costs which must be absorbed by larger revenues generated by larger markets. Advancing technology has made the development of new products that much faster, as we shall see in study session 17 when we talk about the concept of 'lean'.

- *Governmental globalisation drivers.* Governments at the national and international level have introduced trade policies that have brought down barriers and promoted international trade. Some governments actively encourage foreign direct investment (FDI), recognising the positive impact it can have on local economies. The introduction of common technological standards across borders will also encourage globalisation. This has been particularly noticeable in the telecommunications industry where, in the 1990s, the advent of digital telephony brought about compatibility that encouraged communication and the ubiquity of the internet. Similarly, the introduction of globally acceptable standards for advertising has made the job of brands like Nike and Pepsi-Cola easier. Active promotion of particular industries by governments has helped powerful companies who have then been able to market and sell on a worldwide basis. However, protectionism by governments, seeking to protect local industries by their own purchasing policies, will inhibit the growth of globalisation.

- *Competitive globalisation drivers.* The greater the number of players from different countries, the greater will be the degree of globalisation. Any company faced with competition from global companies will, by definition, have to compete globally itself.

A good example of an industry that is becoming increasingly globalised is the airline industry, where the spread of deregulation by governments and the privatisation of national carriers has lead to transnational mergers, cost reduction and greater choice for consumers. There are global alliances between the major airlines where code sharing has made it possible for a consumer to book a ticket with one airline for a multi-stage journey and find themselves on planes owned by a number of different airlines who are partners in the same alliance. For instance, someone booking with British Airways may find themselves travelling with other members of the 'Oneworld' alliance such as American Airlines or Quantas.

Self-assessment question 15.3

Using your industry as an example, refer back Porter's Five Forces model (see study session 3) and describe how the description of the drivers of globalisation fits in with the model.

Feedback on page 186

15.4 Technology – driver or facilitator?

In respect of globalisation the impact of technology cannot be underestimated, as it has underpinned all of the factors we have described so far. Sometimes, however, the effect of technological change has not been as originally predicted. For instance, communication technology, such as satellite television, was forecast to encourage the convergence of tastes and lead to quite uniform products; whilst to some extent this is true, the advent of flexible manufacturing technologies has led to mass customisation and greater product varieties without the sacrifice of economies of scale. Similarly, the dramatic improvement in communication and control brought about by computers has not led to greater centralisation, in the style of multinationals, but has allowed companies to operate along the transnational model with information shared rapidly throughout the organisation.

Learning activity 15.4

Talk to people who have been working for your employer for some time and ask them how technological change has affected the way people now work.

Feedback on page 186

Access to, and control of, technology can afford a company a competitive advantage, but it is worth remembering that advantage may not be sustainable as other firms in the industry imitate the innovator. For global companies, the efficient use of the available technology often becomes a threshold competency, which will only ensure survival and not leadership.

Technology can impact on firms in two ways; either by design technology (product development), or by process technology:

- *Design technology* is about making new or improved products where the consumer will see a difference. For instance, in the global mobile phone industry, international competitiveness depends upon producing a constant stream of new and improved handsets with added features as product life cycles become shorter. It is interesting to note that the largest global manufacturer of cameras is Nokia and the largest retailer of cameras in the UK is the Carphone Warehouse! Similarly, we have already discussed the importance in the pharmaceutical industry of a constant stream of new drugs.
- *Process technology*, however, is about providing the same products and services in a more effective way, and this will be of more concern to us in terms of supply chain strategies. The ability to use technology to control the supply chain and to eliminate waste in the process has become increasingly important over the past few decades. This is where information and communication technologies (ICT) have had their biggest impact. ICT has allowed businesses to coordinate value-adding activities across the world, in diverse geographical locations, whilst still maintaining local responsiveness.

The *integration* of computers and telecommunications via the internet has allowed more rapid, and cost-effective, processing and exchange of information. This has given birth to the fairly recent field of knowledge management. Hardware and software developments have allowed the creation of sophisticated, intelligent databases, decision support systems, neural networks and artificial intelligence, which have made information available to many more managers in a cost-effective manner. These systems have allowed firms to handle increasingly complex, conflicting and voluminous data and be more responsive to rapidly changing markets.

In 1992 it was predicted that, by 2000, there would be over 15 million personal computers installed in businesses with 40% of them connected in far-reaching networks. In fact, these predictions were far exceeded and the rate of change is still exceptional: the computing power of the average PC used at home far exceeds the power available to NASA when the first moon landing was achieved. Additionally, microelectronics and computing have become ubiquitous, with the use of bar codes and radio frequency identification (RFID) to track stock and goods in transit.

Self-assessment question 15.4

Write a memo to the managing director of a chain of clothing retailers explaining three improvements in the management of their supply chain which could be brought about by the use of technology.

Feedback on page 187

15.5 Strategies to address a global supply chain

In study session 5 we discussed the alternative strategies available to a company and said that, according to Porter, competitive advantage could be achieved either through low cost or differentiation. There is usually very little to choose between companies at the functional level and so the main source of adding value in the customers' perception is superior service. The way a company chooses to position itself in terms of customers and suppliers, and its position in the supply network, is of paramount importance and will be a significant driver of overall profitability. Choosing the 'right' relationships and managing them effectively and efficiently can make all the difference, and this is true of both the internal and external supply chain. Increasingly, companies will have to focus on their position in the most effective supply chain networks rather than their position in markets. As the world shrinks, those networks will certainly be in other countries.

Learning activity 15.5

Thinking about your organisation, or one with which you are familiar, examine the global network structure of which that organisation is part.

Feedback on page 187

So what strategies can an organisation adopt to capture value when faced with increasing globalisation? We can consider this in terms of the way the organisation decides to *configure* its activities and the way it *coordinates* them in order to address the drivers as defined by Yip (see section 15.3).

In terms of configuration the firm has two broad choices. Firstly, they can choose to *concentrate* their activities in a limited number of locations to capture the benefits offered by those clusters of advantage relating to availability of resource, government support, or demand conditions. Alternatively, where transport costs for their product are high or where local markets differ significantly, they can *disperse* their activities across the globe. This decision will need to be constantly reviewed since the business environment may change and reconfiguration may be possible or necessary.

How the organisation decides to coordinate those activities will depend, to some extent, on how widely they have chosen to disperse them. The more complex the configuration becomes the more difficult it will be to coordinate activities to ensure that value is added and not lost. At this point, you might want to refer back to the discussion on the impact of technology and whether it was a driver or a facilitator of globalisation. There is no doubt that the increased ease of global communication has allowed (or maybe even encouraged) firms to disperse their activities more since they are better able to coordinate them.

How the firm decides to pursue these strategies will also be an important decision. In some cases, the degree of dispersion will be dealt with by opening factories and offices in other parts of the world to capture a share of the market or cost advantages available. In other cases that may not be possible because of the national governments' approach to multinational firms and it may be legally required that the firm take a local partner. Alternatively, the government approach may be the opposite and actively encourage inward investment by the firm. One thing is certain, the competitive pressures for globalisation are such that, to continue to be successful, companies will have to enter new markets as they open up and be prepared to supply them from the most effective sources available.

Self-assessment question 15.5

Draft a report proposing global sources that would improve supply chain strategies within your organisation, or another organisation with which you are familiar.

Feedback on page 187

Revision question

Now try the revision question for this session on page 259.

Summary

This session has looked at the drivers of change in global supply chain networks, including the concepts of:

- Globalisation of economies, markets, industries, finance and culture.

- The positive and negative effects of globalisation.
- Globalisation drivers of markets, cost, government and competition.
- Technology as a driver or a facilitator of globalisation.
- Product and process technology change.

Suggested further reading

Look at case studies in Johnson, Scholes and Whittington (2007), and identify instances where organisations' supply chains have become global.

Feedback on learning activities and self-assessment questions

Feedback on learning activity 15.1

Depending upon who you work for this could be a big list! Just thinking about the goods and services you have used: you are most probably using a computer which was produced by an American company but manufactured in Taiwan, although the screen was most probably made in Korea. The software was most probably American, produced in the Far East, but developed at a number of sites around the world. However, if the accounting software that your company uses is SAP it is German. So, there are many global elements before you even think specifically about the business you are in.

Feedback on self-assessment question 15.1

As we discussed in study session 8, critical success factors will vary from industry to industry and will also be shaped by the core competences of individual businesses. If we consider the pharmaceutical industry, a global firm will need to achieve a critical mass in terms of market share (the top ten companies account for over 50% of global sales). This means that the firm will need superior access to distribution channels to roll out new products, globally, as quickly as possible. They will also need to have good reputations with the regulatory bodies within the markets to which they are selling. Although the industry is highly regulated, it is quite profitable, with margins rarely below 20%, but cost-efficiency will be a critical success factor, since product life cycles are shortening, R&D costs are escalating and, increasingly, governments wish to bring down the cost of health care. Relationships with regulators, doctors, pharmacists and patient groups (who are now more educated and discerning about available medicines) are of paramount importance.

Feedback on learning activity 15.2

You may find that there are some heated views depending on whom you talk to. Many people when they think about it are benefiting from increased choice, access to foods out of season, and relatively low prices for what had previously been described as luxury goods. By contrast, there may well be people that you talk to who have been affected, directly or indirectly, by the relocation of work to other countries in the process known as 'offshoring'.

15

Similarly, they may be unhappy at the disappearance of smaller companies which have been squeezed out of the market place by the power of larger, transnational, companies.

Feedback on self-assessment question 15.2

Assuming you are living in the developed world, the advantages you claim would revolve around the broader choice that is afforded consumers in terms of products and services and the lower prices of their purchases. You would also refer to the greater opportunities for travel on foreign holidays. In terms of the advantages for businesses, you would discuss the advantages of global sourcing, low-cost production, economies of scale and increased revenue.

The disadvantages you might quote for the consumer would be the decline of traditional cultures, customs and industries. Offshoring could be described as a disadvantage as well if you were employed as a blue-collar worker or in the IT industry. Similarly, for businesses, the impact on smaller firms would be the main difficulty, as larger transnationals forced them out of business by using their strong market power.

Feedback on learning activity 15.3

The answer will depend upon the company for which you work. It is unlikely that your employer will not have been affected in some way by the trend towards increased globalisation. Once you have completed section 15.4 see if you can divide your list into the same categories as Yip.

Feedback on self-assessment question 15.3

You should find that there is a fairly close correlation between the drivers we have described and Porter's model. The impact of customers and their tastes, needs and wants, together with the degree of globalisation of current suppliers can have a big impact on the degree of globalisation that an industry enjoys. The fact that there are already global competitors will cause this to be a 'reinforcing loop' – it is unlikely that the trend to globalisation will reverse but will strengthen as time passes. Barriers to entry to the industry will increase as brands become stronger and economies of scale and the impact of the learning curve kick in.

Feedback on learning activity 15.4

You should get some interesting answers which might not always be positive about the impact of technology! Many people will appreciate the better quality of information that they should now be able to access in a far timelier manner. They should also appreciate the fact that components, stock and goods in transit are easier to locate and to track. Improved forecasting of demand should also be something that they mention. However, they may not be so happy with the fact that mobile telephones have made their working day longer, and that the number of emails they have to deal with has not improved the communication process whatsoever!

Feedback on self-assessment question 15.4

Your answer could include:

- Reduced cost of stock-outs as order procedures are on time and on quantity due to automation.
- Improved performance management as real-time data is collated from stores on a daily basis by an ERP system.
- Higher customer loyalty by the use of loyalty cards, an intelligent database and data-mining techniques.
- Improved demand forecasting by the use of information gathered from loyalty cards and customer relationship management.
- The need for less end-of-season sales as demand and supply are better balanced.
- Reduced cost of inventory.

Feedback on learning activity 15.5

Let's look at an organisation with which most people will be familiar – Microsoft. The company sits in the middle of a network of organisations with which they have a variety of relationships. These include: microchip manufacturers, other software design firms, schools, home users, business users, retailers, systems consultants, internet service providers, training providers and manufacturers of computers and components. Those organisations are spread across nearly every continent.

Feedback on self-assessment question 15.5

Much will depend upon the position of your organisation in the supply network, and even whether it is in a supply network. Hopefully, you will be able to point to issues where a better source of supply could be found. An example with which you might be familiar is Airbus building a factory in China to supply local demand. They are using their traditional European sources as well as some local sourcing. This has been done in anticipation of Chinese engineering and manufacturing 'catching up' with the worldwide aerospace industry. They are currently making a loss on the venture but hope to achieve 'first mover' advantage.

15

15

The global 'supply market'

Introduction

In this study session we look at the concept of global sourcing and some of the regulatory and cultural issues involved.

'The storm that's arriving – the real disturbance in the force – is when thousands and thousands of institutions that exist today seize the power of this global computing and communications infrastructure and use it to transform themselves. That's the real revolution.'

Lou Gerstner, IBM

Session learning objectives

After completing this session you should be able to:

16.1 Identify the location of sources for products or services for which you are responsible.

16.2 Identify and assess arguments for and against global sourcing.

16.3 Assess the impact of regulation on the global 'supply market' in terms of free trade versus protectionism.

16.4 Assess the impact of regulation on the global 'supply market' in terms of regional economic integration.

16.5 Assess the impact of cultural barriers to trade in global supply markets.

Unit content coverage

This study session covers the following topics from the official CIPS unit content document:

Statement of practice

- Assess the role of strategic supply chain management in achieving competitive advantage.

Learning objective

5.1 Assess the validity of global sourcing as a means of achieving competitive advantage.
   - The global supply market as a source of competitive advantage
   - Arguments for and against local, regional, national and global sourcing
   - Regulation of the global supply market by WTO, EU, NAFTA, ASEAN
   - Obstacles to trade imposed by national or regional anti-competitive policies
   - Cultural barriers to trade in global supply markets

16

Resources

Access to the following books is highly recommended for use throughout this session:

- Christopher (2005), chapter 7
- Gattorna (1998), chapters 15 and 20.

Timing

You should set aside about 6 hours to read and complete this session, including learning activities, self-assessment questions, the suggested further reading (if any) and the revision question.

16.1 Global sourcing

Globalisation has been described as consisting of five monopolies based upon: finance, natural resources, mass media, technology and weapons of mass destruction. With the exception of the last category, organisations may be sourcing these locally, nationally, or internationally depending on their size and organisational structure. In each of these industries there are significant gains to be made from *economies of scale* and so the supply is concentrated in the hands of fewer and fewer companies. To take just one example, the number of oil companies, part of the natural resources monopoly, has declined over the past decade and most reserves are in the hands of a relatively few major firms. There is even a quasi-legal cartel acting in this area, OPEC, to encourage the monopoly conditions. If you investigate you will be able to see the same levels of concentration in the other areas as well.

Learning activity 16.1

Thinking about your own organisation, or one with which you are familiar, identify how many of the five categories of monopolies are sourced locally, nationally or globally.

Feedback on page 200

The *features of globalisation* are the ability of transnational companies to exploit arbitrage opportunities across different tax authorities, to reduce transaction costs by developments in communications and transport, and to take advantage of local specialisms – effectively the division of labour has become global. The capacity to do so has been greatly increased by the recent advances in information technology, which has made the speed of transactions so much faster, particularly in the area of financial resources.

Most people are affected by globalisation in a number of ways, some of which they might not recognise. For example, when you finish studying for the day:

- You may decide to read a novel written in the UK, using software developed in North America, which was typeset in India but printed

locally where you live; and it was probably bought using a credit card issued by an international bank.
- You may drink coffee made from Colombian beans, while wearing trainers made in Vietnam, and clothes made in China (or possibly from Egyptian cotton and manufactured locally).
- You may listen to music recorded locally, but played on equipment manufactured in Japan.

In most of those cases, the home country of the brand will not be reflected by the country from which the product or its components was sourced.

Economies and communities around the world are becoming increasingly integrated. Here are a few more facts that show why this story is important:

- *World trade* in goods and services is growing rapidly. Much of this trade is in parts and components, part of an ever-spreading web of a global sourcing network connecting suppliers, designers, producers, distributors and after-sales service providers.
- Many governments have agreed to *lower trade ba*rriers through multilateral trade agreements. This has opened markets and improved access, particularly for manufactured goods.
- The rapid expansion of the *internet* has provided a marketing tool linking buyers to sellers and a business-to-business tool driving supply contacts and contracts across the globe.
- *Lower transport costs*, improved communications and technology are making international trade easier.
- New records are being set in *global people flows*. 130 million people on the planet now live outside their nation of birth. Highly skilled 'experts' take short-term contracts overseas, exporting their knowledge-based services.
- A number of developing countries have joined the global economy and improved their populations' living standards by *reforming* their policies, institutions and infrastructure.

Self-assessment question 16.1

For those products and services sourced locally or nationally that you identified in learning activity 16.1 above, identify any raw materials or components that are sourced internationally.

Feedback on page 201

16

16.2 Is global sourcing a good thing?

There is no doubt that an increasing number of companies are using global sources and an increasing proportion of what they buy is internationally sourced. The decision to source internationally has been identified as a *strategic initiative* which progresses through a number of stages; initially, it may just be that the requirements cannot be met from domestic sources, later it may be a proactive decision to pursue potential new markets and finally it may become a *fully integrated and coordinated system of global sourcing.* It has been argued that this is a natural process of growth in which firms develop knowledge about foreign markets and operations, as well as increasing their commitment of resources to foreign markets.

Learning activity 16.2

List arguments for and against global sourcing.

Feedback on page 201

Naturally, global sourcing is not required in all buying situations and should only be developed by firms who are faced with significant requirements to improve competitiveness. However, firms of all sizes could be, and are, affected. In the initial stages of the introduction of such an approach, domestic purchasing managers will be faced with the problems of evaluating international sources and obtaining bids without the benefit of the usual broad organisational support. The organisation will not, at that stage, have developed the necessary communication links, coordination mechanisms, logistics and personnel capabilities to implement global sourcing on a large scale.

Managers will be trying to:

- meet required levels of *quality*
- meet required *schedule* dates
- meet *cost-reduction* targets
- broaden the *supply base*
- import *new technology*.

Whilst they are attempting some, or all, of these there will be trade-offs that will need to be considered:

- *Cultural barriers* that, at their most basic, may only involve a different language but in some countries will be far more involved.
- *Communication barriers* which may exist where the infrastructure of the country is not fully developed.
- Increased *lead times.*
- Increased *transport costs.*
- Employee *travel and subsistence* costs.
- Perceived *risks* associated with sharing proprietary technology.

Additionally, if the firm is looking to develop just-in-time systems requiring smaller and more frequent deliveries to reduce inventory, the longer lead times and potential logistical difficulties will compound the problems. In addition to transport and employee costs, international buying is also likely to incur:

- *Increased costs* due to damage in transit.
- *Export taxes and other customs duties*, which are likely to increase further as trade blocs such as ASEAN, NAFTA and the European Union gain in prominence. (We will discuss this in section 16.3.)

16

- *Costs associated with longer lead times* such as: reduced flexibility, inflated and obsolete inventories, and reduced responsiveness both to internal requirements and final customer needs. Longer lead times invariably lead to higher inventory.
- *Costs associated with currency fluctuations*: although these costs can be controlled to some extent by negotiating contracts in domestic currencies or by hedging via currency options, futures contracts or previously agreed periodic renegotiation.

In addition to cultural and communications problems we can add:

- *Differing time zones* may compound the communications problem.
- Difficulty in obtaining *technical support* may be increased by both the communications and cultural differences.
- Difficulties with *forecasting and communication* are likely to make the 'bullwhip' effect (see section 14.4) more likely to occur.

The structure associated with global sourcing will vary, and could comprise:

- Dealing with the supplier's representative in the firm's own country.
- Regular buying trips to the supplying country.
- Establishing an office in the supplying country staffed by the firm's employees.
- Establishing an office in the supplying country staffed by foreign nationals.
- Establishing an international procurement office.
- Using an automatic order system.

Each of these degrees of development will have differing degrees of cost and difficulty associated with them.

Self-assessment question 16.2

Assess whether at least three of the products and services for which you are responsible are sourced appropriately in relation to the arguments for and against global sourcing.

Feedback on page 201

Feedback on page 201

16

16.3 Regulation: free trade v protectionism

We can think of all markets as existing somewhere between a totally free market (which is unlikely) and a command economy. *All markets are controlled to some extent* and the mechanisms of control are known as regulation. The intention of regulation is to produce, prevent or modify a particular outcome.

In the context of markets, regulation can exist as the control of: prices, wages, market entry, the size of firms in an *industry* and the control they exercise, employment conditions, pollution, and standards of quality and production. As there will always be a potential conflict between the maximisation of profit and the interests of the people using the good or service, such regulation is necessary.

The term *deregulation* is often misused to describe a process of privatisation or liberalisation of markets. For instance, in the case of airlines, the USA, Europe, Australia and Japan have liberalised their markets and there are a number of airlines operating in those countries. However, those airlines are still subject to a number of regulations concerning safety and employment conditions, although they are now freer to negotiate their own arrangements with airports and other suppliers.

Free trade can be defined as the movement of goods, services, labour and capital without any barriers such as taxation, quotas, subsidies and tariffs to distort the exchange.

Advocates of free trade argue that;

- Free trade tends to make society, in general, richer since the free movement of goods allows for local specialisation. Nations enjoy a competitive advantage by developing a skill base and/or enjoying economies of scale.
- The quality of goods will be better in absolute terms and this will lead to a better quality of life generally.
- Since the trade is voluntary it must also be mutually beneficial.
- Free trade is, arguably, a fundamental right.
- Allowing entrepreneurship and innovation should lead to more rapid growth.
- The fact that countries are trading should reduce conflict.

There are of course, critics of free trade and their views include:

- Countries get hooked into supplying particular raw materials and do not develop alternative, higher value added, goods.
- It is inefficient, since consumer expectations are increased. For example, we now expect to consume fruit and vegetables out of season at high transport cost.
- Protectionism can actually be good for emergent nations.
- The influence of multinationals becomes too strong and can corrupt the political system.
- Outsourcing takes work to countries where the safety legislation is insufficiently developed to deal with the work.
- Free trade undermines national culture.
- Free trade reduces national security by removing or reducing border controls.

Learning activity 16.3

Identify obstacles to trade, imposed by national or regional anti-competitive policies, on products and services in which your organisation (or one with which you are familiar) is involved.

Feedback on page 201

16

Protectionism, in direct contrast to free trade, exists where a country or trade bloc attempts to restrict competition against their home producers. Traditionally this occurred via the imposition of export duties much the same as a purchase tax. This would make the imported goods more expensive and discourage importation. If the goods continued to be imported, the tax would be a source of revenue for the government who would, in theory, invest to make local manufacture more effective.

More modern approaches to protectionism revolve around *restrictive quota systems*, high quality or environmental standards and anti-dumping measures, whereby the product cannot be sold at a price lower than the manufacturing cost of local producers. Again, the purpose is not to raise revenue but to protect local industry. In fact, what tends to happen with quotas is that the restricted supply, faced with continued demand, allows the foreign producer to charge higher prices and make higher profits.

Most developed nations have agreed to *abolish protectionism* and this has been encouraged through organisations such as the World Trade Organisation (WTO).

Immediately after the Second World War, 23 countries negotiated and signed a number of agreements to facilitate the economic recovery of the world. One of those agreements was known as the General Agreement on Tariffs and Trade. In 1995 the organisation was renamed as the WTO; there were 75 member signatories and a number of countries have joined since, the most notable being China. Unlike GATT, the WTO has large administrative offices which are centred in Geneva.

The stated aim of the WTO is to encourage smooth and free trade by promoting lower, or abolished, trade barriers and to provide a platform for negotiated resolution to trade-related disputes between member nations. Therefore its primary purpose is to help providers of goods and services, both exporters and importers, to conduct their business more easily. Not everyone thinks the organisation is a good idea and, together with the World Bank, it has attracted a number of high-profile and often violent protests.

Effectively, the WTO advocates and promotes economic globalisation and, as such, is often accused of bias towards multinational organisations and richer nations.

The WTO tries to ensure that all trading relationships follow these principles:

- A trading system should be *discrimination-free* in that there is no favouritism shown by one country for another in the purchasing or selling of goods and services.
- There should be little, or *no, trade barriers* of any sort (tariff or non-tariff based).
- A trading system should be *predictable* so that governments and producers can be sure that no such barriers will be introduced.
- Whilst a trading system should be competitive there should be provision to allow time for *less-developed countries* to adjust to market forces, to enjoy greater flexibility and to have some privileges.

16

Where there are trade disputes, the WTO has the power to enforce decisions and require member states to impose sanctions on the countries that are at fault. In reality, much depends upon the economic strength of the complainant. When sanctions are applied for, and on behalf of, the EU or USA, they have far more impact than, for example, in the case of members of CARICOM (the trade bloc consisting of the English-speaking Caribbean countries). An example is the subsidy given to small farmers in the EU (the Common Agricultural Policy) which discriminates against farmers in less-developed countries.

Self-assessment question 16.3

In relation to any product or service you source globally (or one with which you are familiar), explain how national or regional anti-competitive policies impact upon its purchase.

Feedback on page 201

16.4 Regulation and regional economic integration

There are a number of parts of the world where countries have joined together, with various degrees of integration, to cooperate in the management of their economies and trade between them. Collectively these groupings are known as trade blocs. Some are quite active in pursuing integration whilst others are partners in name only. In theory, there are five levels of integration:

- *Free trade area.* All barriers to the movement of goods and services between member countries are removed. There are no discriminatory tariffs, quotas, taxes, subsidies or administrative barriers to free trade between the states who are members. However, the member countries are free to decide their own economic policies and trade policies when dealing with non-member states. NAFTA (comprising Canada, North America and Mexico) is a good example of a free trade area. In addition to free trade and no restrictions on FDI between the countries there are pan-national, scientifically based, environmental standards in operation.
- *Customs union.* This is one step further towards political integration – the member countries have a common external trade policy. The maintenance of the external trade policy requires a significant amount of administrative infrastructure and expenditure outside the control of the individual member countries. The Andean Pact (Bolivia, Columbia, Ecuador, Peru and Venezuela) is an example of a customs union. At the time of writing these countries have no internal barriers but impose an import tariff of between 5% and 10% on all goods brought into the region.
- *Common market.* In addition to the characteristics of a customs union, the factors of production (labour and capital) are free to move across the borders of the member countries without regulation. Currently the EU is the only example of this degree of integration, but MERCOSUR

16

(Argentina, Brazil, Paraguay, and Uruguay) has expressed the intent to progress to this stage of integration in the foreseeable future.

- *Economic union.* In addition to the conditions of a common market, there will be a common currency, unified tax rates and common monetary and fiscal policies. As yet no grouping of countries has reached this level of integration but, with the euro accepted by most states, the EU is heading along this route. Such a degree of integration requires significant levels of bureaucracy and the sacrifice of national sovereignty – which is possibly why it hasn't happened anywhere in the world yet.

- *Political union.* The final stage of integration is one of political union. A coordinating bureaucracy is accountable only to the population of the member states and not to the administration of those member states. All national interests are subsumed under that bureaucracy. It can be argued that the EU is heading in this direction with the European Parliament where the members are directly elected by the populations of the nation states. Both Canada and North America have this type of federal structure where, some years ago, the once-independent states were brought together into single nations.

Learning activity 16.4

By talking to your colleagues at work, see how many trade blocs you can identify and consider their degree of integration. Who are their members and how active is each of them in pursuing the stated aims?

Feedback on page 202

Within the more active trade blocs *regulators* will govern the way in which organisations conduct their business, via some form of competition policy. They will put policies in place to prevent practices which restrict fair competition in markets, such as monopolies and the formation of cartels. Regulators will also move against bid-rigging and predatory pricing, dumping, or any other situation where a company (or group of companies) is felt to have abused its market power. Primarily, they will act to break up, or prevent, a monopoly, which is deemed to be against the public interest. In the USA this is known as 'anti-trust' legislation and you will probably be familiar with the ongoing dispute that the US government has with Microsoft.

Monopolies are not always against the public interest. Within the EU, the competition regulator has the power to fine a company (or group of companies) up to 10% of their annual turnover for anti-competitive behaviour such as price fixing, market sharing or forming a cartel. However, they will not act if it can be shown that the behaviour leads to 'consumer benefit or technological progress'.

Not everyone is in favour of anti-trust legislation and Alan Greenspan is quoted as saying, 'No one will ever know what new products, processes, machines, and cost-saving mergers failed to come into existence, killed by

16

the anti-trust legislation before they were born. No one can ever compute the price that all of us have paid for the Act which, by inducing less effective use of capital, has kept our standard of living lower than would otherwise be possible.'

It is worth remembering that there are other global bodies, which play a part in economic regulation. The Organisation for Economic Cooperation and Development (OECD) and the International Competition Network (ICN) also function in this way.

Similarly, you should remember that not all cartels are illegal. Possibly the most famous, legal cartel is OPEC, the Organisation of Petroleum Exporting Countries.

Self-assessment question 16.4

For goods or services that your organisation (or with which you are familiar) sources internationally and that come from different trade blocs, identify the degree of economic integration at which those trade blocs operate.

Feedback on page 202

16.5 Cultural issues

Culture describes the way that people think, feel and act, and differs between organisations, industries and countries. All levels interact with each other and help to shape each other as well. From a business perspective it is useful to think of culture at four different levels:

- *National culture* consists of a distinctive set of shared values, attitudes, assumptions, beliefs and patterns of behaviour that guide the behaviour and are the 'norm' for the population of a particular country. For instance, whilst some countries accept bribery as a natural way of doing business, in other countries it is frowned upon.
- *Business culture* (within a particular country) is, again, an accepted pattern of behaviour which guides the inhabitants of a country. For example, in some countries it is accepted practice to favour one's friends and family in business dealings, whereas in other parts of the world it is regarded as unethical.
- *Industry culture* similarly affects the way that individual firms behave in a particular industry whilst conducting their business, and is usually common across the world. For instance, within universities, there is normally respect for academic independence, regardless of the country in which the university is based.
- *Organisational culture* is driven by a set of values (often the founder's), attitudes, assumptions, beliefs and norms that influence the ways in which the staff of an organisation will conduct business. Since the other three levels of culture also have an influence on this level, it can become quite complicated for transnational organisations. You will remember that we talked about organisational culture and the main contributors to it in study session 4.

16

Learning activity 16.5

Identify obstacles to trade imposed by national or regional cultural differences.

Feedback on page 202

Before continuing with this section, look back at the work you did in study session 4 on organisational culture – the analytical frameworks described will help you in deciding what builds and reinforces a particular cultural paradigm.

Cultural differences will affect consumer behaviour and working practices in organisations that will, in turn, affect the way an organisation is able to transact its business. The nature of the products offered and the strategies pursued will be affected by the cultural norms in the particular country, whether the firm is buying from the country or selling into the country.

Hofstede (1981) devised a framework that can be used to analyse national cultural characteristics. The framework has five dimensions:

1   *Power distance* describes the extent to which people accept that power in society and organisations is distributed unevenly. Where they are willing to accept uneven distribution it is said that power distance is high. Within most western organisations there is a low tolerance of this with the need for participative decisions, but in most Asian cultures the tolerance is higher.
2   *Uncertainty avoidance* defines the lengths to which people will go to avoid uncertainty, and their attitude to risk. A high level of uncertainty avoidance implies that an organisation or society will go to great lengths to minimise risk, and will have rules and laws in place to ensure that. The need for uncertainty avoidance is usually higher in less-developed countries whilst more-developed nations will tolerate more ambiguity.
3   *Individualism/collectivism* as a dimension is based upon the extent to which people stress individual or group needs. Societies which emphasise individualism are driven by self-interest, self-reliance and individual effort, and this is typified by most of American society and organisations. Collectivism is more likely to be found in Asian societies and organisations where, rather than give offence to the group, executives will agree with a decision instead of stressing their own, contrary views.
4   *Masculinity/femininity* describes the extent to which a society values assertiveness and materialism against harmony and supportiveness. A masculine culture is one where a high value is placed upon assertiveness and materialism. The contrast can again be made between largely masculine western cultures and the predominantly feminine eastern cultures.
5   *Long-term orientation* describes the extent to which a culture emphasises long- or short-term goals. Long-term orientation tends to be based on stability, persistence, order and thrift. It has often been argued that the

16

success of Japanese companies up until the early 1990s was due to their long-term focus on investment, the well-being of their workforce and building long-term relationships with their customers.

The cultural differences that exist between nations can be viewed as a potential source of advantage or as a potential source of conflict. Cultural differences can cause friction and difficulties but, equally, the diversity can be an important source of creativity for businesses.

Self-assessment question 16.5

In relation to any product or service you source globally (or with which you are familiar), explain how national or regional cultural differences impact upon its purchase.

Feedback on page 202

Revision question

Now try the revision question for this session on page 259.

Summary

This session has considered a number of issues relating to the global supply market, including:

- Globalisation and the five monopolies of which it consists.
- The benefits and disadvantages of global sourcing.
- Trade blocs and economic policy regarding globalisation.
- Free trade and protectionism.
- The WTO and the major trade blocs.
- The degrees of economic cooperation in trade blocs.
- International cultures and their impact upon business.

Suggested further reading

Look at the corporate websites of a couple of major food retailers. There should be a section relating to their global supply policy. If not, try looking in their annual report.

Feedback on learning activities and self-assessment questions

Feedback on learning activity 16.1

It is unlikely that you are in an organisation sourcing weapons of mass destruction, so you have most probably limited your answer to four monopolies. The answer to this will depend, to a large extent, on the nature of the organisation for which you work. If you work for a large, international oil company, in the exploration part of the business, the natural resources will be locally derived but the finance and technology

16

will be sourced globally. If you work in the refinery part of the business, then finance, technology and raw materials will be sourced globally. If you work for the finished goods part of the business, supplying fuel and oils to business and the general population, then product would be sourced nationally as would the technology; but the mass media and the finance would be sourced internationally.

Feedback on self-assessment question 16.1

Again, this will depend upon the nature of the company for which you work. If you are working in the refinery division of an oil company, the chances are the crude oil will have been sourced internationally. If you work for a company that makes cakes, the dried fruit will have come from abroad.

Feedback on learning activity 16.2

Any decision on sourcing should lead to a company gaining either a cost or differentiation advantage.

Global sourcing may contribute to this by providing.

- Access to materials and supplies at reduced cost.
- Access to technology or expertise not available locally.

However, against this must be set the potential disadvantages of:

- Increased costs due to longer lead times, customs duties and increased transport.
- Cultural and communications difficulties which can impact on both cost and overall quality.

Feedback on self-assessment question 16.2

Your answer should relate to the sources of competitive advantage. Does your company gain significantly in terms of cost from sourcing these products or services from a foreign supplier? Or is it the case that what you purchase is just not available locally?

Feedback on learning activity 16.3

Your answer is likely to include: tariffs, quotas, customs duties, purchase tax, subsidies to local manufacturers, technical or quality standards or simple embargoes.

Feedback on self-assessment question 16.3

This will depend to a large extent on the nature of the company for whom you work. There are two cases that made the news in 2006:

- In the aftermath of hurricane Katrina and Rita and their impact upon the United States, there was an acute shortage of refined sugar in the US. Consumption of packet sugar runs at 2.5 million tonnes annually, and a further 8.5 million tonnes is incorporated in other

16

products. North America, and the EU, has legislation in place which protects local producers by guaranteeing the price of refined sugar and imposing an import tariff on any sugar over 2.7 million tonnes imported annually. The tariff effectively doubles the price of sugar. Confectionery producers faced ruin because of the increased costs of one of their primary raw materials, due to the protectionist measures of their own country.

- Retailers in the United Kingdom were concerned about supplies after the EU Trade Minister Peter Mandelson imposed a quota system on the import of brassieres manufactured in China, which threatened to reduce supply dramatically.

Feedback on learning activity 16.4

There are quite a few! The more active ones include: NAFTA, MERCOSUR, the Andean Pact, and the EU. Other significant ones are:

- ASEAN, the Association of Southeast Asian Nations: Brunei, Cambodia, Indonesia, Laos, Malaysia, Myanmar, Philippines, Singapore, Thailand and Vietnam.
- APEC, the Asia-Pacific Economic Cooperation: 18 member states who surround the Pacific Rim including amongst others North America, China, Japan and Australia.
- GCC, Gulf Cooperation Council: Bahrain, Kuwait, Oman, Qatar, Saudi Arabia, United Arab Emirates.
- CARICOM: the Caribbean Community and Common Market: the English-speaking Caribbean countries.
- SACU, the Southern African Customs Union: Botswana, Lesotho, Namibia, South Africa and Swaziland.

There are others!

Feedback on self-assessment question 16.4

Much will depend upon the organisation for which you work but it is unlikely that you will not source something from the EU, something from North America and something from the ASEAN bloc. You should be able to describe how far along the path to full political union those groupings are, although as you will see in your attempts to describe the EU, things are never clear-cut.

Feedback on learning activity 16.5

There will be examples that you can find in your organisation where the patterns of behaviour have had to be adjusted to 'fit' local conditions. They may be related to the way in which negotiations are conducted, the number of people involved in the negotiations, or the number of levels you have had to talk to until you reached the actual decision maker.

Feedback on self-assessment question 16.5

If you think in terms of the five dimensions that are described in section 16.5, you can see how these might affect all stages of the purchasing process. For instance, in the negotiations the masculine/feminine dimension might make it difficult to reach an agreement with which everyone is happy. In terms of the contract itself, one side might be looking to take a far longer-term view than the other. The contract could also be affected by the power distance dimension with one side wanting a much more definitive specification than the other who might be happy to leave some elements to be resolved later. Whilst one side might be expecting one-to-one negotiations, a more collective approach may be taken by the other side.

16

16

Lean, added value and value chains

Introduction

This study session critically appraises the concepts of 'lean', 'waste', 'value', 'added value' and 'value chain'.

Session learning objectives

After completing this session you should be able to:

17.1 Explain the concepts of 'lean' and 'waste'.
17.2 Assess the application of the concepts of 'lean' and 'waste' to supply chains.
17.3 Critique the lean approach.
17.4 Identify alternatives to the lean approach.
17.5 Critique the concepts of 'value' and 'added value'.
17.6 Critique the concept of 'value chain'.
17.7 Assess arguments as to how value can be added.

Unit content coverage

This study session covers the following topics from the official CIPS unit content document:

Statement of practice

* Distinguish and assess various models of supply chain structures and relationships.

Learning objectives

5.2 Evaluate the concept of lean supply as a means of achieving competitive advantage.
  * The concept of lean
  * The seven types of waste
  * Critique of the lean approach (New and Ramsay 1997)
  * Alternatives to lean (agility) and hybrid approaches (leagility)
5.3 Critically evaluate the concepts of value, added value and value chain.
  * Concepts of value and added value
  * The value chain concept
  * Porter's (1985) value chain model
  * Critiques of Porter's model (Hines 1993)
  * Strategies for adding value: repositioning on the value chain, value constellations

17

Resources

Access to the following books is required for use throughout this session:

- Lysons and Farrington (2006), chapters 3 and 4
- Johnson, Scholes and Whittington (2007), chapter 3.

Timing

You should set aside about 5 hours to read and complete this session, including learning activities, self-assessment questions, the suggested further reading (if any) and the revision question.

17.1 The concepts of 'lean' and 'waste'

The concept of *lean* thinking has been applied to production operations since it was developed by Toyota in the 1980s. It focuses on removing *waste* from the production system – waste being any activity that requires resources, but adds no value (see below). In this respect, lean production has many similarities with business process re-engineering (BPR).

Lean production also seeks to avoid the rigidity caused by functional 'silos', and instead to take a process approach to managing operations. This allows the focus to be on satisfying customer needs, rather than functional objectives. In this respect, lean production has similarities to total quality management (TQM).

Lean production uses *a range of management tools*, including the following:

- Value engineering and value analysis, to remove cost from operations.
- Cross-functional teams, to reinforce the process approach (see study session 11).
- Just-in-time (JIT) systems, to 'pull' inventory through the system in response to customer requirements.
- Target costing, to ensure that the price of the finished good is in line with customer expectations while delivering sufficient profit margin to the producer.

Learning activity 17.1

If 'waste' in a production system is 'any activity that adds no value and is operationally unnecessary', list some different types of waste that might exist in a typical production process.

Feedback on page 216

In the lean thinking approach, authors tend to refer back to the first really lean production system – that of Toyota cars. There are seven commonly accepted wastes, according to Ohno (1995), in the Toyota production system (TPS):

1 overproduction
2 waiting
3 transport
4 inappropriate processing
5 unnecessary inventory
6 unnecessary movements
7 defects.

Overproduction is regarded as the most serious waste as it discourages a smooth flow of goods or services and is likely to inhibit quality and productivity. Such overproduction also tends to lead to excessive lead and storage times. As a result, defects may not be detected early, products may deteriorate and artificial pressures on work rate may be generated. In addition, overproduction leads to excessive work-in-progress stocks which result in the physical dislocation of operations with consequent poorer communication. This state of affairs is often encouraged by bonus systems that encourage the push of unwanted goods. The pull or 'kanban' system was employed by Toyota as a way of overcoming this problem.

When time is being used ineffectively, then the waste of *waiting* occurs. In a factory setting, this waste occurs whenever goods are not moving or being worked on. This waste affects both goods and workers, each spending time waiting. The ideal state should be no waiting time with a consequent faster flow of goods. Waiting time for workers may be used for training, maintenance or 'kaizen' activities and should not result in overproduction.

The third waste, *transport*, involves goods being moved about. Taken to an extreme, any movement in the factory could be viewed as waste and so transport minimisation rather than removal is usually sought. In addition, double handling and excessive movements are likely to cause damage and deterioration, with the distance of communication between processes proportional to the time it takes to feed back reports of poor quality and to take corrective action.

Inappropriate processing occurs in situations where overly complex solutions are found to simple procedures, such as using a large inflexible machine instead of several small flexible ones. The overcomplexity generally discourages ownership and encourages the employees to overproduce to recover the large investment in the complex machines. Such an approach encourages poor layout, leading to excessive transport and poor communication. The ideal, therefore, is to have the smallest possible machine, capable of producing the required quality, located next to preceding and subsequent operations. Inappropriate processing also occurs when machines are used without sufficient safeguards, so that poor quality goods are made.

Unnecessary inventory tends to increase lead time, preventing rapid identification of problems and increasing space, thereby discouraging communication. Thus, problems are hidden by inventory. To correct these problems, they first have to be found. This can be achieved only by reducing

17

inventory. In addition, unnecessary inventories create significant storage costs and, hence, lower the competitiveness of the organisation or value stream wherein they exist.

Unnecessary movements involve the ergonomics of production where operators have to stretch, bend and pick up when these actions could be avoided. Such waste is tiring for the employees and is likely to lead to poor productivity and, often, to quality problems.

The bottom-line waste is that of *defects*, as these are direct costs. The Toyota philosophy is that defects should be regarded as opportunities to improve rather than something to be traded off against what is ultimately poor management. Thus defects are seized on for immediate 'kaizen' activity.

In systems such as the Toyota production system, it is the continuous and iterative analysis of system improvements using the seven wastes that results in a kaizen-style system. As such, the majority of improvements are of a small but incremental kind, as opposed to a radical or breakthrough type.

Self-assessment question 17.1

Identify examples of the seven types of waste in any production process with which you are familiar.

Feedback on page 216

17.2 The lean supply chain

Not only can the 'lean concept' be applied to non-production organisations, it can also be applied to entire supply chains. Lamming (1995) describes lean supply as:

> 'the elimination of duplication of effort and capability in the supply chain, combined with a philosophy of continuously increasing the expectations of performance and self-imposed pressure to excel. This is achieved by recognition of mutual dependence and common interest between customer and supplier – beyond the principle of operational collaboration.'

Learning activity 17.2

Look at a couple of supply chains with which you are familiar. Do you see evidence of them becoming (or having become) leaner? Can you see that the firms have tried to pursue 'the elimination of duplication of effort and capability'?

Feedback on page 217

17

According to Lamming (1993) lean customer–supplier relationships exhibit
a series of characteristics (see table 17.1).

Table 17.1 Lean supply relationships

Factor	Lean supply characteristics
Nature of competition	• Global operations – local presence. • Based on contribution to product technology. • Organic growth and mergers/acquisitions. • Dependent on alliances/collaboration.
Basis of sourcing decisions	• Early involvement of established supplier in new product development. • Joint efforts in target costing/value analysis. • Single sourcing. • Supplier who provides greatest global benefits. • Re-sourcing as a last resort.
Role/mode of data/information exchange	• True transparency on costs, etc. • Discussions of costs and volumes. • Technical and commercial information exchanged. • EDI.
Management of capacity	• Kanban system. • Strategic investments discussed. • Synchronised capacity. • Flexibility to operate with fluctuations.
Delivery practice	• True JIT.
Dealing with price changes	• Price reductions based on cost reduction joint efforts.
Attitude to quality	• Supplier vetting becomes redundant. • Mutual agreement on quality targets. • Continual interaction. • Kaizen. • Perfect quality as the goal.
Role of R&D	• Integrated between assembler and supplier. • Long-term joint development. • Supplier/assembler systems integration.
Level of pressure	• Very high. • Self-imposed.

The main objective of developing a lean supply chain is the complete
removal of waste in order to achieve a competitive advantage. That
advantage can be achieved both by the reduction of costs and the
improvement of quality (whether product or service). Although, in theory,
the competitive advantage should be shared between all the 'actors' in the
supply chain, in reality the share of the benefits will depend on relative
power (see study session 18).

Other benefits of lean supply are (Hines 1994):

• Reduced inventories (and thus improved cash flow and profit).

17

- Shorter lead times, and thus faster delivery to consumers.
- Fewer bottlenecks, so better utilisation of resources, and further improvements to profit.
- Fewer quality problems, so less reworking, lower costs of quality failure, and happier consumers.

Self-assessment question 17.2

Analyse any of your organisation's supply chains and assess the opportunities for removing waste.

Feedback on page 217

17.3 Critiques of 'lean'

In study session 11 we looked at the concept of 'agile' supply chains. One of the arguments for agility was its ability to overcome the inflexibility caused by the pursuit of leanness. Lean supply chains are, apparently, most suitable for high-volume supply in conditions of predictable demand.

Learning activity 17.3

What do you think are the other major criticisms of the lean supply approach?

Feedback on page 217

New and Ramsay (1997) put forward a number of major criticisms of the lean supply chain approach:

- Assuming that the lean approach does give more customers more choice, then this will probably increase the overall level of consumption. This may not be a socially desirable outcome, given the impact on the environment and the possible depletion of scarce resources.
- The ability of lean chains to satisfy customer whims even more quickly may result in overproduction of 'throwaway' goods. This will again have serious environmental consequences.
- Microeconomics suggest that perfect competition leads to the optimal level of efficiency in the market. As the lean supply chain consists of a series of partnerships and 'preferred supplier' relationships, it must represent a sub-optimal solution. With reduced competition comes complacency. The entry barriers created by cooperation will reduce competition and increase the levels of margin earned. This may be 'good' for the organisations concerned, but it is 'bad' for the consumer.
- Concentrating on leanness in the supply chain may lead to 'shakeout' in the industries affected, resulting in an overall reduction in manufacturing capacity and significant job losses. While this may

17

benefit the supply chain, it has significant economic and social consequences.
- Over-leanness may lead to a situation where there is insufficient 'slack' in the system to take account of fluctuations in demand. This issue is related to that discussed in study session 11, as one of the arguments for the development of agile chains.
- The cost burden involved in becoming lean may be too high for many smaller suppliers, and they may be driven away from the supply chain despite, perhaps, being the optimal suppliers.

There are also other arguments against the lean chain approach:

- Large, powerful customers can dominate lean supply chains. Although the ideal situation is that all the actors in a supply chain share the benefits of leanness, in reality the greater share of cost savings will be taken by the most powerful organisation in the chain.
- Most of the leanness tools concentrate on reducing cost rather than improving quality. Any resulting savings may be kept as increased margins, rather than being passed on to the customer.
- Too much concentration on cost reduction may, in fact, worsen quality or at least increase the risk of quality failure.

Self-assessment question 17.3

Assess the validity of the criticisms of lean supply chains, drawing upon evidence from your own experience.

Feedback on page 217

17.4 Alternatives to lean

Generic strategies alternative to lean are summarised in table 11.2 of study session 11. These are kanban, agile and hybrid/leagility. This study session and study session 11 focus mainly on lean and agile.

Kanban means 'visible record' in Japanese and is known for its use on manufacturing lines. The kanban cards or tickets record the part number, supplier and quantity, and are stored in the container that holds the parts. When the bin is emptied, the kanban is used to order more.

Mason-Jones et al (2000) advocate a hybrid approach that combines the lean elimination of waste with agility concepts of exploiting opportunities in markets that are volatile. Up to a decoupling point lean concepts are applied and the product is built to forecasts. After the decoupling point, customer orders drive the supply chain.

This has been used in the car manufacturing industry by Toyota. The base model is made in Japan and additional customer options are added near the port in the United States or at a dealer.

17

Learning activity 17.4

Identify industries or organisations that might and will not suit lean, agile, kanban, hybrid/leagility working.

Feedback on page 217

Self-assessment question 17.4

Compare and contrast the lean, agile, kanban and hybrid/leagility concepts of supply chains.

Feedback on page 217

17.5 'Value' and 'added value'

According to Monden, there are three types of operation in any manufacturing activity:

1 *Non-value-adding (NVA) activities.* These are pure waste, and should be eliminated completely.
2 *Necessary, but non-value-adding (NNVA) activities.* These may appear wasteful, but are essential in order to allow a subsequent activity that adds value to take place. These should be re-engineered to reduce their cost to the minimum.
3 *Value-adding (VA) activities.* These (according to Monden, and in a manufacturing context) involve the conversion or processing of raw materials or semi-finished products through manual labour.

What Monden (in common with many other writers) does not do, is explain what he means by added value.

Learning activity 17.5

In a non-manufacturing context, how would you define 'added value'?

Feedback on page 217

In *marketing*, added value is generally thought to result from four factors:

1 features
2 quality
3 customer perception (or image)
4 exclusiveness.

However, in *financial* terms, added value is the difference between the sales price of a product and its direct cost of manufacture. Thus, there are two ways to increase added value: to increase the price customers are willing to pay, or to reduce the cost of production.

Strategists tend to avoid any precise definition of added value, stating instead that anything that furthers the objectives of the organisation adds value. Furthering the objectives of the organisation, of course, most often means making profits. For this reason, we have a lot of profit-related measures of added value, such as Stern-Stewart's Economic Value Added (EVA®) measure.

> 'Put most simply, *EVA* is net operating profit minus an appropriate charge for the opportunity cost of all capital invested in an enterprise. As such, EVA is an estimate of true 'economic' profit, or the amount by which earnings exceed or fall short of the required minimum rate of return that shareholders and lenders could get by investing in other securities of comparable risk.'

> Stern-Stewart International

So, if we follow Stern-Stewart's logic, added value can be increased by either increasing profit or reducing the cost of capital of the organisation.

Self-assessment question 17.5

Present arguments in bullet point form *against* the claim that added value is essentially about cost reduction.

Feedback on page 218

17.6 The value chain

Michael Porter suggested (1993) that the strategic position of an organisation could best be analysed by looking at how the activities performed by the organisation added (or did not add) value, in the view of the customer. Porter proposed a model for carrying out such an analysis – the *value chain* (see Lysons and Farrington (2006: 102) or Johnson, Scholes and Whittington (2007) for the diagram).

To be included in the value chain, an activity has to be performed by the organisation *better, differently or more cheaply* than by its rivals. Porter, just to contribute further to the confusion of section 17.4, defines added value as 'what the customer pays for'.

The primary activities of the value chain are:

- *Inbound logistics:* the systems and procedures that the organisation uses to get inputs into the organisation – for example, the inspection and storage of raw materials.
- *Operations:* the processes of converting inputs to outputs – for example, production processes.

17

- *Outbound logistics:* the systems and procedures that the organisation uses to get outputs to the customer – for example, storage and distribution of finished goods.
- *Marketing and sales:* those marketing and sales activities that are aimed at persuading customers to buy, or to buy more – for example, TV or point-of-sale advertising.
- *Service:* those marketing and sales activities that are clearly aimed before or after the point of sale – for example, warranty provision, or advice on choosing or using the product.

The secondary (or support) activities of the value chain are:

- *Procurement:* the acquisition of any input or resource – for example, buying raw materials or capital equipment.
- *Technology development:* the use of advances in technology – for example, new IT developments.
- *Human resource management:* improving the use of the human resources of the organisation – for example, by providing better training.
- *Firm infrastructure:* those general assets, resources or activities of the organisation that are difficult to allocate to one of the other activity headings – for example, a reputation for quality, or a charismatic chief executive.

Learning activity 17.6

How do you think Porter's value chain model relates to the concept of a supply chain?

Feedback on page 218

Porter himself stresses that linkages between value chains (that is, between organisations that are customer and supplier to one another) also add value, and proposes that the value chains of related organisations should be viewed as a 'value network' (see Johnson, Scholes and Whittington, (2007) for the diagram).

Peter Hines (1993) recognises Porter's contribution to supply chain management in two respects:

1   Porter places emphasis on logistics, procurement and materials handling as value-adding activities.
2   Porter places the customer at the centre of the added value concept.

However, Hines also makes three criticisms of Porter's model:

1   Although the customer is recognised as central to added value creation, the emphasis of Porter's model is still on profit rather than customer satisfaction – the former is seen as the objective of the latter.
2   Although Porter says that linkages within and between value chains are important, the value chain and value network models both show systems as being divided between functions/activities or organisations.

17

3   The value chain model identifies the wrong functions as important, and
    the arbitrary allocation of functions to 'primary' and 'secondary' is also
    incorrect, particularly classifying 'procurement' as secondary.

For a detailed analysis of Hines' alternative proposals, see Lysons and
Farrington (2006: 104–105).

Self-assessment question 17.6

Assess the validity of Hines' (1993) critique of Porter's model.

Feedback on page 218

17.7 How value can be added

According to Porter, competitive advantage can only be obtained by
pursuing one of the 'generic strategies' (see study session 5). In terms of
value chain activities, this means 'performing those strategically significant
activities better, differently or more cheaply'.

Learning activity 17.7

Given that there are three possible generic strategies – cost leadership,
differentiation and focus – can you think of any other ways that value can be
added in the context of a supply chain?

Feedback on page 218

Normann and Ramirez (1993) suggest that, in the conventional view of
the supply chain, value is added sequentially by each actor before they pass
their product on to the next 'link' in the chain. Thus, they suggest, in this
conventional business world, strategy is about positioning the organisation
at the right stage of the value chain.

They go on to propose that, in the modern business world, strategy is
about 'reinventing' added value by collaboration between supply chain
actors. They propose the concept of value 'constellations' – groups of
collaborating organisations that are not arranged into a sequential chain,
but a complex network. They say that 'successful companies conceive of
strategy as systematic social innovation: the continuous design and redesign
of complex business systems.'

Normann and Ramirez suggest that their 'new logic' of strategy presents
organisations with three strategic implications:

1   The goal of business is not so much to add value, but to mobilise
    customers to create value for themselves. (They quote the examples of
    ATMs and Ikea's approach to furniture retailing.)

17

2 An organisation is no longer able to add value on its own. It therefore has a strategic task to involve its suppliers, customers and partners in new combinations.

3 The only true source of competitive advantage is the ability to conceive of an entire value-adding constellation, and bring it into existence.

Self-assessment question 17.7

Critically evaluate the three 'strategic implications' of Normann and Ramirez.

Feedback on page 218

Supply chains can be used to help develop competitive advantage. An example would be if a company adopted a cost leadership strategy. This corporate strategy could be underpinned by the operations of the company. The supply chain would need to operate as efficiently as possible, buying low-cost product from a potentially global source. Alternatively, a company might need to produce low-cost products efficiently, using lean principles. The whole ethos of the supply chain would be to provide low-cost items that have the potential to under-price competitors. The supply chain would play a crucial role in the overall success of the strategy.

Revision question

Now try the revision question for this session on page 260.

Summary

This session has critically appraised the concepts of 'lean', 'waste', 'value', 'added value' and 'value chain'.

Suggested further reading

Read some case studies, from the internet or magazines, relating to the automotive, fashion and food retail industries.

Feedback on learning activities and self-assessment questions

Feedback on learning activity 17.1

For the answer see the continuation of section 17.1.

Feedback on self-assessment question 17.1

This shouldn't be too difficult, as all processes have some degree of waste, even fairly lean ones.

17

Feedback on learning activity 17.2

Firstly, you need to look for evidence that the firms in the supply chain have been talking to one another. If they don't do that, they're unlikely to have achieved much at all. Then, look for dialogue regarding cost reductions or quality improvements or improvements in efficiency. If you can't find any evidence, that's good – it means there's plenty of scope for you to use your new skills to improve things!

Feedback on self-assessment question 17.2

You can refer back to section 17.1 and look for examples of the 'seven types of waste' outlined there.

Feedback on learning activity 17.3

For the answer see the continuation of section 17.3

Feedback on self-assessment question 17.3

If you have little experience within your own organisation, or find it difficult to get the information you need, try looking at a very 'public' supply chain. The UK supermarkets are widely criticised for promoting leanness in their supply chain at the expense of both suppliers and customers.

Feedback on learning activity 17.4

Some of your suggestions for use will be based around areas such as traditional car manufacturing. The concepts of eliminating waste and exploiting opportunities in markets that are volatile are now transcending into wider areas.

Feedback on self-assessment question 17.4

Lean: long lead times and predictable demand.

Hybrid: long lead times and unpredictable demand.

Kanban: short lead times and predictable demand.

Agile: short lead times and unpredictable demand.

Feedback on learning activity 17.5

'*Added value* refers to the increase in worth of a product or service as a result of a particular activity. In the context of marketing, the added value is provided by features and benefits over and above those representing the "core product".'

Tutor2u.com

17

Feedback on self-assessment question 17.5

Although added value can result from cost reduction, it can also come about as a consequence of:

- improvements in quality
- additional product features
- improved customer service levels
- perceived exclusivity.

Feedback on learning activity 17.6

Porter's model looks inside the organisation, so it is concentrating on the intra-firm aspects of a supply chain, rather than the inter-firm aspects more commonly described. The value chain concept can be used to get some idea of how each actor in a supply chain adds value sequentially to a product or service. Porter's idea for a 'value system' or 'value network' is much closer to the concept of a supply chain, as it is a collection of related value chains.

Feedback on self-assessment question 17.6

Although Hines' criticisms have some merit, Porter can be defended on the following grounds:

1   Commercial organisations exist to make profit, so customer satisfaction is simply a vehicle to achieve this. If an organisation does not make profit, it does not survive.
2   Porter's model was developed primarily to look at how an *organisation* adds value, so it is unfair to criticise it for failing to do something other than that.
3   Porter's model views the 'input/conversion/output' activities as primary. This is consistent with many other models of business. Porter classifies procurement as 'secondary', as it includes the purchase of many items other than raw materials (such as capital equipment and staff), and may thus support any one of the primary activities.

Feedback on learning activity 17.7

In section 17.5 we agreed that added value could come about as a consequence of cost reductions, or the following:

- improvements in quality
- additional product features
- improved customer service levels
- perceived exclusivity.

The first two and the last one are examples of differentiation, whereas the third is related to focus. Porter's generic strategies are so general, that they encompass pretty much everything. That's why they're able to be 'generic'.

Feedback on self-assessment question 17.7

1   Customers will only pay a supplier to allow them to 'create value for themselves' for a finite period. Once customers realise that the supplier

is not adding any value, they will cease to pay, unless there is still no viable alternative that delivers the same value.

2　Normann and Ramirez put forward no convincing argument as to why it is impossible for an individual organisation to add value alone. Indeed, the only examples they cite are those organisations involved in 'constellations'. Logically, if a constellation adds value, that value must be added by the organisations in the constellation, therefore each organisation must add value. There may be synergies, but it is not conceivable that all the added value comes from synergy.

3　Many other authors propose alternatives for achieving sustainable competitive advantage. There is insufficient evidence to support the statement that 'the only true source of competitive advantage is the ability to conceive of an entire value-adding constellation, and bring it into existence'.

17

Power, ethics and the pursuit of socioeconomic goals through supply chains

Introduction

In this study session, we will discuss power in supply chains and will consider the appropriateness of supply chains in achieving objectives other than those of profit.

Just do it!
Nike advertising slogan

Session learning objectives

After completing this session you should be able to:

18.1 Analyse the sources of power in supply chains.
18.2 Analyse the nature and role of power in supply chains.
18.3 Assess evidence on power relationships between large customers and small suppliers in supply chains.
18.4 Assess ethical considerations which may be pursued through supply chains.
18.5 Assess socioeconomic goals which may be pursued through supply chains.
18.6 Justify the use of supply chains to deliver ethical and socioeconomic outcomes alongside commercial goals.

Unit content coverage

This study session covers the following topics from the official CIPS unit content document:

Statement of practice

- Distinguish and assess various models of supply chain structures and relationships.

Learning objectives

5.4 Analyse the sources, nature and role of power in supply chains.
  - Sources of power in supply chains
  - Nature and role of power in supply chains
  - Ways in which power may be exercised in supply chains: overt, covert and structural
  - Power relationships between large customers and small suppliers in supply chains
5.5 Evaluate the use of supply chains to deliver ethical and socio-economic outcomes alongside commercial goals.
  - Ethical considerations in supply chains
  - Types of socio-economic goals pursued through supply chains: environment, employment, equality, small and medium enterprises, prompt payment

18

- Arguments for and against the use of supply chains to pursue non-commercial goals

Resources

Access to the following books is highly recommended for use throughout this session:

- Lysons and Farrington (2006), chapter 17
- Dam Jespersen and Skjott-Larsen (2005), chapter 7
- Christopher (2005), chapters 9 and 10.

Timing

You should set aside about 6 hours to read and complete this session, including learning activities, self-assessment questions, the suggested further reading (if any) and the revision question.

18.1 Organisational power

Organisational power can be defined most simply as 'potential force' – that is, it is the ability to get things done, and to achieve goals and outcomes to one's own standards. We discussed power within organisations in study session 4. We can apply some of those ideas to the supply chain:

- A company can be said to have *expert power* if it is the sole holder of knowledge and expertise within the supply chain – for example, it may hold the patents for a particular part of a process.
- A company can be described as having *referent power* if other members of the supply chain perceive that is has high reputational capital and they would wish to be associated with that company.
- There will be *reward power* if the company is in a position to help other supply chain members achieve their objectives.
- *Coercive power* will be present if the company is large and it is perceived that it will carry out any threats made to other channel members.
- Lastly we can consider whether the *power is legitimate*: is there, for example, a strong position (even a monopoly) in producing or selling a popular product?

You might also want to look back at the discussion of Porter's Five Forces in study session 3.

A supply chain member can be said to be powerful if one of the following applies:

- Other members are dependent upon them for essential components.
- They have control over significant financial resource.
- They play a central part in the network.
- What they supply is not substitutable.
- They have the ability to reduce uncertainty for the other players.

18

It is worth remembering that business strategy is about *appropriating value* for one's own company and stakeholders and, hopefully, building a strategic position where competitors, buyers and suppliers do not pose a threat to that value position. With that in mind, we might want to consider that companies need to find a position where they are able to exercise power over other members of the supply chain. This contradicts much of what is said in the literature about lean supply, which should be based on equity, trust and openness. We can summarise the position in which a buyer may find themselves under four categories: buyer dominance, interdependence, independence and supplier dominance. The position will depend upon the relative utility and the relative scarcity of the goods or services that are being traded:

- *Buyer dominance* is likely to occur where there are few buyers and many suppliers and the supplier is highly dependent upon the buyer for revenue. The buyer will almost certainly have low switching costs relative to the supplier.
- *Interdependence* will occur when there are relatively few buyers and sellers and both have high switching costs.
- *Independence* will occur when there are many buyers and sellers and both buyer and seller have low switching costs.
- *Supplier dominance* occurs where there are relatively few suppliers and the buyer has high switching costs relative to the supplier.

Take as an example a typical supermarket, such as Tesco, Sainsbury or Morrisons, each of which has a considerable market share in the UK. There are many customers going into each of the stores and they are *independent* of those supermarket chains. However, when we look at the relationships that the supermarkets have with suppliers of prepared packaged foods we have an example of *buyer dominance*. The relative size of the supermarket and the likelihood that the supermarket business is a significant percentage of the food supplier's revenue makes the supermarket dominant. When we consider the relationship between the food supplier and the supplier of customised plastic packaging for the product it is likely to be one of *interdependence*. Most probably the food supplier and the packaging firm have collaborated on the design of the packaging and may even have shared the cost of the moulds for manufacture.

For an example of *supplier dominance* from the same industry, we can consider the relationship between supermarkets and detergent manufacturers (such as Proctor and Gamble) in Japan. Here the relationship is reversed, since the supermarkets are relatively small and shop space is at a premium, the Japanese stores are very dependent upon the goodwill of the suppliers to deliver frequently and in small batches.

18

Self-assessment question 18.1

Analyse the power your organisation (or one with which you are familiar) in relation to customers and suppliers in any supply chain.

Feedback on page 232

18.2 The exercise of power

Power as social construct can be considered as arising from three basic conditions:

- the force or the ability to coerce.
- the dependence of one individual upon another.
- the creation of obligations, duty or the calling-in of commitments.

It is worth remembering that power resides with one individual or group because of the beliefs, perceptions and desires of others.

Coercion is the simplest, and most visible, form of power. Typically rewards are offered or withheld or punishments are threatened. There are difficulties with coercion since, if promises or threats are not plausible or not carried out, power is lost.

Dependency arises wherever there is an exchange between two entities. Invariably, it will be an unequal exchange, with one party more dependent on the other for a successful outcome. The more dependent entity will be, relatively, less powerful than the other. However, one could argue that dependency is a subset of coercion, since one party is dependent upon the other not to exercise coercion.

Power also arises from *obligations* because of socially, and legally, accepted norms that bring about compliance. This is about one party doing something because they want to rather than because they have to. In some cultures the power of obligation can be quite strong with the feeling that, once someone has provided a service there is a strong commitment to reciprocate at some time in the future. In the event that the obligation is not met, coercion may well be exercised.

Learning activity 18.2

Identify ways in which power may be exercised in supply chains.

Feedback on page 233

If we now consider the concepts of overt, covert and structural power, we can see that there are elements of overlap in the definitions of these, just as there were for coercion, dependence and obligation. This is not surprising since we are talking about a social system. Remember that power is dependent upon the perceptions of people or groups of people – so we can look at the nature of conflict in each case:

- *Overt power* can be thought of as quite obvious and transparent and, to some extent, brutal. It might arise from relative size, industry dominance and the reputation of the powerful entity. The fact that an organisation is held in high regard will mean that other organisations will wish to be associated with it. The overtly powerful player will be dominant in its behaviour and will, to a large extent, openly dictate the terms of any agreement. Invariably, there will be observable disagreement or conflict and power is exercised to resolve this.
- *Covert power* will be exercised in a more subtle manner and will often arise from things being withheld rather than imposed. One of the strongest tools of covert power is information, whereby a more powerful player will withhold information from the weaker party. By excluding an organisation from a joint venture or alliance, power is denied to that party. Any conflicts of interest are kept from the public domain by excluding them from the discussions or agenda so that they are not apparent to observers.
- *Structural power* is best described by referring back to the work of Porter in describing industry analysis. The situation may arise where relative size and industry concentration will give one player a more powerful position that the others in the supply chain. The main aspect of this type of power is that conflict tends not to exist since the norms and meanings have been institutionalised and are accepted as received wisdom. Those who comply with the power wielder do so because they are not aware of alternative actions that are in their best interests.

As we said earlier, the purpose of business strategy is to *capture value* on behalf of the shareholders; therefore, achieving a more powerful position than the organisations that have to be dealt with must be of prime importance. So how can organisations achieve that?

In terms of the types of power described above, it might be easier to focus on creating *structural power,* by building switching costs into the supplier's product – if the buyer makes its requirements more and more specific, it is unlikely that the supplier will have many alternative customers and it will therefore be more dependent upon the buyer. By increasing the number of sellers who are then able to satisfy the company's needs, the company will build structural power and a resulting dependency.

Self-assessment question 18.2

Give examples of how your organisation (or one with which you are familiar) may use, or be subject to, overt, covert and structural power in supply chains.

Feedback on page 233

18.3 Interdependent relationships

As discussed in section 18.1, the position of the buyer in any transaction can be described as dominant, independent, interdependent or dominated by the supplier. Let's consider the *interdependent relationship* a bit more closely and see what is involved. Effectively, if there is interdependence there should be the elements of a partnership in place. The concept of a partnership should be based on trust, cooperation and seeking mutual benefits. Successful partners should have *shared goals* and work together to improve design, quality, processes and delivery, in order to enjoy a mutual competitive advantage in the market place.

This kind of relationship, however, is not always possible when there is a difference in size between the companies involved since there is often the temptation for the larger company to pursue individual, short-term goals.

Learning activity 18.3

Provide at least three examples of cases demonstrating power relationships between large customers and small suppliers.

Feedback on page 233

To a large extent the likelihood of a partnership existing formally, or informally, can be determined from the *strategic importance* of the product or service being purchased. In general terms, the higher the strategic importance the greater is the chance of partnering. We can consider a purchase to be strategic if:

- There is a *high volume* of purchase on which the final product is dependent.
- There is a *high knowledge* component to the purchase – that is, it is specialised and there is a significant requirement for *training* for its effective use.
- There is a *high search cost* for the purchaser in finding an alternative.
- There is the potential for *mutual benefits* through joint investigation of costs and service quality.

The emphasis in this kind of relationship must be one of openness and trust, with the sharing of risks and benefits and the use of such approaches as open-book accounting and joint development.

To a large extent this poses a significantly higher risk to the smaller player in the partnership since its dependence on the larger player is far greater.

But, as we said earlier, this type of relationship is not always possible or desirable. Whilst this type of relationship is more likely to be found where there is interdependence, it might arise in cases where there is independence or even supplier domination. However, in these cases the relationship might be quite short term or, whilst somewhat collaborative, might still be adversarial. Each situation must be considered, and evaluated, on its merits.

For the large customer dealing with a smaller supplier, regardless of the degree of interdependence, there is the potential for abuse of power and

18

damage to the reputational capital of the firm. That *abuse of power* may manifest itself as excesses in: price control, quality control, inventory management and control over information. Whether that is ethical, and effective, behaviour is open to question. We have looked at the impact of globalisation in study session 16 and there is no doubt that the increasing globalisation of supply chains has added to the ethical dilemmas faced by purchasing departments.

You could reinforce your learning at this stage by looking at the ethical guidance published by CIPS and see how that influences the decisions that the membership, and all staff who wish to be seen as professional, make.

Self-assessment question 18.3

Write a briefing note to your manager: firstly, assessing evidence on power relationships between large customers and small suppliers and, secondly, advocating an appropriate policy for managing such relationships.

Feedback on page 233

18.4 Ethical sourcing considerations

As a number of high-profile cases have demonstrated, there is a strong connection between corporate social responsibility, reputation and supply chain network conditions. The meaning of *corporate social responsibility* (CSR), although a much used term, is open to interpretation. One school of thought argues that in implementing CSR a company should be looking for a win-win result in terms both of business as well as societal benefits, whilst another school of thought argues that it should be done because it is the 'right thing to do'. Similarly, there is a debate about the dimensions of CSR – how far from the boundaries of the firm should the responsibility lie? Should companies be held responsible for the impact of events that occur remotely from their sites and that are only indirectly a result of their business practices?

Some companies are already investing significant resources in actions which appear to further some social good, beyond the immediate interests of the firm and to a greater extent than required by the law. They are introducing ethical sourcing initiatives that should ensure that the firm's purchasing decisions do not contribute to environmental degradation and that the firm only sources from suppliers who can demonstrate that they, and their suppliers, have met required standards for working conditions.

18

Learning activity 18.4

List, in order of importance, the ethical considerations that may be pursued through supply chains.

Feedback on page 233

For many companies, corporate reputational capital and brand image are important sources of competitive advantage. For that reason, non-governmental organisations (NGOs) have targeted these features as a lever for social and environmental change. This may be one of the reasons why firms are introducing ethical sourcing practices or, it may because of a more responsible and altruistic approach to business. In 1999, through the UN Global Compact, Kofi Annan requested that companies commit to ten ethical principles in the areas of human rights, labour, the environment and anti-corruption:

Human rights

- Principle 1: Support and respect the protection of internationally proclaimed human rights.
- Principle 2: Make sure they are not complicit in human rights abuses.

Labour standards

- Principle 3: Uphold the freedom of association and the effective recognition of the right to collective bargaining.
- Principle 4: Eliminate all forms of forced or compulsory labour.
- Principle 5: Work for the effective abolition of child labour.
- Principle 6: Eliminate discrimination in respect of employment and occupation.

Environment

- Principle 7: Support a precautionary approach to environmental challenges.
- Principle 8: Undertake initiatives to promote greater environmental responsibility.
- Principle 9: Encourage the development and diffusion of environmentally friendly technologies.

Anti-corruption

- Principle 10: Work against all forms of corruption, including extortion and bribery.

The likelihood of the introduction of an ethical sourcing code of conduct is dependent upon:

- The number of links in the supply network between the member requiring the code of conduct and the stage of the supply network under scrutiny.
- The diffuseness of the stage of the supply network under scrutiny.
- Power of the different members of the supply network.
- The reputational vulnerability of the different network members.

For instance, there is considerable pressure on the manufacturers of branded chocolate confectionery to ensure that the supply of cocoa is ethically managed. After allegations of cocoa farmers using child and bonded labour, many major retailers, who had codes of practice in place, required the same

18

from Nestlé, Mars, Cadbury and other firms. Consumers also brought pressure to bear. The companies face the considerable challenges of long supply chains, diffuse sources and powerful intermediaries who have little or no concern for such an initiative. In this case, for the chocolate companies to act independently makes little sense; so the development of an industry code would seem the best way forward. Ideally, this would be managed by a combination of representatives of the companies, social organisations and environmental organisations. This will mean that procurement executives will need to engage not only with suppliers but will need to build effective relationships with different members of the supply network and other organisations such as NGOs.

Self-assessment question 18.4

Identify the three most important ethical considerations for your organisation, or one with which you are familiar, and assess how these are being pursued through your supply chains.

Feedback on page 234

18.5 Socioeconomic goals

If we look at the list of principles proposed by Kofi Annan (in section 18.4), we can see that the way it is written proposes a proactive approach by businesses. It doesn't just suggest that firms should be good citizens, it actually encourages them to ensure that those that they deal with are good citizens as well. This means that, in their dealings with other companies, they should try to improve the social and economic conditions of the workforce, population, and country in which their suppliers are based. This can be difficult to achieve, since it will often mean that they are trying to encourage behaviour which is not the cultural norm in the supplier's home territory – not everyone will have signed up for the UN global compact. Companies often get bad press when they 'interfere' in the way a country is run; in this case, it is suggested that they should do so, if it is perceived that one of the ten principles is being broken.

Learning activity 18.5

After talking to your colleagues at work, list in order of importance those socioeconomic goals that may be pursued through supply chains.

Feedback on page 234

18

The area of socioeconomics is, as you will have discovered in learning activity 18.5 above, incredibly broad and often a matter of interpretation. At this stage it would be worth refreshing your memory about culture by looking again at study session 16. Referring again to the ten principles in the global compact, to Western eyes some are fairly clear-cut: most people in those cultures would probably have few issues with principles 1, 2, 4, 5, 6, and 10. However, the other four principles might require more reflection. Principle 3 promotes the position of trade unions and collective bargaining. Whilst some people feel that this is an inalienable right, others feel that unions should not be as powerful as they are in some countries. In most Western democracies, the power of the unions has been declining as socialism has declined as a political ideology. But, even within Europe, there are differences in the power of the unions. In France and Germany, for instance, the importance of the unions and collective bargaining is far higher than it is in the UK.

If we consider the principles 7–9 grouped together under 'environment' all would agree, superficially, that these are a good thing. But what constitutes an environmental challenge? There is no doubt that a process to extract gold, involving potassium cyanide solution, which pollutes the environment for decades to come is an environmental challenge. Similarly, there is no doubt that any process to extract minerals that leaves the countryside scarred and unsightly is a bad thing. Any process that uses excess amounts of fossilised fuels is similarly something that all companies should try to avoid, since these are non-renewable sources of energy. So, is it a good idea for a supermarket to supply its customers with out-of-season fruit and vegetables that have travelled around the world by air freight just to satisfy consumer demand? Might it not be more acceptable to only stock seasonal fruit and vegetables and 'educate' consumers to be happy with local produce? There are similar arguments about packaging and whether it is necessary to use so much plastic, again made from fossil fuel, to contain and display fruit in an attractive manner so that customers will consume more. At one end of the spectrum we have environmentalism, at the other consumerism.

As you can see, whilst all companies, and the vast majority of individuals, will wish to act responsibly, this is not a clear-cut area and much is open to interpretation. Increasingly good corporate citizenship is guided by legislation and firms can be seen to take different approaches to that legislation. Their pattern of behaviour has been described as following five approaches:

*   non-compliance
*   compliance
*   compliance plus
*   commercial and environmental excellence
*   leading edge.

18

Self-assessment question 18.5

Identify the two most important socioeconomic goals for your organisation (or one with which you are familiar) and assess how these are being pursued through supply chains.

Feedback on page 234

18.6 So, are non-commercial goals a good thing?

You might draw the conclusion from the self-assessment question 18.5 above that the main driver for the sawmills to take up the sustainable timber initiative was one of corporate reputation.

Every organisation has a variety of stakeholders whose wishes it must satisfy to a greater or lesser extent, depending upon their power. For a commercial organisation, arguably the most powerful stakeholders are the owners; for a large quoted firm, the shareholders. At its simplest level, shareholders will require that the organisation provide them with an adequate dividend income for the investment they have made and, hopefully, capital growth on their share value. To quote Milton Friedman, the famous American economist, 'the business of business is business' – the implication being that firms should concentrate wholly and solely on making a profit for their shareholders. However, one of the largest types of shareholder in a quoted company is often an investment trust. Over the past few years an increasing number of investment trusts have promised to only invest in ethical companies. So, in these cases, the commercial objective is tempered by one of ethical investing.

Learning activity 18.6

Identify arguments for and against the use of supply chains to pursue non-commercial goals.

Feedback on page 235

Over the last few years there has been strong criticism of UK retailers and their relationships with suppliers in less-developed countries. As a result of media exposure and campaigns by NGOs, retailers and brand manufacturers have been forced to reconsider and restructure their supply chains with respect to both environmental issues and worker welfare. It has become common for retailers and manufacturers to have codes of conduct in place to guarantee minimum environmental and labour standards at sites of export manufacture. Some of the most effective of these codes have been formulated by a multi-stakeholder approach with companies, NGOs, trade unions and national governments agreeing the agenda.

Collective programmes of learning are in place to bring about improved social justice through the workings of the global economy. One of the organisations that has played a large part in this initiative is the Ethical Trade Initiative (ETI), which is the largest and most strategically significant organisation within the UK for promoting ethical ideals. The ETI has the backing of the Department for International Development and has, both philosophically and strategically, sought to introduce the 'triple bottom line' by the introduction of stakeholder capitalism. The triple bottom line implies that companies should be concerned not just with profit but also with goals associated with environmentalism and social needs, in stark contrast to conventional shareholder capitalism. Although the idea of stakeholder capitalism is not new to some parts of the world, notably Japan, it is a

18

relatively new concept within the UK. The idea that interests of a broader group of actors, including company managers, retail buyers, consumers, producers, workers and communities local to export manufacturing sites was, until recently, relatively novel.

However, with the advent of faster and freer communications and the increasing education of the public, can a company afford not to behave ethically? By doing so it would risk its reputation and brand, when it was discovered to have behaved in a way that exploits people or damages the environment. In the long run, what may appear to be non-commercial objectives will have a commercial impact. There will certainly be damage to the bottom line, when reputations are damaged and sales decline because of adverse publicity.

Self-assessment question 18.6

Prepare a brief for your manager arguing in favour of using your organisation's supply chains to deliver ethical and socioeconomic goals.

Feedback on page 235

Revision question

Now try the revision question for this session on page 260.

Summary

This study session has considered what gives rise to power in relationships and specifically in supply chains, and has gone on to consider ethical issues that might arise from the power that customers and suppliers might enjoy. The study session has concluded by considering the suitability of the use of supply chains to achieve socioeconomic goals.

Suggested further reading

Look at case studies from the internet about issues relating to ethical sourcing. (Try searching for articles using, for example, the keywords 'Nike' and 'sweatshop'.)

Feedback on learning activities and self-assessment questions

Feedback on learning activity 18.1

You should be using expert power, referent power, reward power, coercive power and positional power for your examples.

Feedback on self-assessment question 18.1

Much of your answer will depend upon the nature of the organisation and its position in the supply network. You will most probably be able to

18

find each of the relationships described above when you consider all of the companies with which you have dealings.

Feedback on learning activity 18.2

You should be able to identify specific cases of all three of the descriptions of power in section 18.2, particularly if you have watched, or taken part in, some of the negotiations in which your company has been involved. A confrontational approach invariably involves some form of coercion, whilst a more collaborative approach will usually be because of mutual dependence on a successful outcome. Obligations arise because people will want to be seen to do the 'right' thing.

Feedback on self-assessment question 18.2

You should be able to find examples of all three of these types of power in your organisation's dealings with other organisations that either supply you or that you supply. Much will depend on the nature of the supply chain and the position that your organisation occupies within it.

Feedback on learning activity 18.3

You could give the examples of: supermarkets in their dealings with smaller suppliers; the relationship between brand manufacturers such as Nike and smaller manufacturers based overseas; and, thirdly, car manufacturers' relationships with their component suppliers.

Feedback on self-assessment question 18.3

The evidence you present will follow on from learning activity 18.3. In terms of the policy that is appropriate, you might want to draw on:

- Degree of collaboration.
- Degree of mutual benefit sought.
- Level of openness and sharing of information.
- Degree of joint development of products and processes with an agreement over intellectual property rights.
- Degree of joint problem solving.
- Relevance of long-term contracts once a relationship is formed.
- Viability of open-book accounting.

Your policy statement should underline the principles of equity and fairness that will be necessary for an ethical approach to the relationship.

Feedback on learning activity 18.4

Issues that you might include are:

- totalitarian regimes
- child labour
- safe working conditions

18

- rates of pay and equal opportunities for women
- sustainability of resources
- corruption.

In all cases, it would be possible to pursue an ethical approach to the issue by negotiating some form of redress to the situation.

The order in which you place the issues depends upon your point of view. For instance, when South Africa had a government that practised apartheid, one school of thought suggested that buying South African fruit supported the regime, while others suggested that it supported the poor who were employed to pick it.

Feedback on self-assessment question 18.4

Looking at the ten principles that Kofi Annan proposed, identify which ones are most important to your organisation. Does it have a policy statement on some, or all, of them? What sanctions are there against employees who break these policies? What sanctions are there against suppliers who do not comply with the policies that your company has in place?

Feedback on learning activity 18.5

There will always be a debate about what constitutes an ethical goal and what constitutes a socioeconomic goal. The two concepts are not mutually exclusive. Much will depend upon the person from whom you get an answer. For instance, when we look at pharmaceutical companies that have developed treatments for AIDS and the reduced prices that they charge in the African continent, are they answering an ethical imperative or a socioeconomic one?

Your list could include any of the principles proposed by Kofi Annan, the order will be a matter of individual conscience.

Feedback on self-assessment question 18.5

From learning activity 18.5 you will have established a number of socioeconomic goals. You will need to consider how proactive your organisation is in the pursuit of these goals. Just as in section 18.4 you looked at the policies in place and the sanctions that might be exercised, so here you might want to consider the proactive steps that the company takes.

An example might help. B&Q, a DIY store in the UK, sourced much of its wooden merchandise from producers in South Africa where there was no certification regarding sourcing from sustainable forests. At B&Q's insistence their local agent played a crucial role in convincing the South African sawmills, who supplied the producers, to achieve certification. These sawmills were powerful companies in their own right and had not sought certification, considering it an unnecessary expense. As a result of B&Q's agent convincing one of the producers, and talking to one of the larger sawmills who wished to maintain an international reputation as forward-looking and 'ahead of the game', the first certificates were issued and, a

18

few years later, all significant players are now part of the scheme. Is your company that proactive about their approach to their socioeconomic goals?

Feedback on learning activity 18.6

The main argument against non-commercial goals or objectives is that the company is there purely and simply to make a profit for the shareholders. Arguments 'for' can be considered under the umbrella of corporate social responsibility and the fact that companies should also be 'good citizens'.

Feedback on self-assessment question 18.6

To a large extent your answer will depend upon the organisation for whom you work and the nature of its business. But you could probably use an argument along the lines of Howard Schultz when interviewed by the *Sunday Times*:

> 'I am not concerned with Starbucks becoming the most profitable company in the world. That's a very shallow goal, to achieve profitability at all costs. That isn't a zero sum game for me or anyone else at Starbucks. It's very important that we do something that hasn't been done before, to build a different kind of company that does achieve the fiscal issues ... but demonstrates its heart and conscience in giving back to its employees, to the communities we serve, to the coffee growing regions, and then to reward our shareholders.'

Howard Schultz may not have set out to build on the most profitable companies in the world but he has certainly built the most profitable chain of coffee shops in the world.

18

Towards a globalised strategic supply chain model?

'A rising tide lifts all boats.'
Chinese proverb

Introduction

In this study session we shall consider the arguments for and against the concept of a global supply chain and look at the different approaches for the management of such a supply chain.

Session learning objectives

After completing this session you should be able to:

19.1 Explain the concept of 'best practice'.
19.2 Assess claims for the existence of a globalised strategic supply chain model.
19.3 Assess arguments against the existence of a globalised strategic supply chain model.
19.4 Analyse an organisation's strategic supply chains against the contingent and network sourcing models.
19.5 Analyse the appropriateness of adversarial and cooperative strategies in different circumstances.

Unit content coverage

This study session covers the following topics from the official CIPS unit content document:

Statements of practice

- Assess the role of strategic supply chain management in achieving competitive advantage.
- Distinguish and assess various models of supply chain structures and relationships.

Learning objectives

6.1 Assess the validity of the development of a 'best practice' strategic supply chain model.
  - Arguments for and against the existence of a 'best practice' strategic supply chain model
  - Contingent approach to strategic supply chain management (Cox and Lamming 1997)
  - Network sourcing as a 'best practice' strategic supply chain model (Rich and Hines 1997)
6.2 Compare the characteristics of adversarial and co-operative strategies and analyse their appropriateness in different circumstances.

19

- Characteristics of adversarial and co-operative strategies
- Partnership
- Appropriateness of adversarial and co-operative strategies in different circumstances

Resources

Access to the following books is highly recommended for use throughout this session:

- Lysons and Farrington (2006), chapters 7 and 14
- Dam Jespersen and Skjott-Larsen (2005), chapter 8
- Christopher (2005), chapter 7
- Gattorna (1998), chapters 15 and 20.

Timing

You should set aside about 5 hours to read and complete this session, including learning activities, self-assessment questions, the suggested further reading (if any) and the revision question.

19.1 'Best practice'

The concept of 'best practice' originated in the private sector as a tool to 'benchmark' performance against competitors and thereby engender improvement. Best practices are model practices that are goal-oriented and replicable. They contribute directly towards the achievement of a given goal, using appropriate resources in a cost-effective manner. Network sourcing, covered in section 19.2, is often seen as a 'best practice model of sourcing behaviour'.

19.2 Network sourcing

Rich and Hines (1997), and a number of other authors, argue that *all firms should take a structured approach to purchasing and supply*. Broadly similar to the lean enterprise approach, much of the work is based on research into the Japanese automobile industry. These authors suggest that success for the organisation will be achieved by implementing lean enterprise thinking.

The concept of *network sourcing* is typical of automotive, electronics and other mass production industries within Japan. In these systems, the focal company assembles components supplied by their first tier of suppliers, who manufacture components and sub-assemblies, which are supplied by a second tier (or even a third or more) of manufacturing specialists. The focal company will have managerial relationships with all tiers. This leads to a much narrower structure than typical Western manufacturers who may have as many as 2,500 direct suppliers in contrast to the usual more 300 of a Japanese firm.

After developing a clear understanding of the dynamics of the markets and the competitive pressures that the firm faces, *working practices must be aligned* to deal with them. Purchasing staff will be involved in internal processes such as order fulfilment and quality control and will need to integrate these with their external relationships, by integrating their suppliers in their 'open systems'. This means there will be an 'open systems', learning approach to the relationships with suppliers. Rich and Hines summarise this as 'The three pillars of strategic alignment':

- policy deployment
- cross-functional management
- supplier integration.

The authors argue that this will lead to a truly global market with a network of supply from the various clusters of expertise, as described in study session 15.

Learning activity 19.1

Identify organisations where you feel a network sourcing approach to supply is in operation.

Feedback on page 245

Policy deployment is a form of strategic management that argues for the integration of day-to-day activities into the overall goals of the organisation, by means of support systems and *continuous measurement specific to policy goals.*

Cross-functional management argues for the integration of different product or functional areas on a company-wide scale to remove the silo mentality and internal competition that arise from conflicting objectives. Senior management are involved in the process of improving the daily operations of the business rather than handing down strategic imperatives to be implemented by those further down the hierarchy.

Supplier integration and development means that the first two pillars will be applied beyond the external boundary of the firm as well as within the firm.

The benefits claimed for this approach are:

- There is *faster adaptation* to changing market conditions.
- *Lead times are reduced.*
- *Transaction costs are lower* due to closeness of suppliers.
- *Longer-term stability* for all players leads to more rational capital investment.
- Shared knowledge *reduces working capital* by increasing stock turn, usually assisted by EDI.
- Joint learning *reduces product development costs* and final product costs.

19

239

The emphasis on the *learning approach* means that there is a need to take a more consensual approach to agreements between suppliers and internal customers. Relationships need to be longer term and the focal firm needs to invest in the development of their suppliers' competencies and their integration into the systems of the firm. Many of the principles of *knowledge management* will be appropriate, with the development of associations, knowledge transfer by group socialisation, and collective focus on the strategic imperatives of the focal firm.

Under these assumptions, the strategic role of purchasing staff will rise by virtue of their ability *to coordinate and develop players across all organisational boundaries*, both internal and external to the firm.

Self-assessment question 19.1

Write a proposal explaining how an organisation with which you are familiar, would benefit from a 'globalised' approach to supply chain management.

Feedback on page 246

19.3 To partner or not?

Partnerships can exist in a number of forms but are usually *cooperative non-equity-holding arrangements*. These can range from an agreement on a shared 'destiny', through a minority shareholding to a strategic alliance. They will fall short of a formal joint venture. Their increasingly popularity has brought about the idea of *win-win relationships* and underpins many of the decisions to outsource particular aspects of an organisation's functions which they consider to be non-core activities. In these terms, the firm that decides to outsource their logistics, for instance, is *focusing on their core competences* and concentrating on the things that they believe they are good at. The development of these close relationships is a feature of the lean supply approach favoured by companies such as Toyota and Benetton. For example, in North America, Toyota uses only one core firm to transport its finished vehicles, whereas General Motors uses seven.

Learning activity 19.2

Using your own organisation, or one that you know well, identify where the boundaries are between the firm and suppliers for all functional areas.

Feedback on page 246

19

From what we have said here, and in previous study sessions, you can see that the argument presented by Cox and Lamming (1997) is that 'one size *doesn't* fit all'. There continues to be a conflict between the need for effective performance in terms of cost reduction and the 'best' result for the firm, and the idea that there can be cooperation and a 'win-win' outcome.

Within large firms, at least, there is likely to be a range of approaches to supply chain management. Core areas will enjoy a greater degree of *vertical integration*, *market-focused sourcing* will be used for fairly standardised products, whilst specialist inputs are more likely to be bought in under *close partnership arrangements*.

Some of those people who currently work in purchasing and supply have an opportunity to play a part in the strategic direction of the firm. However, to take up this part they will need to develop the flexibility to apply different approaches to different situations and the ability to recognise which approach is appropriate in different circumstances. Those circumstances are dependent upon industry structures, national cultures, the rate of change in an industry and government policies, all of which we have discussed in previous study sessions.

Proponents of the *contingent approach* argue that much of the research for the opposing view, which we shall discuss in section 19.3, is based on the success of Toyota, and that the automotive supply chain has specific characteristics. The flow of components is fairly standardised, regular and frequent, which cannot be said of, for instance, service supply chains. Additionally, when comparing Japanese suppliers to those based in Western countries, it is worth noting that the Japanese supplier is more likely to be more deferential whilst those in the West are likely to be more opportunistic.

This means that all business relationships should be managed in an *appropriate* way and there is no single approach that is 'ideal' for the relationships that the company has to manage. At one extreme the buyer will merely *select a supplier* after some form of beauty parade (invitation to bid or whatever) and the relationship will be managed at arm's length. The process will be more involved if it is necessary to *supply chain source* from a number of tiers in the supply chain. Although the relationships are unlikely to develop much further than that of 'selecting a supplier', the process will be more time-consuming since there will be more searches, evaluations and negotiations involved as the process will be repeated for each tier. In both these cases, the buyer will rely on market forces to encourage suppliers to be innovative and cost-efficient.

However, in some cases it is necessary for the buyer to take a more proactive role in the relationship and bring about a closer more collaborative approach. Where this involves the procurement of first-tier products or services, it is described as *supplier development* and there will be joint investment in both the product or service and the logistics. Hopefully, the degree of innovation that arises will surpass the level that could be expected from a reliance on market forces. If the same degree of proactiveness is applied across the supply chain, then this is described as *supply chain management* whereby the buyer will undertake proactive supplier development across a large proportion of the supply chain. Cox and Lamming argue that, although this approach potentially offers significant

19

benefits to both buyers and suppliers, in reality it is very difficult to achieve for the reason explained above.

Self-assessment question 19.2

Write a proposal explaining how an organisation with which you are familiar would benefit from a contingent approach to globalised supply.

Feedback on page 246

19.4 So, who is right?

The two schools of thought that we have discussed, *network sourcing* and the *contingent approach*, agree that there should be a focus on effective management of the total supply chain, and that there should be careful selection of suppliers so that they can assist in cost reduction, quality improvement and the transfer of innovation. They also agree that there should be active development of supplier capabilities and that there will be joint evaluation of any relationship that that is built up between them. Similarly, proponents agree that the purchasing function should be represented at board level and that there should be cross-functional operational requirements.

Whether either approach will lead to a global supply chain is still open to debate, since there are relatively few companies who are able to take a truly global approach to business. Globalised industries are typified by centralised, scale-intensive manufacturing and R&D, leveraged through worldwide exports of standardised products.

Learning activity 19.3

For your company, or one with which you are familiar, assess its relationships with approximately three suppliers against the contingent and network sourcing models.

Feedback on page 246

Although both schools of thought argue that their approach could lead to purchasing achieving strategic significance to the organisation, it is worth considering this in more detail. You will remember that a sustainable competitive advantage is only possible if the firm is implementing a value-adding strategy that cannot be duplicated, over time, by other firms. This means that *firms cannot expect to 'purchase' a sustainable competitive advantage in the marketplace.*

A sustainable competitive advantage can only be obtained by doing something which is valued by the customer and which others cannot emulate. It is impossible for this to be merely a purchased asset – others could purchase the same assets.

The core competence approach highlights the decision to 'make or buy' as a strategic decision – once core competences have been identified all other combinations of activities and assets should be bought in. This is because, by definition, someone else can do it better. But once that decision has been made, the buying in becomes an operational consideration. So, to develop a strategic role, purchasing must develop hard-to-imitate resources that contribute to the firm's competitive advantage. There are three ways that they might do this:

1   *Identify and develop unknown suppliers.* This will only work for as long as the buyer can keep the existence of the supplier secret.
2   *Enclose known suppliers.* This is possible if a jointly developed product or process can become the subject of a confidentiality agreement. These are often quite difficult, and expensive, to negotiate and enforce. Varying degrees of backward integration will also enclose suppliers – short of actually acquiring the supplier.
3   *Buy in a hard-to-imitate manner.* Some buyers may be able to do this through market power in one form or another, but it is always in the supplier's interest to seek out sales with other customers. The buyer's competitors will always constitute the most attractive target market, since their requirements are similar and the supplier is already some way down the learning curve. The competitors, seeing the company has gained an advantage, will pressure the suppliers for business. If buyers are able to do this, they will have persuaded suppliers to do something that is not in their best interests. This means that the supplier will have been rewarded for this in some way, unless the buyer is very powerful and able to impose the terms of the deal.

So, where does this leave us in our discussion about the contingent or network sourcing approach? We can see that, if purchasing is to be of strategic significance, as both schools of thought suggest it can, realistically it must develop strong market power and pick and choose the situations where it wishes to exercise that power, or it must buy in a hard-to-imitate manner which means managing the whole supply chain.

Self-assessment question 19.3

For an organisation of your choice, prepare a discussion justifying either a contingent or network sourcing approach to its suppliers.

Feedback on page 247

19.5 Adversarial and cooperative strategies

The traditional approach in most Western organisations, when purchasing decisions are made, tends to be based on quantified and financial considerations. As we have seen from the preceding sections, the network sourcing approach additionally focuses on the 'softer' side of the relationships with suppliers.

We can summarise these contrasting approaches in a table (see table 19.1). As you can see there is quite a difference between the two approaches.

Table 19.1 Traditional and partnership approaches to purchasing

Traditional approaches to purchasing	Partnership approach to purchasing
Emphasis on price.	More than one criterion.
Short-term contracts.	Longer-term contracts.
Periodic evaluation of bids.	Continuous evaluation.
Many, competing suppliers.	Few, specially selected suppliers.
Most powerful partner reaps benefits of improvements.	Sharing of benefits of improvements.
Improvements sought periodically.	Improvements sought continuously.
Supplier required to deal with problems.	Joint problem solution.
Information is proprietary.	Information is shared.

Learning activity 19.4

Thinking about an organisation with which you are familiar, identify whether its approach to purchasing is mainly adversarial or cooperative.

Feedback on page 247

It is worth considering that these are two extreme descriptions of the relationships that companies may have with their suppliers. If we accept the contingent approach to supply chain management, we must accept that a firm will have different relationships with different suppliers depending on the importance of the good or service being procured. Where the assets being acquired are of high specificity and contribute to the core competences of the firm, then they will almost certainly be dealt with in-house, since they are part of the source of the firm's competitive advantage. Remember that, as discussed in study session 10, it is the combination of assets and the way a firm uses them (routines) that leads to competitive advantage.

However, where the assets are of medium specificity there is likely to be a far more cooperative approach to sourcing, with strategic alliances, network sourcing or, at the very least, single sourcing from preferred suppliers.

For those assets of low specificity and therefore low importance, it is likely that the firm will adopt a far more adversarial approach to its suppliers seeking to leverage any market advantage that it can and obtain the best possible deal available.

This means that the relationships, and the drivers, at the extremes of this continuum can be described as shown in table 19.2:

Table 19.2 Adversarial and cooperative approaches

	Adversarial	Cooperative
Attitude to change	Reactive	Proactive
Basis of transaction	Little or no trust	Trust
Flow of information	One way	Two way
Business relationship	Contractual obligations	Mutual obligation
Time horizon	Short-term focus	Long-term focus
Negotiating stance	'Take advantage'	Honour-based mutual benefit
Objective	Survival	Co-evolution

This will present different challenges for the people involved in the purchasing process and, as we said earlier, their strategic importance will depend upon their ability to manage different relationships with different suppliers.

Self-assessment question 19.4

Select one of your employer's suppliers and prepare a short business case, advocating a more cooperative (or a more adversarial) approach to that supplier. Your answer should justify your choice of supplier.

Feedback on page 247

Revision question

Now try the revision question for this session on page 260.

Summary

In this study session, we have compared the contingent and network sourcing approaches to supply chain management. We have looked at the adversarial and cooperative stances and shown that, rather than being two alternatives, they represent opposite ends of a continuum.

Suggested further reading

Look back at the case studies you collected for study session 13 and see if you can identify examples of the different approaches discussed in this study session.

Feedback on learning activities and self-assessment questions

Feedback on learning activity 19.1

Rich and Hines argue that the success of network sourcing is due to the cooperative approach to the relationship with suppliers and that the most effective way to proceed is via the Japanese model of policy deployment, active supplier integration and cross-functional management. The joint

19

learning approach to supplier relationships means that all participants will gain, as the supply chain in which they operate enjoys competitive advantages over alternative supply chains. It could be argued that this essentially cooperative approach might to lead to more and more 'layers' being integrated into a particular focal company's supply chain management system.

You may have identified an organisation like Microsoft, which sources its R&D from a large number of countries. What do you feel they gain from doing that? Look at those relationships again and decide whether they are, in reality, treating all of their supply chain in exactly the same way.

Feedback on self-assessment question 19.1

Your answer will depend on whether you believe the arguments or not. Do you agree, in the case of the organisation that you have chosen to discuss, that one size does fit all? Is it possible to treat the whole of the supply chain as one entity? Or will there need to be different approaches used for different parts of it?

Feedback on learning activity 19.2

Cox and Lamming (1997) state that organisations and their structure are in a time of radical change and it may no longer be possible to think of the clear boundaries between departments and between the firm and its environment. Whereas purchasing decisions and even outsourcing decisions have traditionally been taken at an operational level, they have now become of strategic importance to successful firms, due to the pressures of technology and increased competition. It is necessary to take a view of the whole supply chain and the relationships between the different players. They argue that 'chain' is most probably the wrong metaphor since many successful companies are actually in a network of suppliers rather than a linear chain, with few alternatives at each stage. The management of those relationships becomes crucial and successful firms will be skilled at managing external as well as internal functions. With that in mind, successful firms will need to take a flexible and contingent approach to their own management, deciding case by case where the effective boundary of the organisation lies.

Feedback on self-assessment question 19.2

The advantages offered by Cox and Lamming revolve around the idea that the firm is trying to accrue advantage to itself, rather than to share it with those with whom it deals. You may well have chosen a company like Wal-Mart as an example of a firm taking a contingent approach to supply, since it has different relationships with different suppliers – depending on the power relationship. Wal-Mart is certainly a firm with a global reach.

Feedback on learning activity 19.3

You should be looking to see how cooperative those relationships are, how many suppliers your organisation uses and how closely they work together.

19

When there are meetings between your company and its suppliers, is there an attempt to arrive at a win-win solution, or are your purchasing managers performance rated on how well they do in the negotiations? How involved is your organisation with the suppliers of your suppliers? Are there supplier associations in operation? Are your suppliers involved in joint development of components that you buy in?

Feedback on self-assessment question 19.3

You have seen the arguments presented for both approaches; the real test in this question is which organisation you chose. If you chose an organisation where there were a variety of different types of supplier with varying degrees of power, and you revised study session 18 thoroughly, you most probably talked about the contingent approach. However, you might have chosen an organisation with a very structured supply system, where it was possible for the focal firm to use layers of suppliers to prepare sub-assemblies for them and where it was culturally acceptable to have cooperative relationships between suppliers and buyers. In this case, you most probably advocated network supply.

Feedback on learning activity 19.4

From table 19.1 you can see that there will be evidence of a far more collaborative approach if a network or partnership approach is taken. This means that all the characteristics of a win-win series of negotiations will be necessary. As we saw in section 19.2 there will need to be greater openness, equitable treatment and an approach to open learning if a cooperative approach is to succeed.

Feedback on self-assessment question 19.4

You should be able to identify a suitable supplier in terms of the strategic importance of the asset(s) which they are supplying your firm. To what extent do those assets contribute to the core competence of your organisation? How dependent are you upon their expertise? Don't forget if the assets are of critical importance you will be producing them in-house.

19

Competence-based and lean supply approaches to the strategic supply chain

Introduction

In this session we look again at the concept of the lean supply chain, and ask whether it really is the panacea to supply problems and a true source of sustainable competitive advantage.

'Communication is everyone's panacea for everything.'
Tom Peters

Session learning objectives

After completing this session you should be able to:

20.1 Explain the 'core competence' approach for determining supply chain structures and relationships.
20.2 Explain the resource-based view in relation to replicable and non-replicable competences.
20.3 Assess the appropriateness of lean supply for an organisation.

Unit content coverage

This study session covers the following topics from the official CIPS unit content document:

Statement of practice

• Distinguish and assess various models of supply chain structures and relationships.

Learning objectives

6.3 Understand and apply competence-based approaches for determining supply chain structures and relationships.
   • Hamel and Prahalad's core competence model
   • Core, complementary and residual competences
   • The resource-based view, especially in relation to replicable and non-replicable competences
6.4 Assess the lean supply model as a prescription for supply relationships.
   • Partnership and lean supply
   • Trust in buyer–supplier relationships
   • Appropriateness of lean supply and partnership for different organisations

Resources

Access to the following books is highly recommended for use throughout this session:

• Lysons and Farrington (2006), chapters 3 and 4
• Johnson, Scholes and Whittington (2007), chapter 3.

20

Timing

You should set aside about 4 hours to read and complete this session, including learning activities, self-assessment questions, the suggested further reading (if any) and the revision question.

20.1 Core competences and the supply chain 'strategy'

A *competence* is an activity or process through which an organisation deploys or utilises its resources. It is, as mentioned earlier, something the organisation *does*, rather than something it *has*.

Strategic competences can be classified as follows:

- *Threshold competence* is the level of competence necessary for an organisation to compete and survive in a given industry and market.
- A *core competence* is something the organisation does that underpins a source of competitive advantage.

A key tool for identifying core competences is Porter's 'value chain'. This was covered in study session 17.

Learning activity 20.1

Reread study sessions 3, 6 and 10, where they relate to core competences and the resource-based view of strategy. How does the core competence approach to strategy determine the structure of supply chains?

Feedback on page 254

Prahalad and Hamel's original work (1990) on core competences led to a flurry of articles on what was termed 'strategic sourcing' or 'strategic outsourcing'. Almost all of these seemed to conclude that the role of purchasing was anything but strategic, as the only items that would be bought in would be, by definition, non-core. According to Ramsay (2001) 'the only strategic part of this description of "strategic outsourcing" is the process of deciding which activities are core'.

Self-assessment question 20.1

Write a briefing paper for your manager outlining the implications of the core competence approach for one of your organisation's supply chains.

Feedback on page 254

20.2 Replicable and non-replicable competences

In section 20.1 we concluded that each organisation in a supply chain should 'stick to the knitting' and concentrate on utilising their core competences. This leads to a model of the supply chain where every input can be freely purchased by any of the organisation's rivals. In this situation, it is inconceivable that an organisation could gain any kind of sustainable competitive advantage from the supply chain. It may be possible to gain a short-term advantage, but rivals will soon source the same parts or components from the same suppliers, and erode the competitive advantage.

Learning activity 20.2

Can you see any ways in which an organisation might gain a sustainable competitive advantage from its supply chain?

Feedback on page 254

According to Ramsay (2001), a sustainable competitive advantage might be gained from an organisation's supply chain in the following circumstances:

- If the organisation can identify and develop *unknown suppliers* that its rivals cannot track down and use.
- If the organisation can *enclose* a supplier, to cut it off from the wider market. This may be done by means of a joint venture, or sole supply agreement.
- If the organisation can *purchase in a hard-to-imitate manner*. This might be relevant, for example, to a very powerful customer with more bargaining power, or to a purchasing manager with a 'special relationship' with a supplier.

Despite these arguments, Ramsay concludes: 'the buyer's competitors are likely to make it as difficult as possible for the purchasing function to protect any competitive advantage it has found or developed in a factor market.'

In a detailed criticism of Ramsay's article, Mol (2002) suggests some other situations in which a competitive advantage might be obtained from an organisation's supply chain:

- Two organisations that combine resources in a unique way may gain a mutual competitive advantage that is unavailable to other combinations of firms. An example of this is the exchange of (particularly tacit) knowledge.
- All factor markets are imperfect, so the relationship and supply to one customer will never be exactly the same as to another. Even firms sharing the (apparently) same source of supply may experience different relationships.
- Social structures are more important in business-to-business markets than in business-to-consumer, so a supply can be differentiated by virtue of 'soft' aspects of the exchange. Firms interact through a series of unique inter-organisational relations.

20

251

To conclude, Mol cites Barney's (1991) view that sustainable competitive advantage can only arise if all the following conditions are met:

- Resources are valuable.
- Resources are rare.
- Resources are imperfectly imitable (because they are history-dependent, causally ambiguous or socially complex).
- Resources are not substitutable.

Mol claims that 'in purchasing management, many examples arise of these conditions', and cites the specific examples of: a reputable or knowledgeable purchasing manager that suppliers are more willing to deal with and give good service to, or an exclusive deal with a best-in-class supplier.

Self-assessment question 20.2

Identify a unique and critical supply input or source of supply in any of your organisation's supply chains, and assess the risk of that supply/source being 'stolen' by a rival.

Feedback on page 254

20.3 Lean supply chains – conclusions

In table 17.1 we looked at Lamming's (1993) prescription for lean supply as an 'ideal state' – that is, something to be aimed for. Cox (1996) disagrees, and says:

> 'Lean supply is not an end state; it is what proactive firms should do at all times. In attempting to achieve lean supply, sensible firms will use whichever external relationships – from leverage to partnerships and networks – provide them with the greatest competitive and profit-making advantage.'

Bath and Warwick Universities concluded, in a study for CIPD, that there are three phases of lean development, as follows:

1 *Leanness as transition*: where efforts are made by the organisation to become lean.
2 *Leanness as an outcome*: where flexibility is achieved as a result of de-layering, downsizing and outsourcing.
3 *Leanness as a process*: where the organisation focuses on those aspects that allow it to respond to environmental change.

Learning activity 20.3

Do you think that leanness is the right approach to take for all supply relationships?

Feedback on page 254

In study session 19 we discussed whether the lean approach could form the basis of a universal or globalised supply chain strategy, and concluded that a contingency approach was more appropriate. We need to tailor, in each situation, a unique approach that draws upon all our experience, with the aim of seeking an optimal solution.

In section 11.5 we discussed the limitations of lean supply in the context of developing agility, and looked at Christopher's four 'generic supply chain strategies' (see table 20.1):

Table 20.1 Generic supply chain strategies

Strategy	Supply characteristic	Demand characteristic
Lean	Long lead times	Predictable demand
Hybrid	Long lead times	Unpredictable demand
Kanban	Short lead times	Predictable demand
Agile	Short lead times	Unpredictable demand

These are examples of how a contingency approach might be developed, but it is likely that real situations are too complex to be adequately catered for by only two variables.

If we are to attempt to use a lean strategy to gain a sustainable competitive advantage, we must firstly be sure that the resources and competences underpinning the lean supply chain are replicable or unique (see section 20.2). If it is possible to copy lean supply techniques, and to acquire or develop the resources on which they are based, then any competitive advantage must be at best short term. More likely is that the lean approach will provide the supply chain with some improvement in operational effectiveness, which will be gradually eroded as other supply chains learn from it.

Self-assessment question 20.3

Discuss the circumstances in which you might recommend supply chain strategies of leanness or agility.

Feedback on page 255

Revision question

Now try the revision question for this session on page 260.

Summary

In this session we looked at the concept of the lean supply chain, and asked whether it really is the panacea to supply problems and a true source of sustainable competitive advantage.

20

Feedback on learning activities and self-assessment questions

Feedback on learning activity 20.1

You should consider the 'boundary of the firm' arguments that we discussed in section 10.3. If we accept the core competence principles, each organisation in a supply chain should concentrate on activities related to its own core competences, and outsource every other activity to the supply chain actor best suited to perform it.

Feedback on self-assessment question 20.1

Take the approach that each actor should 'stick to the knitting', and see whether the resulting supply chain looks anything like reality. Quinn and Hilmer (1995) state four advantages of what they term 'strategic outsourcing':

1   Managers can concentrate their efforts on what the enterprise does best, and therefore get the best returns on internal resources.
2   Well-developed core competences provide barriers to entry that can be used to protect competitive advantage.
3   Firms can fully leverage the investments, innovations and capabilities of their suppliers, which would be prohibitively expensive or even impossible to duplicate in-house.
4   Such collaborative strategy decreases risk, shortens life cycles, and creates better responsiveness to changing customer needs.

In order to gain these benefits, Quinn and Hilmer suggest, organisations need to resolve three key issues:

1   What exactly are their core competences?
2   Having identified the core competences, does that mean everything else should be outsourced?
3   How can managers identify and manage the risks of those activities that it is desirable to outsource?

Feedback on learning activity 20.2

There are opportunities, as we shall see in the continuation of section 20.2.

Feedback on self-assessment question 20.2

If you can't find a 'unique and critical' material or component, look at the 'soft' relationship aspects of the supply. Those are, of course, much more difficult for a rival to 'steal'.

Feedback on learning activity 20.3

In section 17.3 we identified a series of criticisms of the lean approach:

• Assuming that the lean approach does give more customers more choice, then this will probably increase the overall level of consumption.

This may not be a socially desirable outcome, given the impact on the environment and the possible depletion of scarce resources.

- The ability of lean chains to satisfy customer whims even more quickly may result in overproduction of 'throwaway' goods. This will again have serious environmental consequences.
- Microeconomics suggest that perfect competition leads to the optimal level of efficiency in the market. As the lean supply chain consists of a series of partnerships and 'preferred supplier' relationships, it must represent a sub-optimal solution. With reduced competition comes complacency. The entry barriers created by cooperation will reduce competition and increase the levels of margin earned. This may be 'good' for the organisations concerned, but it is 'bad' for the consumer.
- Concentrating on leanness in the supply chain may lead to 'shakeout' in the industries affected, resulting in an overall reduction in manufacturing capacity and significant job losses. While this may benefit the supply chain, it has significant economic and social consequences.
- Over-leanness may lead to a situation where there is insufficient 'slack' in the system to take account of fluctuations in demand. This issue is related to that discussed in study session 12, as one of the arguments for the development of agile chains.
- The cost burden involved in becoming lean may be too high for many smaller suppliers, and they may be driven away from the supply chain despite, perhaps, being the optimal suppliers.
- Large, powerful customers can dominate lean supply chains. Although the ideal situation is that all the actors in a supply chain share the benefits of leanness, in reality the greater share of cost savings will be taken by the most powerful organisation in the chain.
- Most of the leanness tools concentrate on reducing cost rather than improving quality. Any resulting savings may be kept as increased margins, rather than being passed on to the customer.
- Too much concentration on cost reduction may, in fact, worsen quality or at least increase the risk of quality failure.

Feedback on self-assessment question 20.3

You should base your arguments on Christopher's generic strategies, shown in tabular form in section 11.5.

Revision questions

Revision question for study session 1

Explain why an organisation, despite having a clear strategic plan, might eventually adopt a course of action completely different from that envisaged in the plan.

Feedback on page 261

Revision question for study session 2

Your managing director, a very 'hands-on' man who is very close to day-to-day activities, has given you an academic research paper that appears to justify its title 'Long-term strategic planning is dead'. He uses bureaucratic, long-term strategic planning processes that he manages himself, but see few benefits. Your company is losing market share and responds slowly to an increasingly dynamic hostile environment.

He requires you to write a short memo advising him on the usefulness of long-term strategic planning processes and recommend improvements to the organisation's approach to strategic management.

Feedback on page 261

Revision question for study session 3

Binary Ltd is a manufacturer of PC hardware. Explain to Binary how SWOT analysis can be used to summarise the results of any strategic analysis carried out during the planning process.

Feedback on page 261

Revision question for study session 4

Write a memo to your organisation's director of procurement explaining the following:

- The concept of national and regional cultures.
- How national and regional cultures might affect customer/supplier negotiations.

Feedback on page 262

Revision question for study session 5

Your organisation has decided that one of its key suppliers has developed too much bargaining power. The supplier makes, to your organisation's design, a specialised component part. There are believed to be three possible strategies to address this problem:

1   Open a new SBU to produce the component previously bought in from the supplier.
2   Acquire the supplier organisation.
3   Find a new supplier with less bargaining power.

Evaluate these strategic alternatives.

Feedback on page 262

Revision question for study session 6

X plc is a manufacturer of office furniture. It currently produces and sells its products within a single European country. X plc has decided to expand its sales to the rest of Europe.

Identify the resources that might be required to support this strategy, and explain why each might be useful.

Feedback on page 262

Revision question for study session 7

Doctors with Wings is a registered charity that raises funds to send volunteer doctors and nurses to medical emergencies around the world. Those emergencies can arise for any reason, ranging from famine to war or major outbreaks of disease. Funding primarily comes from government agencies and corporate donations, although the charity seeks donations from the public, as well as medicines and other supplies from manufacturers. The majority of volunteers are recruited, often with the support of teaching hospitals, immediately after qualification. These new doctors are persuaded to donate their time to charity during presentations made by volunteer doctors who have just returned from a medical emergency.

Evaluate the principal stakeholders in the organisation and analyse the nature of the influence and importance that they hold in their relationship with the charity.

Feedback on page 262

Revision question for study session 8

Genus Inc. has just changed its procurement policy. In future, all 'low-value items' will be bought through an electronic trading room on the organisation's website. Genus will post a specification in the trading room for any items it wishes to buy, and suppliers will be invited to tender. The software will allow procurement staff to see all the tenders submitted, without knowing to which supplier they belong. Staff will decide solely on the basis of price and availability.

Recommend to Genus what changes should be made to support the implementation of this new strategy.

Feedback on page 263

Revision question for study session 9

Explain how attitudes to change might be classified, and how resistance to change might be overcome.

Feedback on page 263

Revision question for study session 10

Identify situations where 'adversarial procurement' might be an appropriate supply chain management strategy.

Feedback on page 263

Revision question for study session 11

Contrast the features of the 'lean' and 'agile' approaches to supply chain management.

Feedback on page 264

Revision question for study session 12

Discuss why there has been an increase in cross-functional and inter-organisational working in supply chain management.

Feedback on page 264

Revision question for study session 13

Discuss alternative approaches to supply chain management, illustrating your discussion by reference to a range of different organisations.

Feedback on page 264

Revision question for study session 14

Compare and contrast the nature of supply chains in the private and public sectors.

Feedback on page 264

Revision question for study session 15

Discuss the roles of government and technology in the globalisation of supply chains.

Feedback on page 264

Revision question for study session 16

Identify and discuss the issues to be considered when deciding whether to source a key component locally, or from another country.

Feedback on page 265

Revision question for study session 17

Contrast Porter's 'value network' concept with the concept of a 'supply network'.

Feedback on page 265

Revision question for study session 18

Discuss the various objectives that organisations might seek to achieve through the management of their supply chains.

Feedback on page 265

Revision question for study session 19

Discuss the circumstances in which you believe an adversarial approach to purchasing might be more appropriate than a partnership approach. Advise a large financial services company, looking to acquire a new headquarters office building, whether an adversarial or partnership approach might me more appropriate.

Feedback on page 265

Revision question for study session 20

Your manager has been to a conference where one of the speakers seemed to suggest that 'all supply chains can learn from the lean approach developed by Toyota'. Write a report to your manager that discusses the validity of this statement.

Feedback on page 266

Feedback on revision questions

Feedback on revision question for study session 1

Organisations are not machines. Various factors contribute to the 'realised' strategy not being the same as that 'intended'. You might mention: strategic drift, changes in the environment, management incompetence or 'emergent' strategy.

Feedback on revision question for study session 2

Start by providing a basis for your discussion: describe the rational intended model and its advantages and disadvantages, noting that in application process, context and content need to be used in a balanced way; describe the systems behaviour of strategic management and describe the nature and consequences of dynamic, complex and hostile environments. You can now argue for modifications to existing process for use in the described environments.

The nature and usefulness of Quinn's 'logical incrementalism' model for the environment can be presented and briefly compared with the rational intended model. You have bases for process improvements.

An appropriate strategic leadership style is needed to complement appropriate processes. Analysis of the managing director's style may show that he has insufficient time for strategic thinking, given his preoccupation with the strategy process at the expense of strategy content and day-to-day activities. You might recommend involvement of a wider community for strategy development, perhaps with greater capacity for information gathering and analysis.

Don't forget to use a memo format. If the examiner asks for one, there will be marks available as a reward.

Feedback on revision question for study session 3

Having a clear structure for an answer really helps. Try something like this:

- Briefly explain the rational planning model, mentioning particularly the roles of internal and external analysis, and highlighting the stage at which SWOT is used.
- Explain why SWOT is necessary (lots of data collected).
- Illustrate S, W, O and T, each with an example relevant to Binary.

- Briefly explain how SWOT could then be used to identify strategies.

Feedback on revision question for study session 4

Base your answer on the factors given in study session 4:

1 attitudes to work
2 attitudes to authority
3 attitudes to equality
4 working hours and attendance levels
5 degree of bureaucracy
6 the nature of decision making.

For each point, give an example that demonstrates its relevance to customer/supplier relations. Point 6, for example: in one country, sales and purchasing staff might agree the price of a supply between themselves, following a fairly friendly negotiation, whereas in another they might have to refer the decision back to their management teams 'away from the negotiating table'.

Don't forget the memo format.

Feedback on revision question for study session 5

In any exam question that uses the verb 'evaluate', a structure for the answer will really improve your marks. The following steps seem reasonable:

(a) For each option:
  - Briefly explain it.
  - Discuss the advantages of it.
  - Discuss the disadvantages of it.
  - Conclude whether, on balance, you think it's a good idea.
(b) Finally, conclude by saying which option you feel would be the most reasonable.

Feedback on revision question for study session 6

Pretty much all the resources of the organisation will be affected by such a major shift in strategy. Plan your answer first, by simply listing all the organisation's resources, and then brainstorming how each might be affected. Annotate your list with your ideas, then cross out anything on your list that has no annotations. Write up the remaining points as your answer.

Feedback on revision question for study session 7

Examiners have a nasty habit of 'hinting' at a theoretical model, without specifically naming it. This is a question on Mendelow's stakeholder mapping tool. There's no need to 'invent' stakeholders, just use the ones mentioned in the scenario. The steps in your answer should be:

1 Identify the stakeholder (say who/what they are).
2 Discuss how much power they might have (high or low).

3 Discuss how much interest they might take (high or low).
4 Conclude which quadrant of the matrix you would thus place them in.

The stakeholders and their places in the 'map' should be as follows:

- Key players: government agencies, large corporate donors, volunteer doctors.
- Keep informed: small corporate donors, individual donors.
- Keep satisfied: medicine manufacturers.

Feedback on revision question for study session 8

Remember that this question is about 'aligning' organisational activities with strategy. If you are looking for an appropriate structure, or are short of ideas, think about the various issues considered in this session. Discuss how the organisation might support their strategy by changing:

- The mission and objectives: new performance measures; cost reductions in purchasing, system performance, and so on.
- The communication structure: policies and guidelines to purchasing staff, for example.
- The reward systems: it might be decided to give staff a bonus, based on the savings made by the new system, to maintain motivation levels.
- The '7-S' factors: for example, 'shared values' to get buy-in to the new system; 'skills' to train the staff to use the system; and 'staff' perhaps by reducing staff numbers. These are all to fit in with the new 'strategy' and 'systems'.

Feedback on revision question for study session 9

There are two ways to answer this question. The first, and more difficult, is to brainstorm loads of ideas, structure them into a coherent plan, and then write out the answer. The second, and easier, is to learn the theoretical models, and then build and answer round the two appropriate frameworks:

- Inactivists, reactivists, proactivists and interactivists.
- Education, collaboration, intervention, direction, coercion.

Feedback on revision question for study session 10

What a strange question! Of course, it's easy to assume that all customer–supplier relationships should be partnerships, but that's by no means the case. It's a little bit like the management styles debate. We all think that participative management is the only way, but that's not true either. Just look at the army, or a game of football!

To answer this question, you need to review the content of study session 10 and then brainstorm situations where, for example, price is the only purchase criterion. Think about one-off purchases, where developing a relationship isn't an issue, or buying 'off-the-shelf' commodities, where there are many different suppliers.

Feedback on revision question for study session 11

For answer, see section 21.11, reproduced for convenience as table 21.1 below.

Table 21.1 Lean v agile

Feature	Leanness	Agility
Purpose	Meeting predictable demand as efficiently as possible	Meeting unpredictable demand as quickly as possible
Focus	Improving utilisation	Deploying capacity effectively
Inventory	Minimum inventory	Holding buffer stocks to allow responsiveness
Lead time	Shorter	Shortest
Selection criteria	Cost and quality	Speed, flexibility and quality
Linkages	Long-term partnerships	Virtual and temporary
Performance measures	Quality and productivity	Delivery promises met
Organisation	Standardised	Responsive
Planning and control	Synchronisation and waste reduction	Instantaneous response

Feedback on revision question for study session 12

To answer this question, you will probably need to reread sections 12.3 and 12.4 very carefully. You will find a number of causal factors 'buried' in the text, though there isn't a list anywhere that you can learn. Consider such issues as the increasing complexity of business, the growth in joint ventures, and the increased specialisation between functions (within organisations).

Feedback on revision question for study session 13

This is a very broad question, but shouldn't cause you any real problems if you've done the activities and questions in study session 13, particularly those in section 13.3.

Feedback on revision question for study session 14

In any question that asks you to 'compare and contrast', it helps if you look for similarities and differences. Reread sections sections 14.5 and 14.6, and note down the essential characteristics of private and public sector supply chains. Then look for similarities and differences. End your argument with a conclusion as to whether they are fairly similar or very different.

Feedback on revision question for study session 15

Section section 15.3 contains lots of information on the role of government, and section 15.4 is all about the role of technology. Base your answer on those sections.

Feedback on revision question for study session 16

See learning activity 16.2 and the content of section 16.2. 'Identify and discuss' implies that much more than just a list of points is required. A paragraph about each of the following would suffice:

- costs (including transport and currency)
- lead times
- risks (including exchange rate risk)
- cultural barriers
- availability of supply, both locally and globally
- quality.

Feedback on revision question for study session 17

This is a question that is designed to test your intellectual dexterity. Don't be intimidated by it; simply break it down into a series of steps that you can address one at a time:

- Explain what Porter meant by a value network (a collection of linked and related value chains), and perhaps draw a diagram and/or give an example.
- Explain what is meant by a supply network (see study session 12), and again draw a diagram and/or give an example.
- Identify and explain any differences between the two concepts. For example, Porter's model is much closer to a conventional supply chain than it is to a supply network, as it looks at a series of firms.

Feedback on revision question for study session 18

This is a simple question with a diverse answer. To get the full range of possible objectives, you would need to reread study sessions 10, 13, 14 and 17, as well as study session 18. It is clearly unnecessary to discuss all objectives, so just make sure that you have a reasonable range and number of suggestions. Five or six would be fine, possibly including: cost reduction, improved quality, greater certainty of supply, shorter lead times, improved customer satisfaction, or competitive advantage. As the question asks for a discussion, you should make it clear that the various objectives are alternatives, though they can be pursued collectively. Identify any conflicts between them, and conclude as appropriate.

Feedback on revision question for study session 19

As well as basing your answer on section 19.4, you might also look at your answer to revision question 10. Of course, your answer to this question should be much more sophisticated, as you now know so much more! Because this question is based on a specific context (a financial services company acquiring a new building), all of your suggestions should be relevant to this. In such a question, it is always a good idea to make a couple of suggestions that are *really* specific to the context. In this question, you might consider the fact that any cost savings (from an adversarial approach) are likely to be very significant, or the fact that the company is unlikely to want a long-term relationship with its supplier if it is buying the property, but may wish to create one if it is leasing.

Feedback on revision question for study session 20

This has really been the big issue in supply chain management in the last decade, and you may have noticed that this text keeps returning to the 'lean supply' concept. In particular, reread sessions study sessions 13, 17 and 20, if you need a reminder of all the issues.

- Explain what the lean approach is, and the benefits claimed for it. (See sections 17.1 and 17.2.)
- Explain the criticisms and potential drawbacks of the lean approach. (See section 17.3.)
- Explain the alternative(s) to it, and the way they address the weaknesses of the lean approach (agile supply, for example). (See section 20.3.)
- Conclude as appropriate – probably by saying that, while many supply chains can learn from Toyota's approach, overall a contingency approach is more appropriate (unless you happen to work for Toyota!).

Don't forget to use a report format (header, introduction, content, conclusion, recommendation) as there will be marks available as a reward for an appropriate format.

References and bibliography

This section contains a complete A–Z listing of all publications, materials or websites referred to in this coursebook. Books, articles and research are listed under the first author's (or in some cases the editor's) surname. Where no author name has been given, the publication is listed under the name of the organisation that published it. Websites are listed under the name of the organisation providing the website.

Ansoff, HI (1965) *Corporate Strategy*. Penguin.

Ansoff, HI (1991) 'Critique of Henry Mintzberg's "The Design School"' *Strategic Management Journal,* 12, pp449–461.

Balogun, J, and V Hope-Bailey (1999) *Exploring Strategic Change*. Prentice Hall.

Barney, JB (1991) 'Firm Resources and Sustained Competitive Advantage', *Journal of Management,* 17(1), pp99–120.

Burgelman, RA (1983) 'A Model of the Interaction of Strategic Behaviour, Corporate Context and the Concept of Strategy', *Academy of Management Review,* 81(1), pp61–70.

Christopher, M (2005) *Logistics and Supply Chain Management.* Pearson.

Cox, A (1996) 'Relational Competence and Strategic Procurement Management: Towards an Entrepreneurial and Contractual Theory of the Firm', *European Journal of Purchasing and Supply Management,* 2(1), pp57–70.

Cox, A, and R Lamming (1997) 'Managing Supply in the Firm of the Future', *European Journal of Purchasing and Supply Management,* 3(2), pp53–62.

Crosby, PB (1979) *Quality is Free.* McGraw Hill.

Cyert, RM, and JG March (1963) *A Behavioural Theory of the Firm.* Prentice Hall.

Dam Jespersen, B, and T Skjott-Larsen (2005) *Supply Chain Management.* Copenhagen Business School.

De Witt, B, and R Meyer (1999) *Strategy Synthesis.* Thomson.

Drucker, PF (1961) *The Practice of Management.* Mercury.

Emmett, S (2005) *Supply Chain in 90 Minutes.* Management Books 2000.

Floyd, SW, and B Wooldridge (1994) *The strategic middle manager.* Jossey-Bass.

French, J, and B Raven (1959) 'The Bases of Social Power', in Cartwright, D (1959) *Studies in Social Power.* University of Michigan Press.

Gattorna, J (1998) *Strategic Supply Chain Alignment.* Gower.

Goold, M, and A Campbell (1987) *Strategies and Styles: the Role of the Centre in Managing Diversified Corporations.* Blackwell.

Goold, M, and A Campbell (2002) *Designing Effective Organisations.* Jossey-Bass.

Hakansson, H (1982) *International Marketing and Purchasing of Industrial Goods – an Interaction Approach.* Wiley.

Hamel, G, and CK Prahalad (1994) *Competing for the Future: Breakthrough Strategies for Seizing Control of your Industry and Creating Markets of Tomorrow.* Harvard Business School Press.

Handfield, RB, and EL Nichols (2002) *Supply Chain Redesign: Transforming Supply Chains into Integrated Value Systems.* Prentice Hall.

Harland, CM (1996) 'Supply Chain Management: Relationships, Chains and Networks', *British Journal of Management,* 7(1), pp63–80.

Harrison, R (1972) 'Understanding your Organisation's Character', *Harvard Business Review,* 50(3), pp119–128.

Hines, P (1994) *Creating World Class Suppliers: Unlocking Mutual Competitive Advantage.* Pitman.

Hofstede, G (1991) *Cultures and Organisations: Software of the Mind.* McGraw Hill.

Johnson, G, K Scholes and R Whittington (2005) *Exploring Corporate Strategy.* Pearson.

Juran, JM (1988) *Juran on planning for quality.* Free Press.

Kay, J (1997) *Foundations of Business Success: How Business Strategies Add Value.* Oxford University Press.

Kraljic, P (1983) 'Purchasing Must Become Supply Chain Management', *Harvard Business Review,* 61(5), pp109–117.

Lamming, RC (1993) *Beyond Partnership: Strategies for Innovation and Lean Supply.* Prentice Hall.

Lamming, RC (1995) 'Purchasing and Supply Relationship Management Between Small Customers and Their Large Suppliers', *Proceedings of the 4th International IPSERA Annual Conference,* University of Birmingham.

Lamming, RC, et al (2000) 'An Initial Classification of Supply Networks', *International Journal of Operations and Production Management*, 20(6), pp675–691.

Lewin, K (1943) 'Defining the "Field at a Given Time"', *Psychological Review*, 50, pp292–310. Republished in *Resolving Social Conflicts & Field Theory in Social Science* (1997), Washington, DC: American Psychological Association

Lindblom, CE (1959) 'The Science of Muddling Through', *Public Administration Review*, 19, pp79–88.

Lynch, R (2005) *Corporate Strategy*. Pearson.

Lysons, K, and B Farrington (2006) *Purchasing and Supply Chain Management*. Pearson.

Mintzberg, H (1979) *The Structuring of Organisations*. Prentice Hall.

Mintzberg, H, and A McHugh (1985) 'Strategy Formation in Adhocracy', *Administration Science Quarterly*, 30, pp160–197.

Mintzberg, H (1987) 'Crafting strategy', *Harvard Business Review*, 65(4), pp66–75.

Mintzberg, H (1994) *The Rise and Fall of Strategic Planning*. Prentice Hall.

Mintzberg, H (1997) *Strategic Safari*. Prentice Hall.

Mol, MJ (2002) 'Purchasing's Strategic Relevance', *Journal of Purchasing and Supply Chain Management*, 3(2), pp1–8.

Monden, Y (1993) *Toyota Production Systems: An Integrated Approach to Just-In-Time*. Industrial Engineering and Management Press.

New, S, and J Ramsey (1997) 'A Critical Appraisal of Aspects of the Lean Approach', *European Journal of Purchasing and Supply*, 3(2), pp93–102.

Normann, R, and R Ramirez (1993) 'From Value Chain to Value Constellation: Designing Interactive Strategy', *Harvard Business Review*, 71(4), pp65–77.

Nonaka, I, and H Takeuchi (1995) *The Knowledge Creating Company: How Japanese Companies Create the Dynamics of Innovation*. Oxford University Press.

Pascale, RT (1991) *Managing on the Edge*. Penguin.

Peters, T (1987) *Thriving on Chaos: Handbook for a Management Revolution*. Macmillan.

Peters, T, and R Waterman (1982) *In Search of Excellence: Lessons from America's Best-Run Corporations*. Harper and Row.

Porter, ME (1980) *Competitive Strategy: Techniques for Analysing Industries and Firms*. Free Press.

Porter, ME (1985) *Competitive Advantage: Creating and Sustaining Superior Performance*. Free Press.

Prahalad, CK, and G Hamel (1990) 'The Core Competence of the Organisation', *Harvard Business Review*, 68(3).

Quinn, JB (1980) *Strategies for change*. Irwin.

Quinn, JB, and FG Hilmer (1995) 'Strategic Outsourcing', *Sloan management review*, 36(3).

Ramsey, J (2001) 'Purchasing's Strategic Irrelevance', *European Journal of Purchasing and Supply*, 7(4), pp257–263.

Reve, T (1990) 'The Firm as a Nexus of Internal and External Contracts', in M Aoki, ME Gustafsson and B Williamson (1990) *One Firm as a Nexus of Treaties*. Sage.

Rich, N, and P Hines (1997) 'The Three Pillars of Strategic Alignment', in A Cox and P Hines (1997) *Advanced Supply Management*, pp74–93. Earlsgate.

Schein, EH (1997) 'Three Cultures of Management: the Key to Organisational Learning', *Sloan Management Review*, 38(10), pp9–20.

Simon, HA (1960) *The New Science of Management Decision*. Prentice Hall.

Stalk, G, et al (1992) 'Competing on Capabilities', *Harvard Business Review*, 70(2).

Watts, CA, KY Kim and CK Hahn (1995) 'Linking Purchasing to Corporate Competitive Strategy', *International Journal of Purchasing and Materials Management* 31 (2), pages 2–8. (Available by logging in to the CIPS website, then following the link to the IPS website and searching their articles database.)

Yip, GS (1992) *Total Global Strategy – Managing for Worldwide Competitive Advantage*. Prentice Hall.

Index

competence *see also* core
competence
corporate strategy, 35
definition, 120, 250
non-replicable, 251
replicable, 251
types, 120
competitive advantage
added value, 215
core competence, 121
corporate strategy, 70
globalisation, 189, 242
leanness, 249, 252
replicable/non-replicable
competences, 251
competitive architecture, 71
competitive globalisation drivers,
181
competitive performance, 71
competitive rivalry, 33
complementary competences, 120
computers, 182
conformity to requirements, 130
conglomerate integration, 63
consultants, 111
contingent approaches, 241, 242
cooperative relationships, 127, 240,
243
core competence
competitive advantage, 121
corporate strategy, 34
definition, 120
supply chain strategy, 250
types, 120
corporate social responsibility
(CSR), 54, 227
corporate strategy
alignment, 95, 101
commitment, 95, 99, 101
communications, 98
competitive advantage, 70
core competences, 34
culture, 50, 52
hierarchy of objectives, 96
innovation, 126
objectives, 96
position importance, 29
power, 49
process review, 85
resources, 34, 69, 72
stakeholders, 36
strategy levels, 72

structures, 44, 48
supply chain strategy, 116, 118
support resources, 69
SWOT analysis, 37
cost globalisation drivers, 180
cost improvements, 128
cost leadership, 60, 61, 215
costs of conformance, 130
costs of global sourcing, 192
covert power, 225
critical success factors (CSF), 97
critiques of leanness, 210
cross-functional management, 239
cross-functional teams, 144
CSF *see* critical success factors
CSR *see* corporate social
responsibility
culture
barriers to sourcing, 192
change management, 108
corporate strategy, 50, 52
globalisation, 177, 179, 198
customs union, 196
data exchange, 209
debt finance, 78
decentralisation, 142, 148
dedicated asset specificity, 120
defects, 208
deliberate strategy, 7, 17
delivery practice, 209
demand forecasting, 166, 167
Department for International
Development, 231
dependent power, 224
deregulation, 194
design technology, 182
differentiation, 60, 61, 215
difficult links test, 47
direction in change management,
109
diversification, 62
dividends, 78
divisional structures, 45, 48
dominance, 223
downstream links, 152
drivers of change, 175, 176, 178,
182, 183
economic conditions, 229
economic union, 197
Economic Value Added (EVA)
measure, 213
economy globalisation, 176